DESIRE WORK

DESIRE WORK

EX-GAY *and*
PENTECOSTAL
MASCULINITY
in South Africa

Louise –

Thank you for all your
support over the years.
It has always meant the
world to me.

— Melissa

Melissa Hackman   Duke University Press   Durham and London   2018

Printed in the United States of America on acid-free paper ∞
Designed by Courtney Leigh Baker and typeset in Minion Pro
and Gill Sans by Graphic Composition, Inc., Bogart, GA

Library of Congress Cataloging-in-Publication Data
Names: Hackman, Melissa, [date] author.
Title: Desire work : ex-gay and Pentecostal
masculinity in South Africa / Melissa Hackman.
Description: Durham : Duke University Press, 2018. |
Includes bibliographical references and index.
Identifiers: LCCN 2018000187 (print)
LCCN 2018008203 (ebook)
ISBN 9781478002314 (ebook)
ISBN 9781478000648 (hardcover : alk. paper)
ISBN 9781478000822 (pbk. : alk. paper)
Subjects: LCSH: Gays—South Africa—Cape Town. |
Ex-gay movement—South Africa—Cape Town. |
Pentecostal churches—South Africa—Cape Town. |
Masculinity—Religious aspects—Pentecostal churches.
Classification: LCC HQ76.3.S62 (ebook) | LCC HQ76.3.S62 C343
2018 (print) | DDC 306.76/609687355—dc23
LC record available at https://lccn.loc.gov/2018000187

COVER ART: Robin Wong, *At the Corner*, 2016. Courtesy of the
photographer.

To the memory of Bernice Brice

CONTENTS

The idea for this book project began over fifteen years ago when I was a divinity school student. I was working on an ethnography of LGBTI youth, access to health care, and spirituality, when I met a young man at the local LGBTI youth center who informed me that he was "ex-ex-gay." I had never heard of being ex-gay, much less being "ex-ex-gay" and I asked him to tell me about his experiences. He narrated for me how he had attempted, albeit in his case unsuccessfully, to transform himself into a heterosexual through a nearby Boston-area live-in program. He had left/dropped out of the program in frustration when his work to transform his same-sex desires did not lead to a change in his sexual attractions. This conversation got me interested in the ex-gay movement—in what motivations, pressures, and incentives might lead people to attempt to be heterosexual. The rabbit hole of Google led me to international ministries working all over the world, and I landed on a Pentecostal ministry in Cape Town—I call it Healing Revelation Ministries (HRM)—that is the subject of this book.[1] HRM, like other ex-gay ministries, advertised that it could "heal homosexuality through the power of Jesus Christ."

I worked with HRM members and ex-members between 2004 and 2013, including one continuous year of fieldwork in 2007–2008. This time period spanned much of the ministry's thirteen-year existence between 1997, when it was founded, and 2010, when it closed its doors. Thirteen years is a long period of time for any ex-gay ministry to exist,[2] as these organizations are plagued with challenges to their missions—including leaders' "sexual falls," an ex-gay term for sexual activities with people of the same sex, and financial competition with other organizations, like those targeting HIV/AIDS, that are able to generate more local and international donors. I tell you about HRM's closing up front not to predispose you to seeing HRM and its members as failures, but rather to situate the story within a historical context, which is detailed below and in this book's introductory chapter.

A white American man whom I call Brian began HRM. He first came to South Africa in 1996 as a missionary because he believed that God had "called" him to help "save" gay men and women in Africa's "gay capital,"

Cape Town. Brian was originally from southern California and grew up in a strict Pentecostal household. He had lived as an openly gay man until he "recommitted" himself to God in his thirties. In his forties, he spent five years in Europe as a missionary. It was while he was there that he felt the "call" to go to Africa. He first affiliated with Christian Uplift,[3] the first ex-gay ministry in South Africa, which was headquartered in Johannesburg and run by two white South Africans. Brian founded HRM in the Western Cape in 1997 and situated its headquarters in a local Assembly of God church, the Church of the Reborn, in 1998, which allowed it access to a broader Christian community and a physical location to offer classes, support groups, and counseling sessions.

HRM closed its doors in 2010 when Brian moved back to the United States and most of the leadership team had "returned to the lifestyle," an ex-gay term indicating when ex-gays decide to live openly gay lives. Brian subsequently opened a branch of HRM in the United States. The ministry is now American based, with affiliations with a large secular university (where Brian acts as a chaplain) and a Christian fraternity. HRM still offers classes, support groups, and counseling for men struggling with same-sex attraction but no longer does any work in Africa.

The ex-gay movement claims to "heal homosexuality through the power of Jesus Christ." It began in the 1970s in southern California in response to larger conservative Christians' fears about the influence of feminism, gay rights, and other identity-based movements they saw as "taking over" America (Gerber 2012; Davies 1998). It is a montage of biblical inerrancy, self-help rhetoric, psychology, and science. The nonprofit ministry Exodus International was officially founded in 1976, and although marred by a number of scandals in the 1980s, including the defection and then public love affair of two founders, it continued to grow until 2013 when it closed its doors. The closure came a year after Exodus publicly admitted that homosexuality was not a curable condition and reparative therapy was harmful (Eckholm 2012b). Exodus president Alan Chambers also apologized to the gay community for unintentional harm (Steffan 2013). Although Exodus is now defunct, there are still many other ex-gay ministries around the world. There is Exodus Global Alliance,[4] a Canadian ex-gay organization with member ministries in Latin America and Asia, and the Restored Hope Network, an American ministry that broke off from Exodus International in 2012 when Alan Chambers declared that ex-gay recovery was largely unsuccessful. Many of these ministries, like HRM, were started by Americans or have American affiliations (Jones 2013; Queiroz, D'Elio, and Maas 2013).

Ex-gay ministries have historically dealt with a variety of named "sexual sins" and dysfunction. These include homosexuality, masturbation, internet pornography use, prostitution, pedophilia, voyeurism, sadomasochism, pre-marital sex, and extramarital sex (Dallas and Heche 2009; Ankerberg and Weldon 1994). Internationally, such ministries share theologies and ideologies of "God's divine plan for heterosexuality," as well as ways of structuring and running their programs. The story in this book, therefore, is not just a story about South Africa. It is a transnational story that shows the long-standing links between places in the United States and Africa and the ways that scientific, biblical, and moral ideas and knowledge often travel a trans-national route.

I started this project with one driving question: Why was there an ex-gay ministry in South Africa, the only African country to legally protect gay rights? South Africa is unique in Africa because sexual orientation is pro-tected in the Bill of Rights in the Constitution, and gays and lesbians can marry and adopt children. Yet despite these legal protections the majority of South African people—many of whom are religious—do not support these rights. Studies have consistently found that many Africans across the conti-nent strongly disapprove of homosexuality and rights being extended to gay community members. In places like Nigeria, as much as 98 percent of the population believes that society should not accept homosexuality (Pew Research Center 2013). In South Africa, this number is between 60 and 80 percent, depending on the study (Pew Research Center 2013; Roberts and Reddy 2008). In a moment where much of African Christianity and African public life is reputed to be marked by homophobia, this book examines how HRM offered men in the late twentieth and early twenty-first centuries personal and individual religious solutions to same-sex desires, understood widely as "sinful" and morally wrong. In this book I do not seek to answer the question, does the ex-gay process work (other studies have shown that it has only limited success long-term). But rather I ask: How does it work? What techniques does the ex-gay movement employ to transform desire? Why do some men (mostly white and some coloured) in South Africa seek to alter their gender and sexual selves in the postapartheid period? And how do they define success for themselves?

Despite a large amount of polarized literature on the ex-gay movement, written either by its members and supporters or by those who oppose it, there are few ethnographies on the ex-gay movement. We do know ethno-graphically that American ex-gay ministries are mostly evangelical Chris-tian, male, and often segregated by race. We also know that there are ex-gay ministries on every continent but Antarctica and that they are growing in so-called Third World/Global Southern countries, where homosexuality is often linked to Westernization and immorality. (The ex-gay movement itself is also linked to the West.) We currently have four full-length ethnographies on ex-gay ministries, all on the United States, although one has a chapter on the ex-gay movement in Uganda (Waidzunas 2015). Tanya Erzen documents a live-in ex-gay program in northern California (2006). Michelle Wolkomir examines the lives of gay and ex-gay Protestants as they attempt to reconcile or alter their religious and sexual selves (2006). Lynne Gerber compares evangelical weight-loss ministries with evangelical ex-gay ministries, documenting what addressing these two groups together can tell us about contemporary evangelical life in America (2012). Tom Waidzunas (2015) looks at the science of the ex-gay movement and practices like reparative therapy. All four of these texts narrate ethnographically what the contemporary American ex-gay movement looks like. My study fills in what the ex-gay movement looks like outside the United States in a postcolonial context. Besides a study by Annie Wilkinson on the ex-gay movement in Ecuador (2011) we know little ethnographically about what the ex-gay movement looks like beyond the borders of the United States.

This book sheds light on African Pentecostalism, Africa's fastest-growing form of Christianity (Hefner 2013; Freeman 2012). I use the definition of Pentecostalism that my subjects adhered to and that is similar to what most Pentecostals believe and practice in other parts of Africa. Their beliefs included substitutionary atonement (the belief that Jesus died for humanity's sins), biblical inerrancy, belief in the virgin birth of Jesus, the necessity for adult full immersion baptism, the idea that Jesus died and was divinely resurrected, gifts of divine healing, the indwelling of the Holy Spirit, a close personal relationship with God, and conservative social values. There are two different groups of Pentecostals in South Africa. One is traditional Pentecostals, a group mostly segregated during apartheid into black- and white-only churches (Anderson and Pillay 1997). The second is neo-Pentecostals, which includes HRM, who differentiate themselves from older Pentecostal groups by claiming racial inclusivity and engagement with the world, not separation and isolation. I use the term "Pentecostal" instead of "neo-Pentecostal" throughout this book because that was how subjects self-identified. African Pentecostalism is heavily invested in transforming sexual acts, gender roles, and sexual subjectivities, so HRM was one part of a larger trend in the faith that addresses reforming sexualities. However, HRM was unique in that instead of only outright condemning homosexuality, it sought to acknowledge and alter it.

The ministry was made up of two groups of Pentecostal men: white and coloured. A note on racial terms: I use self-referential racial terms throughout this book. During apartheid, South Africans were categorized as white, coloured, or black African. As a separate racial category under apartheid, coloured Africans had higher status than black Africans but were much lower than white Africans. Afrikaners/Afrikaans people are white. There are two groups of whites in South Africa. The first are Afrikaners/Afrikaans people and the second are British South Africans. The differences between the two have to do with history and language: the first language of British South Africans is English, not Afrikaans. The coloured community is descended from racial and cultural mixing of Europeans, the local Khoisan peoples, and enslaved populations from other parts of Africa and Asia (Loos 2004). Today, Afrikaans, a mix of indigenous, Dutch, and English languages, is the first language of most of the Cape coloured community and of white Afrikaans people.

Understanding why white South African men joined an ex-gay ministry in their country during democracy means also holding on to the idea that the ministry is a hybrid in that it links together African and American Christian ideas on what constitutes "sin," what "sin" looks like, and how to "heal" from it. It also means looking at whiteness in South Africa, a contested and controversial topic. The ministry's leaders and members were mostly white South Africans, with some coloured men, and in their early twenties to midthirties. Many of the men were Afrikaans. Their whiteness was a key piece of the ex-gay selves they formed. These men grew up in small towns in the Western Cape or in Cape Town's suburbs and attended racially segregated schools. They held a variety of working- and middle-class jobs. They were all part of larger shifts in sexual discourses and practices in democracy. The ministry's position in Cape Town is also important, as the city is known as and sells itself as Africa's "gay capital." Many also know it as the "most racist" place in South Africa.

The ministry was full of men whose subjectivities were in flux personally and socially. They drew on some ideas of what it meant to be men in the twenty-first century, in the "new" South Africa, and they disputed or rejected other notions. They differentiated themselves from other South African men, seeing themselves as better, more equitable, and more committed to caring for women and children, at the same time that they viewed and talked about women as lesser than men and in need of male leadership. They were men seeking access to hegemony in the new South Africa, fighting against being gay in a society that largely sees homosexuality as meaning that men lack masculinity. They were white men in a society where whiteness is largely linked to racism. In these pages, I explore the *why* and the *how* of the men in this South African ex-gay ministry, focusing on the types of selves they sought to build through hard desire work.

First and foremost, I would like to thank the leadership and membership of Healing Revelation Ministries for their openness to this project and to me. Thank you for answering my always-evolving questions and for your friendship, laughter, and thoughtfulness over many years.

Thank you to Duke University Press and its anonymous readers for helping me to make this book stronger and clearer. Thanks to Courtney Berger and Sandra Korn for navigating with me through the process.

This project started off as my dissertation, and I would like to thank my dissertation committee, Carolyn Martin Shaw, Don Brenneis, and Sue Houchins, for their guidance and support over the years. Special thanks to Carolyn for her mentorship and friendship.

I'd like to thank my transnational network of friends for their support as I researched, wrote, and edited. This book could not have been written without the support of friends Kate Chabarek, Rachel Engmann, Garth Hammer, Mahri Irvine, and Shelia McMahon, who kept my spirits up from Boston, Indianapolis, Accra, Basque Country, and Cape Town. Heather Smith has been amazing every step of the way and has made Atlanta a place I can call home. Thanks to Jason Alley, Jon and Ulka Anjara, Lynne Gerber, Diane Hoffman, Naomi and Jason Rodriguez, and Kate Wilkinson. Thanks also to Sharon Kaplan and Aurit Lazerus for their guidance. Special thanks to my dog, Evans-Pritchard, for his love and for forcing me to leave the house and to laugh.

Thanks to my friends at Brown University and Emory University. At Brown, thank you to Jennifer Stampe, Rebecca Carter, and Louise Lamphere. At Emory, Kristin Phillips has been writing partner extraordinaire. Michael Moon and Elizabeth Wilson have been friends and mentors who helped me to navigate the publishing process and supported me each day as I wrote and edited. Thanks also to Jonathan Goldberg, Taryn Jordan, Chelsea Long, Sean McAlister, Ingrid Meintjes, Neema Oliver, Jessica Reuther, and Pamela Scully.

Thanks to audiences at the American Anthropological Association, Association for African Studies, the University of Florida, Leeds University, Bates

College, University of California, Berkeley, Brown University, and Emory University for their comments and questions.

Thanks to the Wenner Gren Foundation, the University of California, Santa Cruz's Anthropology Department, and to Brown University's Anthropology Department for their funding and support.

This book is dedicated to the memory of Bernice Brice, who would not have been surprised that I ended up as an anthropologist.

Portions of this book appeared in *Ethnos*, *Social Analysis* and the edited volume *Sexual Diversity in Africa: Politics, Theory and Citizenship* and are reproduced with permission. Parts of chapter 2 are taken from "'Ex-Gay' Subjectivities: Tracking Cultural Convergences in Post-Apartheid South Africa," in *Sexual Diversity in Africa: Politics, Theory and Citizenship*, edited by Sybille Nyeck and Marc Epprecht, 109–128 (Montreal: McGill-Queen's University Press, 2013). A section of chapter 4 is derived from "A Sinful Landscape: Moral and Sexual Geographies in Cape Town, South Africa," *Social Analysis* 59, no. 3 (2015): 105–125. Portions of chapter 5 are from "Desire Work: The Production of Heterosexuality among South African Pentecostal Gay Men," *Ethnos* 81, no. 3 (2016): 508–534.

ADRIAN'S DESIRE WORK

Adrian was a member of Healing Revelation Ministries (HRM), an ex-gay
ministry in Cape Town, South Africa. He was thirty in 2008 but looked
closer in age to someone still in college with his unlined chubby face and
quiet, earnest way of expressing himself. He was a self-identified coloured
man who kept his hair cut short and neat, and he favored roomy shirts
and slacks that hid his body. He was easily embarrassed and avoided group
gatherings when he could. I first met Adrian in 2004 when he was in his
midtwenties; he often seemed to be on the margins of conversations and was
very socially awkward. I was surprised when a ministry leader told me that
by the time I met him, Adrian had made significant social progress. When
he first started attending a weekly support group for ex-gay Pentecostal men
he could not look anyone in the eye, even in one-on-one conversations,
and he stared at his hands or the table on the rare occasions when he spoke.
Besides attending groups for Christian men with "same-sex attraction," or
sexual desire for other men, Adrian also underwent weekly individual counseling sessions for over a year with Brian, the ministry's white American
founder.

Adrian was in his early twenties when he first came into the ministry
offices at Church of the Reborn, a Pentecostal Assemblies of God church.
Adrian had decided to undergo a sex change operation and entered the
ministry without any hope that he could change his sexual preference. He
went to his initial counseling appointment to prove to himself that he had
exhausted all other "healing" options. He had already investigated the process for transitioning and planned to meet with a psychologist to begin liv-

ing as a woman. Adrian spent his childhood being teased and bullied for being different. In his high school years he thought he was a *moffie*[1] or that he was born in the wrong body. At their first counseling session Brian told Adrian that if he wanted to heal from his "same-sex attraction" he would have to work on drastically changing his self-presentation, beginning with his voice. At various times Adrian described his voice as sounding "like a woman," "effeminate," and "thin." He was shocked when Brian explained that he himself was the one making his voice "thin"—he spoke like a woman because he spent so much time with women, learning to mimic their characteristics and mannerisms. Adrian thought he had a physiological problem and had never gone through puberty; he believed his voice had never broken. Brian told him that he could make his voice "thicker," but it would take time and practice.

Adrian's voice had always been a major source of shame for him and he was ecstatic at the idea that he could deepen it. When Adrian and I met for lunch in 2007, he explained how, with effort and constant attention, his voice was changing and "starting to become normal." With practice in the past year it had become easier for him to change his voice without always having to think before speaking. However, he said that when he "gets a fright" or is very upset he loses his self-control and his voice becomes high-pitched. When people began to notice the change in how he spoke, he pretended not to know what they were talking about. Laughingly, he told me that he knew Christians were not supposed to lie, but he was too embarrassed to admit to anyone outside of his ex-gay support group that he was practicing to become more masculine. The other men in the ministry also sometimes participated in "helping" him change his self-presentation, occasionally mocking him for being effeminate. If he spoke in a high voice, they would sometimes sarcastically repeat back what he had just said in a very exaggerated, camp manner, and they also made fun of him when he was absent, which he knew.[2]

Besides controlling his pitch, Adrian also consciously changed how he walked; his high-pitched voice was accompanied by what he referred to as "effeminate walking," which involved swinging his hips. He learned through careful attention to move his body differently when he walked and to reposition when sitting. During most of our lunch Adrian had his legs crossed at the knee. Halfway through telling me about his transformation, he glanced down and stopped talking for a few seconds. He quickly uncrossed his legs, opening them up much wider and placing both feet flat on the floor. He leaned into the back of his chair and took a more relaxed sitting posture.

His arms rested on his upper thighs instead of his knees. His body took up more space and he remained in this stereotypically masculine position throughout the rest of lunch.

Adrian believed his masculine interior would continue to grow and transform as he naturalized his masculine exterior through posture and walking. He told me, "I think I have worked that [effeminacy] off. I don't even know how I used to walk because I've totally lost the ability to walk like that [pause] I think." Through practice Adrian had returned to what he referred to as his "natural" voice and gait. The language that Adrian used is notable—that of work, practice, and "forcing" himself to speak and walk differently. He believed that working on his exterior would initiate an interior working—that his masculinity would grow with each deeper voice intonation and time spent sitting with legs wide, taking up space.

Adrian was working to cultivate his ideal self—a deep voice, masculine walk, and heterosexual desires. He had an intimate relationship with God, who he believed would guide him to express himself in a manner that was read by others as masculine. Adrian felt that with God's love he could transform himself in body and spirit. God would eventually lead him to heterosexual desire and marriage. With God's guidance, he could begin to sexually desire women, not men, and have a transformed affect and comportment.

Adrian was part of a diverse group of men who entered the ministry in an effort to transform their gender and sexual selves. Men are the majority in most ex-gay ministries throughout the world, including HRM. One reason for this is that men are conceptualized as "naturally" sexual and said to "act out" sexually, while women are claimed to be "naturally" emotional and to "act out" through emotionally damaging interpersonal relationships. Women and their sex lives are marginalized and usually rendered invisible in ex-gay ministries like HRM. The men in HRM were white and coloured. They were mostly single and lived in apartments with roommates in town. The small number of men who were married lived with their wives and families in the suburbs. A few had been to technical colleges or to university. Some worked or sought to work in the ministry or at a church full time. Others were specialists in the fields of photography, piano repair, insurance, security, and construction, or they worked in the service industry as waiters, restaurant managers, and travel agents. All sought to answer God's "call" for their lives and focused on sexual salvation as a way to achieve a new and better saved Christian self. Few of these men had been in "the [gay] lifestyle"; instead they usually watched a large amount of gay pornography, sexually fantasized about other men, or had secretive, anonymous sexual encounters. Most had grown up in some kind of a Christian household, with some in mainstream denominations like the Dutch Reform or Anglican churches, and others in Pentecostal or nondenominational Christian churches. These men had often let their faith slip over time. They used HRM as a way to recommit their lives to Christ. A lack of church attendance or a lapse in a relationship with God was often a result of their same-sex sexual attractions. Before HRM, men frequently interpreted their desires as evidence that they were "bad" Christians or did not deserve God's love and compassion. HRM provided men with a new way to be good and morally righteous Christians. They learned to tell different stories about themselves and their desires, to recenter their social and moral trajectories, and to turn to God and HRM for the tools to become heterosexual. This book details this journey, one that often led to years in HRM but also frequently led the men to "come out" as gay, as discussed in chapter 5.

Between 2004 and 2013, I worked with white and coloured ex-gay men at Healing Revelation Ministries (HRM), an ex-gay Pentecostal ministry in Cape Town, known by many as Africa's "gay capital." These men sought to transform their homosexual attractions through intense work on their desires. Ex-gay men like Adrian who strove to be heterosexual engaged in what I call "desire work," or a process of emotional, bodily, and religious discipline and practices with the end goal of heterosexual marriage. Although Pentecostals around the world believe that God and the Holy Spirit perform miracles every day, instantaneously curing people of diseases, disabilities, and addictions such as alcoholism, there is no miracle in desire work; *one must learn to do "what comes naturally."* Ex-gay belief systems rest on this paradox: opposite-gender desire is "natural" but sometimes also needs to be learned and embodied through purposeful effort. For ex-gay men, eliciting desire was hard work, and it was the most difficult part of forming and maintaining the heterosexual self.

"Desires" are historically and culturally located forces that are produced through a multitude of engagements with social norms, public life, political economies, and cultural forces; they are more than what individuals wish for or feel (see for example Rofel 2007; Smith 2006; Sinnott 2004; Carrillo 2002). Rachel Spronk has written of young middle-class professionals in Nairobi who drew on a "therapeutic ethos" from popular media to form sophisticated, sexually knowledgeable, and intimate selves in romantic partnerships that often challenged established moral authorities such as elders (Spronk 2011: 146). Shanti Parikh documents young Ugandans in the "Bentu class" (as having "been to" outside of Uganda and back) who act as cultural desire brokers, linking sexual knowledge and the enactment of sexual desires to what it means to be cosmopolitan and modern (Parikh 2015: 35). In South Africa, the men in HRM produced heterosexual desires in a larger context of national desire work, in which dominant male heterosexuality is often patriarchal and abusive and men are encouraged to work on themselves (see for example Morrell, Jewkes, and Lindegger 2012; Hunter 2010; Jewkes et al. 2009). In this book, I examine how ex-gay Capetonian Pentecostal men attempted to transfer their desires from men to women through emotional, bodily, and religious work. I ask: how do men learn to desire different kinds of sexual and gendered relationships? What are the micropractices of thought, feelings, and action involved? What kinds of new selves emerge? Is ex-gay desire work successful, and if so, to what ends?

Men with same-sex attraction joined HRM because they felt that their desires and sexual practices did not align with their conservative Christian values, in which homosexuality is interpreted as a "sin" and heterosexuality as "God-ordained." They believed their "sinful" desires were leading them toward unhappy lives in which they would be alone, ostracized from their families and God, and eventually end up in hell, which is a literal place in the Pentecostal worldview. The ministry promised that men who "struggled" with same-sex attraction could achieve their heterosexual ideal through hard work; they could be reintegrated into their families and the larger Christian community to have fulfilling and joyful lives. They were told that a new self was possible through hard work.

Many Christians, including the ones I worked with in South Africa, interpret the body as outer proof of an inner state. In her work on devotional diet culture in the United States, Marie Griffith details how "body type, among assorted possible signifiers, has come to seem a virtually infallible touchstone of the worth of persons about whom one knows nothing else, as well as the value—indeed, the deepest truths—of one's own self: a vital component of subjectivity" (Griffith 2004: 7). Devotional dieters believe that people are fat because they cannot control themselves. A fat body is read as proof of a lack of religious commitment because the person is seen as more concerned with feeding the body than nourishing the soul. Similarly, HRM members saw the effeminate body and actions, for example, waving a hand when speaking or snapping one's fingers in ways that were read as stereotypically "gay," as proof that little "healing" from homosexuality had occurred. They interpreted effeminate affect as the lack of hard work on the self.

The work of ex-gay men in HRM, however, corresponded to a more complex interplay between the outer and inner self. Adrian employed works of bodily change not only for the purpose of exhibiting a changed exterior to outsiders. He believed that altering his exterior would also transform his interior. In her work on women in the Egyptian piety movement, Saba Mahmood challenges the idea that conduct is itself an expression of emotion, the body being the vehicle to express interior feelings and desires. Like Adrian, the Egyptian women employed and repeated actions to create interior states of piety. She writes, "Instead of innate human desires eliciting outward human forms of conduct, it is the sequence of practices and actions one is engaged in that determines one's desires and emotions. In other words, action does not issue forth from natural feelings but *creates* them" (Mahmood 2005: 157, italics in original). Instead of bodily acts being indicators of an evolved interior state, the two are necessarily intertwined with each other. Seen through this perspective, Adrian's bodily acts could be reinscribed from foolish or as trying too hard to being an important part of his new masculine self-formation, where actions help form feelings, not merely express them.

Mahmood discusses a young woman named Amal who desires to become shy. Some may read this as hypocritical. Is Amal pretending to be shy to prove to herself and others that she is a pious woman? Mahmood offers an alternative reading. "Instead, taking the absence of shyness as a marker of an incomplete learning process, Amal further develops the quality of shyness by synchronizing her outward behavior with her inward motives until the discrepancy between the two is dissolved. This is an example of a mutually constitutive relationship between body learning and body sense" (Mahmood 2005: 157–158). Amal's behavior, like Adrian's, was not inauthentic but rather constituted her attempt to interiorize outward exhibitions. Work was necessary to align interior and exterior when they are "mutually constitutive" (Mahmood 2005). Adrian's sitting, standing, and change in voice pitch were all necessary to achieve, through discipline, new heterosexual affect, feelings, and piety. Men needed to practice desire work to achieve heterosexuality in what was a self-making project that took years. However, Muslim piety work seems to have been more successful than ex-gay desire work long-term. Ex-gay men frequently failed in their attempts to achieve heterosexuality, despite constantly working on themselves.

Seen through the prism of Mahmood's work, ex-gay Pentecostal men disciplined themselves not only to limit their effeminacy and camp but also to produce heterosexual affect and embodiment. In this way, desire work is not only restrictive but productive of new ways of being, of conceptualizing and actualizing the self. This production often had unintended consequences, including leading some men to use their time in HRM to eventually come out as gay. Foucault's work on "technologies of the self" helps elucidate the work on the self that ex-gay Pentecostal men undertook in their quest toward heterosexuality, a journey that often did not lead to the desired goal. Foucault defined "technologies of the self" as "a certain number of operations on their own bodies and souls, thoughts, conduct, and way of being, so as to transform themselves in order to attain a certain state of happiness, purity, wisdom, perfection, or immortality" (Foucault 1988: 18). Desire work is a technology of the self in its focus on active processes of constant attention, care, and correction of the self. Ex-gay men repeatedly engaged in bodily and emotional performances to establish an inner state of purity of soul that would make evident their transformed masculinity and heterosexuality.

Self-Making in Millennial South Africa: Race, Sexuality, and Masculinity

Desire work did not take place in a historical vacuum. Democracy brought changes in economics, sexual and racial discourses, masculinities, and potentialities for self-making. Selves, like nations, have histories and sociocultural contexts (Giddens 1991; Taylor 1989). They are intimately affected by social, historical, economic, national, and transnational contexts. Public life profoundly shapes inner processes. The African National Congress (ANC), led by Nelson Mandela, was jubilantly elected through peaceful national elections that were broadcast all over the world as evidence of the hopeful beginnings of the "new" South Africa, known as the "Rainbow Nation." The new democratic government promised equality and accessibility for all citizens, especially those who had been marginalized and oppressed under National Party rule. Most citizens entered into democracy with hope for its ability to usher in a more equitable distribution of resources, multiracial representations in government and the public sphere, and equality across races, classes, and genders.

However, since its inception in 1994, democracy in South Africa has been plagued by upheaval and accompanying citizen disappointment and disapproval. By the time the nation celebrated twenty years of democracy in 2014, many South Africans believed that local and national governments were unable or unwilling to provide communities with the necessary physical and material support they were repeatedly promised by the ANC (Reddy 2015). Many critics believed that the postapartheid government was failing its citizens, with politicians putting their own personal gains and needs before those of their constituents. Land was not redistributed to those from whom it had been taken during apartheid. Service delivery protests, often violent, had become a ubiquitous part of democratic life (Von Schnitzler 2016).

The implementation of the Growth, Employment, and Redistribution Plan (GEAR) in 1996 led to the privatization of utilities and poor service delivery to impoverished areas (Dugard 2008; Miraftab 2004).[3] This, combined with the continuation of apartheid-era structural inequalities, led to a postapartheid economic downturn and a growing disillusionment with the ANC. Democratic South Africa has some of the highest unemployment rates in the world (Campbell 2013; Berkowitz 2013), alongside some of the highest crime rates globally (Mthethwa 2008). Its sexual violence rates are also some of the most extreme in the world for a country not at war, but reporting and prosecution rates are low (Smythe 2015). Widespread economic reparations never materialized. All these factors have contributed to "a politics of hope and despair, characterised by a repeating cycle of unrealisable political promises and citizen despair" (Wale 2013: 19). HRM members, like many other South Africans, shared these sentiments with their fellow citizens in the period covered by this ethnography. No one in the ministry expressed satisfaction with the ANC government, its policies, or its provision of resources.

The men in HRM focused on themselves in a postapartheid context where public life seemed out of control and full of what they considered to be "sin" and hopelessness. The ex-gay Pentecostal men in this study focused on introspection, work on the self to reach an ideal, the embrace of therapeutic techniques, flexibility, self-surveillance, and self-mastery. They shared this in common with others in the neoliberal context, where there is a focus on the entrepreneur as an ideal postcolonial citizen. For example, Carla Freeman writes about Barbadians involved in "an ongoing process of envisioning and becoming, as opposed to a given position, status, or state of being that is achieved and established through economic means alone" (Freeman 2014: 2). For the women in Freeman's work and the men in mine, self-making was always in flux and never achieved once and for all—there was always more self-work to do. The men in HRM subjected themselves to constant self-examination and tried to perform mastery of the self's desires. They had this in common with a diverse group of people, including educated youth in Turkey (Ozyegin 2015), American college-aged Facebook users (Gershon 2011), and Russian talk show listeners (Matza 2009). Desire was processual in nature. Ex-gay Pentecostal men did not call themselves terms like "newly straight." Instead, they used "ex-gay" because this self was always in process and never achieved, due to the pull of same-sex desires and activities that could lead one to "sin." I focus on the ex-gay process because it was not something that had an end point. Ex-gay men never arrived completely at heterosexuality or referred to themselves as such. Despite often spending years in the ministry, men still discussed their "struggles" with same-sex attraction and the importance of working on themselves to address their unmet emotional needs (which they believed they sexualized) and their periodic "sexual falls."

However, while the men in HRM were flexible, intent on altering same-sex desires through hard work, and always ready to try new techniques to achieve the goal of heterosexuality, they were also inflexible at the same time. By this I mean that while the men saw themselves as pliable subjects, they were also rigid in their ideas about the rightness and sanctity of heterosexuality. They were willing to be flexible in terms of their behaviors toward achieving heterosexuality but not in their beliefs about its rightness and "ordination" by God. For these ex-gay men God and the Bible were their main sources of authority. They were malleable in their work to achieve a goal, but there was not a question of this goal's morality and sanctity.

HRM was one part of a larger democratic cultural shift in sexual discourses. Ex-gay men discussed sex and sexuality in depth and in great detail, something they shared in common with much of the rest of the nation. A drastic change occurred in South Africa at the end of apartheid in how and where sexual activity and subjectivities were discussed. The government's constitutional protection of gay rights and rise of NGO HIV-prevention messages led to a proliferation of public discourses related to sexuality. Although their work to build a heterosexual self was unique, HRM members also shared with other members of the nation a focus on a new self that was more sexually informed and made conscious sexual decisions. Deborah Posel writes of the new national context, "Sexuality is presented as a site of rational, individual choice and agency—an opportunity for empowerment and 'healthy positive lives.' And the health education campaign is an effort to constitute an essentially modern sexual subject, one who is knowledgeable, responsible, in control, and free to make informed choices" (2005b: 134). HIV/AIDS made democratic sexual subjectivity and its practices— having "safe sex," preaching about and employing the ABCs (abstain, be faithful, use condoms)—key to what it meant to be modern and cosmopolitan. This link between personal empowerment and sexual decision-making became an important piece of what it meant to be a democratic citizen. One problem with this development, however, is its silence about the fact that many South Africans are unable to enact this prescribed sexual self due to unequal power relations and structural oppressions. Ex-gay Pentecostal men shared with other citizens in South Africa in the postapartheid context a focus on being agents in charge of their sexual decisions. For the men in HRM, like for other South Africans in democracy, being a modern citizen meant identifying, speaking about, and analyzing their sexual desires in new ways. The ministry offered a cultural space for men to be public about their desires and to work on them.

Race and Racism

Apartheid was a system of white supremacy based on the strict separation and segregation of the races. Black and coloured South Africans were geographically segregated into townships on the peripheries of urban centers. During apartheid, Afrikaners represented themselves as being "under siege" (Retief 1995: 109), which led to severe legal and social penalties for any white person who challenged the heteronormative and racist status quo. Legally, the Immorality Act regulated interracial sex and homosexuality, as both were understood to disrupt the maintenance of a puritanical Christian nationalism, whereby whites understood themselves as the keepers and guardians of a strict Calvinist morality that needed to be strictly policed (Klausen 2015: 4–10). White women were also subject to public hygiene messages on sex, as they were exhorted to reproduce to stop the so-called black communist onslaught. The Bible was used by Afrikaners to uphold racist, sexist, and homophobic doctrines. Afrikaners saw themselves as God's chosen people, who had come to claim their own promised land, with black and coloured Africans representing non-Christian "others" who were not entitled to human rights and the land on which they lived (Bloomberg and Dubow 1989; Moodie 1975).

White men saw themselves as the guardians of morality and as the linchpin of this white supremacist homophobic system because of a patriarchal lens in which they were the authoritarian leaders of families and the nation. Kobus Du Pisani explains that during apartheid, "there is only one correct way of thinking and behaving. Many men are guilt-driven to obey higher authority. There is a high level of respect for leaders and authority, the adherence to rules, the self-image of moral superiority and the tendency to place people into separate compartments by classifying them as 'different' or 'other'" (Du Pisani 2001: 165). Gays and lesbians fell into the "other" category and were understood as being dangerous to white hegemony. Homosexuals were seen as a threat to the maintenance of apartheid because they were covert and did not lead to the reproduction of the white family, seen as key to the continuation of white rule. White citizens' lives were full of sexual policing.

Although democracy ended the official segregation of apartheid, there were many carry-overs from the apartheid era in the racist views of South African whites toward black and coloured South Africans and in the economic powers of whites, who were allowed to keep their "apartheid loot" (Steingo 2005: 197). While white privilege was rather consistently bound up with political and economic privilege, white South Africans were still a diverse group. Some embraced democratic principles and interracial relationships based on equality and freedom (Besteman 2008). However, for many white South Africans, the white self was an embattled self because they felt that the racial and moral superiority they had enjoyed under National Party rule was under attack. These white men, like those in HRM, felt threatened by democracy and ANC dominance and used the language of "crisis" to reflect their discontent. A South African bumper sticker expresses this well: "Forget about the whale, Rather save the white male" (Morrell 2001: 26) .

Many white men viewed themselves as "victims" of the ANC and its decisions. One ex-gay HRM leader told me, "They [the ANC] stole the rainbow from us," gesturing toward South Africa's construction as the "Rainbow Nation" and the ANC's supposed theft of the nation from white rule (there is an overlap of symbolism here, as the rainbow is also the symbol of gay pride). Ex-gay men, like many white selves in contemporary South Africa, rejected the past and had an attitude of "ignore-ance" (Steyn 2005: 129) toward the past and how it continued to affect and alter the present. Melissa Steyn explains that for many white South Africans, "Being placed in more equal footing is presented as marginalization; the binaries that underpin whiteness are seen to be simply reversed. Whites, it is averred, are now in the same position as black people were in the past under apartheid" (Steyn 2005: 131). The white selves that HRM members developed were part of larger trends of white selves' self-definition as morally righteous and separated from apartheid and its continuing legacies like economic privilege. These white men were dismissive of the ANC government, saying that it was "ruining" the country.

White and coloured ministry members expressed similar views during apartheid about black men as criminal, violent, and oversexed, and coloured men as weak, irresponsible, and predisposed to sexual deviance because of their mixed-race heritage. I often heard that "black" or "African culture" was inferior to white culture and that racial differences had "natural" sexual characteristics. The white men in HRM explicitly constructed their racial and religious selves in relationship to a particular racist sexualization of African and coloured masculinities. Coenraad, an HRM leader who was Afrikaans, explained that sex outside of marriage was central to black masculinity and that black men were "messing up the country"; he pointed to President Jacob Zuma as evidence. Coenraad claimed that black men were less likely to become born-again than whites because, "You will lose some status because it means you can't sleep around playing. It's [sex outside of marriage] very socially acceptable. You [black men] almost have to prove yourself. You must make a woman pregnant. Look at [President] Zuma. It's a social status thing. So many women and so many children." (These ideas are not supported by statistical or academic literatures.) Similarly, white ministry leader Glen said that black and coloured men "have more issues and they have more sex. So I think they are different [than whites]." Bianca, a white woman who is married to a white ex-gay man, said that black men are "very extreme. They have to control. They choose these weak women to dominate them." For these ministry members, there was a link between what they believed were "natural" and well-defined races, cultural contexts, and sexual morality.

The coloured men in the ministry also frequently differentiated themselves from black men, othering this group and constructing them as the abject. These coloured men aligned themselves with the moral and sexual discourses of white HRM members on the dangers of black male leadership in the public realm and the assumption that all black men sought to oppress and rule over black women in the private sphere. To me, it at times seemed like the coloured men in HRM were equally, or even more racist, than the whites. Coloured subjectivities have a complicated history in South Africa, particularly in Cape Town, and they were historically and are still today often associated by community outsiders with promiscuity, miscegenation, and the so-called dangers of racial mixing understood to have begun during colonial conquest. Zimitri Erasmus explains that being coloured is often associated still with "sexualised shame" (Erasmus 2001: 14), with coloured community members talked about as inherently sexually immoral, a topic that was often alluded to and joked about in the ministry. During apartheid, coloured people had less social and political power than whites but more than blacks. Many middle-class coloured men and women sought to differentiate themselves from blacks and were complicit in putting forth racist stereotypes of black men and women in a politics of respectability

(Ruiters 2009: 114–115). Coloured men in the ministry who sought to alter their same-sex desires had to both perform desire work and also fight back against stereotypes, often put forth by the ministry itself, that they were more "sexually broken" due to their racial subjectivities. To counter ideas that positioned them as socially and morally lesser than whites, as well as inherently prone to "sexual sin," this group of coloured men often positioned themselves as ethically superior to unsaved coloured and black men.

White and coloured ministry members said they felt ostracized by the African National Conference (ANC) government because it supported "immorality" through the protection of homosexuality in the constitution, the legalization of abortion, and religious pluralism. Damon, a longtime coloured HRM member, was one of many Pentecostals who were nostalgic for the Christian nationalism of the apartheid government and laws banning same-sex sexual activity and relationships. He told me, "[The] apartheid years were horrible. [silence] A lot of things happened and a lot of people suffered severely. But this [ANC government] is even worse than the whole apartheid era. This crime and constitution [which enshrined gay rights] and all that, is even worse. It scares me. It really does." Many Pentecostals in Cape Town referred to the ANC government as "morally bankrupt" and chose not to engage in politics. These Pentecostals, including the white and coloured men in HRM, reanimated racist and homophobic apartheid-era beliefs by using language such as "sin," "immorality," and "decadence" in reference to the ANC and black individuals and communities.

Many white South Africans have tried to distance themselves emotionally and physically from democracy's multiculturalism. Racism in South Africa has been expressed differently in the postapartheid period. For example, whites' discussions of criminals, street traders, street children, and *bergies*, the homeless, "often serve as new ways to talk about old problems, interests, and conflicts" (Samara 2005: 220). Many white South Africans attempted to veil racist ideas with language such as "order," "safety," and "security" (Samara 2010: 646). Like some, though not all Afrikaans people, the white men in HRM sought to detach themselves from apartheid, its legacies, and its privileges, at the same time that they reinscribed its racist tenets like the link between race and so-called natural moralities. They shared this in common with middle-class white Afrikaners in Bloemfontein, who also sought to "sanitize" white identity, as they "recycled key discourses underlying racist apartheid ideology, particularly discourses of black incompetence and whites under threat " (Verwey and Quayle 2012: 560). These Afrikaners felt that being overtly racist was something to be frowned upon in democracy, so instead they employed images and language of "uncivilized chaos, decay, or barbarism" (Verwey and Quayle 2012: 569) to describe the ANC and to justify their withdrawal from racial mixing and engagement with racial others. Both these whites and the ones in HRM were involved in projects of Afro-pessimism and racial retreat into democracy's ubiquitous gated communities.

The men in HRM did something similar. However, their coded racism was based on gendered and sexual stereotypes of black and coloured men. They sought to be morally superior to these groups of men, continuing apartheid-era beliefs, detailed above, that coded these men as inherently inferior to white men. Instead of seeing themselves as racist, coded as negative in democracy, the men in HRM sought to repackage and recycle Afrikaner narratives of moral masculine superiority. Due to their same-sex attraction, their own masculinities were suspect and could be questioned by others. Through their discourses on black and coloured masculinities as immoral, they reinscribed their own masculinities as superior. Ex-gay men sought to naturalize racial masculine borders as a way to shore up their own masculinities, put into question by their desires for other men. Their racism was heightened due to their own questionable masculinities. They needed to "other" black and coloured men to feel better about themselves. These white selves situated themselves as morally and sexually superior to black and coloured communities.

Cape Town has a special place in the history of white withdrawal from democracy, which is played out in current politics; Cape Town has been the only city in South Africa that was not predominantly black in democracy and whose provincial and city governments were not governed by the ANC in the period covered in this book.[4] Many Capetonian Pentecostals participate in "moral semigration," or withdrawal from the state because of its perceived moral and spiritual bankruptcy. The term "semigration" was originally used in South Africa to describe white disengagement from the state and physical isolation from contact with nonwhites in the postapartheid era (Ballard 2004). Many whites spatially reproduce apartheid's geographies in their choices of where and how to live.

Masculinities

Besides race, transforming masculinity was a key part of ex-gay work on the self in the democratic context. The South African government, local and international NGOs, and public health campaigns publicly advocated for a change in how all men desired and performed heterosexual masculinity (Dworkin et al. 2012; Morrell, Jewkes, and Lindegger 2012). Statistically, the country was one of the most dangerous places on the globe at the beginnings of democracy. It had one of the highest documented numbers of rapes (see, for example, Jewkes, Sikweyiya, and Dunkle 2009; Wood 2005; Jewkes et al. 2002). Coupled with low levels of reporting, poor police response, and inadequate prosecution, "over 90% of rapists and nearly two thirds of men who kill their intimate partner go unpunished in South Africa" (Barker and Peacock 2009: 11). At the time I conducted my year of fieldwork in 2007–2008, the United Nations named South Africa as being within the top five most murderous nations in the world (Mthethwa 2008). The country was in the midst of a self-declared national crime epidemic, much of it consisting of violence within communities and between family members.

The men at HRM generated and authenticated heterosexual desires in a larger context of national desire work, where pervasive violence has led masculinity to be declared in crisis. HRM was only one group in South Africa that proposed to interpret and solve problems arising from the cultural effects of changing laws and social norms in democracy. Despite the number of academic and public conversations on the necessity for men to drastically change, there was little information on the micropractices men should employ to produce more equitable selves (for exceptions, see Peacock 2013; Robins 2008). Men's desires were a national preoccupation, but little was known about desires in terms of process. How were men supposed to change their desires? Ex-gay Pentecostal men were one part of a larger shift in postapartheid national life that attempted to push men to discipline and reform their own sexual desires through self-conscious and directed effort.

South Africa's new democracy was full of gendered extremes. Everyday life was starkly different from the government's wishful decrees of equality. Legally, the Bill of Rights in the Constitution protected the bodily integrity of all citizens. Section 12, subsection 2 of the Bill of Rights states, "Everyone has the right to bodily and psychological integrity, which includes the right (a) to make decisions concerning reproduction; and (b) to security in and control over their body" (1996). However, this ideal often remained out of reach. Helen Moffett contrasts the human rights discourses of democracy with what happened in the private sphere between men and women. She writes, "The flattened and transparent structures associated with democratic practice are eschewed in the domestic, and even more so, the sexual realms" (Moffett 2006: 142). Democracy had different inflections and expressions in public and private contexts.

For women, there was a deep divide between government rhetoric and representation and daily life, which was similar to the stark contrast one finds when comparing the legal protections for gays and lesbians with their social marginalization and frequent victimization by violent hate-crimes (HRW 2011; Mkhize et al. 2010). There were distinct splits between public and private. The constitution may have rhetorically protected women and gays and lesbians, but real life was very different from legal discourse.

Men were said to be destroying the country through their inability to lead, provide, and make and sustain emotional connections (see for example Morrell and Richter 2004; Walker, Reid, and Cornell 2004). When I was in the field in 2007–2008, the South African media was full of stories of sexual violence, detailing what men were doing to women, children, and the nation: the gang rape of lesbians in townships by men, high rates of child abuse, baby rape, and other crimes by South African men crowded the headlines. A headline from the *Sowetan* read, "Woman Killed Dad Who Gave Her HIV-AIDS" (Seleka 2008). The *Daily Sun* had "Rescued, Then Raped" on their front page, which detailed how a woman who was standing on train tracks to commit suicide was stopped by a man who then raped her (Stamier and Kekana 2008). A woman wrote a letter to the editor of *Drum* titled "Wanted: Good Black Men" to ask where she could find a nonabusive partner (Hlaka 2007). In all these examples, men were indicted for the ruin of other citizens and the nation. These public discourses on sensationalized masculinities affected more mundane performances of masculinity for ex-gay men, who sought to be "better" men than those often depicted in the media. Ex-gay men frequently contrasted themselves with the rest of South African men, using the kinds of articles mentioned above as proof of the need for saved men like themselves to "save" the nation from moral ruin. The rise of the ex-gay movement emerged from this convergence of cultural scripts, public discourses, and the availability of new masculine self-making practices in democratic South Africa.

Pentecostalism

Christianity has been significantly transformed in the past hundred years. In 1910, 1.4 percent of the world's Christians lived in sub-Saharan Africa. By 2010, this number had skyrocketed to 23.6 percent (Pew Forum on Religion and Public Life 2011: 9). Pentecostalism is the fastest growing form of Christianity today. More than one-fourth of all Christians are now classified as Pentecostal or charismatic (Hefner 2013).[5] This Pentecostal explosion began in the 1980s in Africa (Freeman 2012). South Africa is a predominantly Christian country and has been for many years. Both the 2001 South African census (Statistics South Africa 2004) and a 2011 Pew Research Study (Pew Forum on Religion and Public Life 2011: 54) found that around 80 percent of South Africans were Christian.[6]

Pentecostalism is now a large part of postapartheid life for many South Africans. In South Africa, there have been distinct changes in religiosity during democracy, with mainstream Christian churches losing members and a soaring rise in Pentecostalism. Pentecostal churches have experienced the greatest increase in adherents since 1994, with a 48 percent growth from 1996 to 2001 (Schlemmer 2008: 24–25). Depending on how one defines "Pentecostal" and which denominations are included, estimates ranging from 10 to 40 percent of South Africa's total population was Pentecostal during the period covered by this ethnography (Anderson 2005: 67); 10 to 20 percent of this group lived in urban areas (Pew Forum on Religion and Public Life 2009; 2006).

Christian conversion has historically provided Africans with a sense of individual agency. Missionaries in the twentieth century offered converted Africans direct access to God's supreme power, instead of working through the ancestors (Ashforth 2005). Many converts to Christianity in sub-Saharan Africa had the least social capital and power, and these women and younger men sought to build subjectivities different from their pasts and the prescriptive identities of "traditional" life, where male elders often had the most social power (Thomas 2000). These converts had the opportunity to shape new selves based on personal relationships with God, Jesus Christ, and the Holy Spirit. Self-reflective subjectivities and interiority are important outcomes of Protestant conversion (Keane 2007). This continues in Pentecostalism, where personal agency and the opportunity to construct a new, improved self is a key part of life for Pentecostal church members.

Pentecostalism is commonly described as a faith of "rupture" beginning with the conversion experience (Thorton 2016; Robbins 2007; Engelke 2004). This Pentecostal project, as David Maxwell categorizes it, is one of "constant emphasis on permanent internal revolution" (Maxwell 2005: 18). It provides a way for many Africans to split from prior ties of ethnicity, tribal affiliation, and kinship and to initiate a new self (van Dijk 1998; Meyer 1998). Becoming a new, improved self is consistent with a long history in Christianity of radical personality changes via conversion, especially for those considered social deviants like alcoholics, criminals, and prostitutes (Wanner 2003; Lovekin and Maloney 1977).

However, postconversion self-making involves work, and although people commonly describe their born-again experience as a rupture, it is more complicated than that. Katrien Pype explains, "Connections with the divine need to be established repeatedly. Christian selves are constantly emerging; they persistently need to be actualized" (Pype 2011: 281). Pentecostal self-making is process-oriented because Pentecostals believe that they live in a "fallen" world where demons and Satan attempt to get Christians to embrace "sin" and stop living a morally righteous lifestyle. Pentecostal self-making is never complete. Achieving salvation is a part of everyday life, a part of constant work on the self. Ex-gay men drew on Pentecostalism's focus on constantly working on the self to remain saved and filled with the Spirit to assist them in becoming heterosexual.

Pentecostals conceive of the faith as a place where they can significantly transform all aspects of their lives as individuals with agency. For many social scientists, Pentecostalism today offers solutions to the traumas of neoliberalism, structural adjustment, and government instability (Maxwell 2005; Comaroff and Comaroff 2000). Pentecostal churches and ministries in Africa are frequently discussed as providing adherents with opportunities for personal authority, honor, and dignity in the face of the negative economic and social effects of neoliberal reform (Cole 2010; Meyer 2007; Newell 2007). These churches offer tools that allow Africans to view and experience themselves as empowered and respected agents in spite of massive unemployment, a lack of social services, and little government accountability. For example, Zambian Pentecostals form intimate social ties that assist them emotionally and materially and allow them to bypass the unfulfilled promises of the state (Haynes 2012). This constant self-work allows Pentecostals to move from "the unredeemed state of being a victim" to "the redeemed status of being a victor" (Maxwell 2006: 194). Pentecostalism offers opportunities for empowerment and agentive decision-making in spite of structural domination.

In particular, Pentecostals believe that conversion and living a sanctified life can have worldly rewards in economic prosperity, transformed gender roles, improved relationships, and even better sex lives, all of which are discussed throughout this book. This new sense of self is primarily effected through changes in family and interpersonal relationships, which include avoiding alcohol, being faithful to one's spouse, maintaining fellowship with church members, and accepting guidance and inspiration from the word of God. Pentecostalism offers a new way to be an empowered self, with increased self-esteem and tools to reach personally defined goals based on religious values, not the values of "the [sinful] world." It supplies the theological language and practical tools that provide entrepreneurial, individualized solutions to economic, social, and familial problems. Pentecostal churches afford concrete ways for many Africans to redefine themselves with Pentecostal, not worldly, criteria, such as abstinence, fidelity, and obedience to the church's teachings. The Pentecostals I worked with in Cape Town did not seek to overthrow the government or work collectively for political change. Instead, they believed that working on themselves and trying to get ahead as individuals was key to thriving in what they considered as democracy's moral laxity and the ANC's political and economic corruption.

Although the Pentecostals I worked with and those around the world believe in the End Times and the importance of reaching heaven after death, much of the focus of their self-work was on what Paul Gifford calls "this-worldly victory" (Gifford 2014: 47), or individual religious empowerment in the here and now. For many African Pentecostals, the economic realm was a key place where they sought to be agentive and to receive God's blessings. Unlike Liberation Theology's privileging of the poor, in Pentecostalism, whether one lives in poverty or in abundance is linked to the Prosperity Gospel, also known as the "health and wealth gospel." In this theological system, poverty is an individual, not a structural problem. Being poor is linked to demonic blockages, or as a punishment for participation in sinful activities and the withdrawal of God's favor (Heuser 2015). The therapeutic ethos of Pentecostalism also affected the Prosperity Gospel in that what was promised to Christians was physical, financial, and emotional prosperity. Prosperity was also linked to happiness; salvation promised material and affective rewards. "Worldly success" is therefore not divorced from trends in the faith that link contentment and empowerment to what God promises to the born-again believer (Soothill 2014). Although the Prosperity Gospel is important for many African Pentecostals (Agana 2016; Omenyo 2014), for the men in HRM, the focus was on gender and sexual empowerment. They felt that it was only through God's help that they could achieve new heterosexual masculine selves. Though they may have believed in Pentecostal doctrines like the Prosperity Gospel, they focused and honed in on religious and ethical ideologies and practices that were key to sexual and gender self-making. While these individuals may have tithed to the church, I did not hear a lot of focus on religious economies or economic reasons for conversion. Instead, ministry members were more focused on the parts of Pentecostalism that offered gender and sexual, not financial, salvation.

Pentecostal churches work directly on the sense of self and the improvement of congregants' personal relations to build happier and more assured members. In South Africa, studies have found that Pentecostals "are characterized by a moving sense of spiritual encounter and a corresponding sense of joy, happiness, and optimism . . . [and] feelings of self-confidence, self-esteem, and a sense of viability" regardless of economic hardship or social marginalization (Johnston 2008: 25). However, these new optimistic Pentecostal selves in South Africa embodied a paradox; the men in HRM often felt agency in their personal lives but felt disenfranchised in the public realm because of democratic laws based on racial, sexual, and gender equality and social norms of integration. Churches and ministries such as HRM have provided a way for some South African Pentecostals to retreat from public life and simultaneously claim to change it. They used Pentecostal beliefs and practices to resist democracy's new legal and cultural norms of racial and social integration. These Pentecostals sought to discount and avoid the state and politics. This was similar to what Ruth Marshall found in her work with Nigerian Pentecostals. She writes, "In its programmatic form, the Born-Again project does not refer to a revolution to create a new institutional order, found a constitution, or elaborate new laws. Rather it represents itself as providing the conditions for the redemption of the religious and political tradition, which were promised in colonial and post-colonial rule, and ruined through it" (Marshall 2009: 204). Pentecostalism offered alternate forms of sources of affiliation, "moral" community formation, and tools to live sanctified lives despite postcolonial problems.

In Cape Town, ex-gay men transformed their moral despair about democracy into hopefulness for personal empowerment through their desire work. They learned that there was a process that they could follow for individual moral "redemption" and for rebuilding themselves despite the more liberal and secular surrounding environment. These Pentecostals looked to themselves to perform personal transformation because public interventions seemed an ineffectual waste of time.

Pentecostal Gender and Sexuality

Pentecostalism offered Africans the language and tools to enable new ways of being a cisgendered man or a woman and ways to embody a saved sexual self (van de Kamp 2016; Burchardt 2015; Frahm-Arp 2012). HRM was one part of a larger trend in African Pentecostalism, discussed in more detail in chapter 4, whereby the faith was a way to have a gendered and sexual conversion experience. Men and women learn new vocabularies, ways of relating to each other, how to categorize desires as "godly" or not, what to do with the "ungodly" feelings, what kinds of sex were "ordained" by God, what sex acts He disapproved of and why, and the "appropriate" ways to be a godly woman or man in a "fallen" world.

For men, Pentecostalism often meant growing in prestige in the eyes of other religious men but losing much of the respect of secular masculine peers.[7] Transnationally, many Pentecostal men constructed what they saw as superior masculine selves through Pentecostal conversion and practices (van Klinken 2012; Smilde 2007; Wilcox 2004). Evangelical men in Colombia stopped hegemonic masculine activities like violence, drinking, smoking, gambling, and pre- and extramarital sex to form selves that were more oriented toward their homes and churches, viewing themselves as "better" than their unsaved contemporaries (Brusco 1995). In Tanzania, many Pentecostal men expressed in their postconversion testimonials "relief and pride" in being "proper and responsible" husbands and fathers who could embody Christian respectability (Lindhardt 2015: 7). The men in HRM also felt personally enabled through embracing and embodying Pentecostal gender roles. They were taught about gender complementarianism, where men and women both had "God-given" gender roles but men were the leaders and had more power in interpersonal and public contexts. For ex-gay men, who were often ridiculed for being effeminate and who also felt less than masculine, learning that they were biblically, theologically, and biologically built for leadership made them feel empowered. It also helped them gain in prestige in the eyes of other Christians as the men in the ministry were publicly proclaimed to be moving from "sin" to salvation in leaving behind same-sex desires and behaviors.

Ex-gay Pentecostal men in South Africa also believed that they became improved masculine selves through their desire work, but they felt threatened by domestication or anything linked to women because they already felt feminized by their same-sex desires. Their masculinity was more focused on self-control, particularly of sexuality, than the domestic sphere. They sought to be "better" than the men around them through constructing sexual self-control and abstinence as evidence of possessing a moral masculine character. This is similar to what Adriaan van Klinken found in his study of Zambian heterosexual Pentecostal men. These men saw themselves as superior to secular men because "holiness requires self-control. In contrast to their peers who cannot control themselves and simply follow their desires, for born-again men the ability to control the self becomes a way of proving male strength" (van Klinken 2012: 225). Similarly, in Benin, Pentecostal men were taught gendered self-control in order to avoid engaging in polygamy or cheating on their wives (Quiroz 2016). Ex-gay Pentecostal men in South Africa also conceptualized desire work as evidence of masculine vigor, instead of viewing it as the loss of masculine prestige. The men in HRM saw themselves as stronger, not softer, than unsaved men because they could exercise self-control. For men like Adrian, with whom I began this chapter, sexual self-control was recoded as masculine. Pentecostalism was key to gendered and sexual self-making.

In a Christian framework where men are supposed to lead the family and nation, masculinity that is "broken" leads to major societal breakdown. South Africa's declared "crisis in masculinity" at the time I did my fieldwork (Hunter 2010; Jewkes, Sikweyiya, and Dunkle 2009) was one part of a larger continental "crisis" in masculinity occurring in the postcolonial context because of violence and HIV/AIDS (Wyrod 2016; Smith 2006). Pentecostal churches often positioned themselves as key actors in these conversations, offering conversion and church membership as the solutions to "immoral" masculinities (Lindhardt 2015; van Klinken 2013; Soothill 2007). These churches claimed to provide men with new selves that were less violent and more nurturing and loving toward women and children.

South African Pentecostals said the lack of father figures was one of the key reasons for the nation's moral crisis. Popular Christian self-help writer Leanne Payne writes, "When enough individuals are out of touch with the masculine, a whole society is weakened on every level of existence" (Payne 1995: 82). The Pentecostals I worked with believed that apartheid's destruction of the family contributed to a nation of wounded men incapable of intimacy who used sexual conquests, fathering children without support, and crime as ways to prove masculinity.[8] Pentecostals in HRM and the Church of the Reborn used the language of "brokenness" in their explanations for why individual men acted "immorally," for example, participating in "ungodly" sexual behaviors and harming women and children. They applied the same concepts to societal problems and the nation itself, calling South Africa a "broken nation."

David, a coloured man who worked at the church and took HRM classes, believed that the nation's high rates of violence and moral failures were linked to a lack of fathers in the home. He told me, "So the core problem of our nation is the house. If you break down the family, you sort of break down the nation. Because then all the social ills of society will flow from that. From brokenness in the family." HRM offered ministry members and those who attended their classes a unique form of Pentecostal masculinity that provided a specific and masculine response to the postapartheid period. They were actively and self-consciously working on achieving new masculine selves. They believed that new kinds of men would "save" South Africa from the "depravities" of democracy. The ex-gay Pentecostal men I worked with differentiated themselves from non-Christian men by claiming that the latter focused on externals to achieve masculinity like sports, sexual prowess, and drinking. Desire work was characterized by men taking the role of "spiritual warriors" for their families, and taking control, initiating, and having emotional strength. These Pentecostal men also thought they should be integrated beings with emotions that they felt deeply and could express without shame.

Throughout this book, I examine the intersections and disjunctures in discourses and practices of sexuality, masculinity, and morality that occur during the formation of the ex-gay Pentecostal self. Men sought to express and temporarily resolve personal and cultural anxieties through the formation of new selves. Desire work was a way for men to personally respond to a national crisis in masculinity through a focus on individual transformation of the self via hard work.

The Politics of Homosexuality in Africa

Homosexual behaviors and relationships have a long history in Africa that predates colonialism (Hoad 2007; Epprecht 2004). Marc Epprecht explains that same-sex sexual activities in much of southern Africa were not understood contextually as sex because they were divorced from fertility. Privacy and discretion allowed same-sex activities to exist without community-wide condemnation (Epprecht 2004: 132). African cultural norms of respectability and propriety led to "de facto tolerance"—sex was not generally discussed (Epprecht 1998). The sexual subjectivity of the "homosexual" or "gay" person sometimes replaced and sometimes existed alongside prior models for same-sex sexual activity in southern Africa after contact with Europeans. Colonialism brought with it judicial regulation and a tightening up of cultural restrictions. Under National Party rule, legislation and cultural policing only intensified.

As stated earlier, for the National Party, homosexuality was a threat to white hegemony and rule. The government began increasingly to scrutinize gay men after apartheid was established and its power entrenched. The authorities periodically policed homosexuality with sweeps and arrests in public areas during the 1950s, for example where men were cruising for sex. As the National Party gained more control of the country in the mid-1960s,[9] white homosexuality came under intense surveillance and punishment, a trend that continued as apartheid cemented its hold on the nation (Du Pisani 2012). What motivated the change from minor enforcement to moral crusade had little to do with a change in the public's knowledge about or the visibility of homosexuality. Instead, "led by Prime Minister Verwoerd's clampdown on liberation movements and the formalization of apartheid South Africa, South African authorities consolidated Afrikaner 'Christian nationalism' control over the country, expelling from the *laager* anything that was deemed threatening to white civilization" (Gevisser 1995: 30). White men in positions of power believed that those white men who participated in same-sex sexual activities contributed to the moral degeneration of white society.

Whites originally passed the Immorality Act in 1927 (and amended it in the 1950s) in an attempt to quell sexual expression outside of racially homogenous heterosexual unions. They made so-called illicit sexual acts and subjectivities illegal. Despite these legal restrictions and moral sanctions, gay communities and organizations existed in cities like Cape Town, Durban, and Johannesburg during apartheid (see, for example, Tucker 2009; De Waal, Manion, and Cameron 2006; Hoad, Martin, and Reid 2005). Much of black and coloured South Africans' sexual activities flew under the radar during apartheid as long as they did not affect white society (Jones 2008: 404). However, not everyone in coloured and black communities accepted same-sex sexual activities. Many communities believed that *moffies*, *isitabane*, *sekswanas*, and gay men and women were immoral, unnatural, and un-African.

In the coloured community, men who self-identified or were designated as *moffies* (which could alternatively mean someone who was effeminate, gay, a drag queen, or transgender) were often visible parts of the community (Tucker 2009). However, heterosexual coloured elites did not usually accept *moffies* or *moffie* culture. Cody Perkins explains, "Coloured elites felt that *moffies* threatened Coloured social standing within South Africa and hampered Coloured men's claims to respectable ideals along the lines of those accepted by White South Africans" (Perkins 2015: 153).

Despite coloured elites attempts to silence those who they felt threatened the social order, *moffies* were often a visible and vibrant part of coloured working-class subcultures in places like Cape Town, at least before the forced removals of the Group Areas Act in 1950 demolished neighborhoods such as District Six (Chetty 1995: 117). For example, gayle, or *moffietaal* (gay language), is a well-studied part of coloured culture. Gayle was a way to discuss and conceal gay life during apartheid.[10] Many believe that the language (a mix of Afrikaans and English) originated in the Western Cape, in coloured communities. A variety of speakers across racial lines used gayle (Cage 2003: 18–19). Though frowned upon by elites who were invested in racial respectability, *moffies* were a visible part of coloured communities during apartheid and continue to be so today.

The international antiapartheid movement changed the range of possibilities for self-making offered at home and in the larger world for black South Africans with same-sex desires. These South Africans understood themselves differently as apartheid progressed. In particular, the 1980s and early 1990s led to the emergence of new models for same-sex sexuality that focused less on gender identity and more on having a self that was based on sexuality. The emergence of a gay subjectivity in black communities in South Africa in the last decades of apartheid had local and international sources, such as the addition of sexuality by exiled ANC leaders to their non-discrimination rhetoric, a new awareness by many that there was an international and supportive gay community, and the first Gay Pride March in the country in 1990 in Johannesburg (Donham 2002: 418–419). Before this time, effeminate individuals or those known to participate in same-sex sexual activities were usually called *isitabane*,[11] and they often became socially reinscribed as women, hermaphrodites, or intersex. Amanda Lock Swarr explains, "In Soweto and other South African rural and township areas, slippage among bodies, sexual practices, and identification was notable among those who are labeled as stabane" (Swarr 2009: 530). For example, Linda Ngcobo was an openly gay Zulu antiapartheid activist. Although born with male genitals, Ngcobo saw herself and was raised by her family as a girl. She had designated female chores, clothing, and social roles—even singing as a soprano girl in her father's Zionist church choir. The above changes in South African social and political life had an important effect on individuals like Ngcobo, who stopped identifying as a woman and reconceptualized himself as a gay man at the end of apartheid (McLean and Ngcobo 1995: 169). In black communities, new sexual selves became possible in the waning days of National Party rule; a diversity of gender and sexual selves continues today.

Contemporary Africans largely view homosexuality and gay rights in a negative light, despite a history of same-sex sexual behaviors and gay selves in South Africa and other parts of the African continent. Homosexuality is currently illegal in thirty-eight countries in Africa (Amnesty International 2013: 7). Campaigns like the "Kill the Gays" bill in the Ugandan Parliament have garnered international attention in the past few years to the politics of African LGBTI lives. A member of the Ugandan Parliament came up with the "Anti-Homosexuality Bill" in 2009, proposing that people should be imprisoned and even killed for being homosexual (Cheney 2012; Sadgrove et al. 2012). The constitutional court struck the bill down in 2014 for a legal technicality. Lawmakers then drafted more legislation to replace it: the Prohibition of Promotion of Unnatural Sexual Practices bill (Smith 2014). Gay Ugandans still remain under threat of arrest and imprisonment.

Gays and lesbians are vilified as being outside the moral fabric of the nation, un-African, and not deserving of rights in countries such as Malawi, Senegal, Zimbabwe, and Namibia (see, for example, Lorway 2015; Thoreson 2014; Msibi 2011). To oppose this, African gay rights activists have argued that gays and lesbians should be protected by universal human rights and that being gay is historically part of the African social fabric (Epprecht 2013). Condemnation of homosexuality seems to be part and parcel of a politics of scapegoating in Africa, what Sylvia Tamale calls a "politics of distraction" whereby leaders attempt to divert attention away from political and economic crises by focusing on the supposed national dangers of homosexuality (Tamale 2013: 39).

Many Africans across the continent understand the West as trying to import a neocolonial "moral imperialism" to Africa veiled in the language of human rights (Kaoma 2014: 236). Politicians in many African nations have sought to distance themselves from South Africa's legally progressive stance and its constitutional protection of sexual orientation. Leaders like Robert Mugabe of Zimbabwe have made clear that homosexuality is un-African and should be punishable. For example, in a speech in 2011, Mugabe stated, "It is condemned by nature. It is condemned by insects and that is why I have said they are worse than pigs and dogs" (quoted in Laing 2011). The ANC leadership does not consistently support gay rights either, despite constitutional protection. South African president Jacob Zuma said in 2006 at a Heritage Day celebration (before he became the nation's president), "When I was growing up an *ungqingili* (a gay) would not have stood in front of me. I would knock him out," along with stating that gay marriage was "a disgrace to the nation and to God" (quoted in Robins 2008: 148).

Many Christians, particularly Pentecostals, are at the forefront of African homophobia, joining other Africans in their beliefs that homosexuality is unnatural and un-African (Chitando and van Klinken 2016a; van Klinken and Chitando 2016). There is a convergence of religious and political leaders' homophobic rhetoric in much of Africa (Gunda 2010: 37). Pentecostals frequently believe gays and lesbians should be punished by the state. Public officials often join religious leaders and everyday believers in their calls for LGBTI Africans to be marginalized, change themselves, hide, and/or be punished for same-sex attractions and activities. Conservative Christians add another layer of antigay beliefs in their ideas that homosexuality is unbiblical and demonic. Passages used to say that homosexuality is unbiblical are called "clobber passages" because they are used to beat the LGBTI community with the Bible. Christians frequently use Genesis 19:15, Leviticus 20:13, Romans 1:26–27, and 1 Timothy 1:9–10 as biblical proof that God condemns homosexuality. Some religious leaders deny that homosexuality exists at all in their societies,[12] while others blame it on a diversity of causes like Western imposition,[13] colonial holdover, the supernatural, and/or recruitment by the LGBTI community. In Cameroon, for example, homosexuality is linked to the devil and the End Times, with LGBTI visibility understood as evidence of Satan's international growth and dominance (Lyonga 2016: 60).

So why does homophobia (which of course has national and local inflections) seem to be a hallmark of much of African Christianity in the early twenty-first century? The meteoric rise of Pentecostalism has made religious competition a key piece of the African religious landscape and raised the stakes of moral rhetoric. Adriaan van Klinken states, "Making homosexuality a major issue in public debate, Pentecostals also make it difficult for other churches to take a more nuanced position as this could easily be used against them on a highly competitive religious market" (van Klinken 2015: 145). The export of the American culture war on homosexuality has also led to an increase in religiously motivated homophobia in Africa (Kaoma 2009: 4). Kapya Kaoma explains that there is an "insidiously inverse relationship between LGBTI rights in the United States and in Africa; any advancement toward full equality in the United States is depicted as evidence of a growing homosexual threat to the world" (Kaoma 2013: 78). Politicians and religious leaders frequently tell other Africans to fear the growing "homosexual agenda" that seeks world domination. In Uganda, for example, homosexuality is closely linked to Western values and the possession of an inauthentic national identity (Valois 2016: 39).

Debates on homosexuality are also hotbed issues in more mainstream African churches. In the Anglican Communion, homosexuality has been extremely divisive and has set the stage for other churches to fight against more liberal branches of their denominations (Chitando and van Klinken 2016b: 6). Anglican bishops censured homosexuality at the 1998 Lambeth Conference (held every decade). African religious leaders spurred the vote to outlaw gay ordination and for clergy to be prohibited from performing LGBTI commitment ceremonies (Hoad 2007: 51). The Anglican Communion has kept up the pressure on not accepting and welcoming gays and lesbians, and in January 2016, it disciplined the Episcopal Church for three years because of its open and affirming stance, its consecration of gay bishops, and its performance of same-sex marriages (Domonoske 2016). However, some churches in Africa are progressive toward gay rights. This includes South Africa's Anglicans and, perhaps surprisingly, the Dutch Reformed Church (known by many as the church of apartheid), which in 2015 voted to recognize same-sex relationships (though not call them marriages) and to ordain gay ministers without requiring them to take a vow of celibacy (DeBarros 2015; Ngubane 2015).

The nation of South Africa stands out as an exception on the African continent because gay rights are legally protected. Since becoming democratic in 1994, South Africa has formed a government based on the concept of universal human rights, with equality for gay people and the rights of women enshrined in the Equality Clause of the Constitution (Cock 2005; Stychin 1996). Gay men and women are also able to legally marry (Berger 2008). However, public attitudes and interpersonal behavior are not in line with governmental protections. Intense moral disapproval toward same-sex sexuality contrasts sharply with the ideologies of the Equality Clause. In democratic South Africa, homosexuality represents larger social anxieties about social change brought on by the new human rights–based constitution, its accompanying discourses, and social movements calling for its implementation. HRM members shared with the majority of South Africans the attitude that homosexuality is wrong, including black nationalists who think that homosexuality is un-African as well as a Western colonial import (Epprecht 2004). Lesbian women frequently experience verbal harassment and assault, which they usually do not report to police (Nel 2008; Reid and Dirsuweit 2002). So-called corrective rape of lesbians is a well-known and commonly used tactic, sometimes endorsed by families, to punish lesbians and "fix them" in black townships (Currier 2012; Gontek 2009; Muholi 2004).

Between 2003 and 2007, studies found that 80 percent of South Africans over sixteen years of age believed that sex between two people of the same sex is "always wrong" (Roberts and Reddy 2008).[14] In the Western Cape, slightly lower numbers of the population held this opinion, at 68 percent, suggesting that the province that includes Cape Town is more liberal in its attitudes toward homosexuality. A 2013 Pew Research Center study found that 61 percent of South Africans surveyed answered the question "should society accept homosexuality" negatively. I am unsure how to account for the 20 percent difference in these statistics between 2008 and 2013. Part of it may be who did the survey, who was surveyed, and how the question was worded. Despite this discrepancy, these numbers still stand in sharp contrast to other African countries surveyed. For example, 98 percent of Nigerians, 96 percent of Ugandans and Ghanaians, and 90 percent of Kenyans believed that society should not accept homosexuality. Public disapproval is lower in the United States, where only 33 percent of the population said that homosexuality should not be accepted (Pew Research Center 2013: 1).

South Africa has a history of homosexuality, gay selves, and homophobia. HRM was not the first group of people to try to "cure" same-sex attraction and behavior in South Africa. Beginning in 1969 the South African Defence Force (SADF) had a psychological unit to "cure" white soldiers who were categorized as "homosexual." These "cures" included electro-shock treatment, hormone prescription, and sex-reassignment surgery, which frequently occurred without patient consent (Vincent and Camminga 2009: 685; Van Zyl et al. 1999). Outside of formal institutions, individuals also sought a variety of "cures" and went to a variety of "experts." For example, black antiapartheid activist Simon Nkoli wrote about telling his parents that he was gay in the mid-1970s. They took him to three separate kinds of healers for treatment—four separate *sangomas* (traditional healers) with various opinions (two who said he was bewitched, and two who said there was no problem), a Catholic priest who told him to repent, and finally a psychologist who told him to accept himself as gay (Nkoli 1995, 1993). Although this is the anecdotal account of one person, I note it because it illustrates, along with the SADF hospital example above, that not only were there people identifying as "gay" during apartheid but also that there were a multiplicity of local solutions to homosexuality from various community "experts" at the same time.

The history of homosexuality in South Africa is intimately linked to Cape Town. During apartheid, the city and surrounding areas had "protogay neighborhoods," including Sea Point for white gay men, where HRM was located, and District Six for coloured men (Gevisser 1995: 27). The communities had little contact until the 1990s due to apartheid's institutionalized racism and geographic separation (Tucker 2009; Leap 2005). HRM could only be public and flourish during the postapartheid period because gayness was protected and public. A diversity of "cures" are still available for homosexuality beyond HRM. I've picked up tracts in downtown Cape

Town that advertise healings by *sangomas* (traditional healers) for a variety of problems that include homosexuality, erectile dysfunction, and other forms of "misfortune." Many of the men I knew in HRM had gone for a variety of other "cures," including deliverance (the casting out of demons and demonic cleansing) at their local churches, before learning about and joining the ministry.

This book is about sexual and gendered self-making for men who were at the intersections and margins of both LGBTI and Pentecostal communities. The ex-gay movement gained traction in South Africa, particularly in Cape Town, Africa's "gay capital," because of LGBTI visibility in democracy. Despite violence and social stigma, there are vibrant LGBTI communities in Cape Town, although they are segregated by race. These communities were key to HRM's formation and growth in democracy because LGBTI visibility generated space for the growth of new sexual and gender subjectivities, politics, and group memberships. Events held by the Triangle Project (Cape Town's LGBTI center), marches for rights, annual Pride Parades, and parties like the Mother City Queer Project all made space for LGBTI Africans to be public about their desires and engage in their own self-making projects. South African LGBTI demands for recognition and rights made it possible for the members of HRM to do the same, to be public about who they were without apology and advocate for their rights as members of the new democratic nation. The men in HRM feared gay men but also were enabled by gay visibility to make claims for rights, for the ability to name their own subject-positions, and to construct a narrative of sexual liberation—even though this narrative was in opposition to the LGBTI one.

Ex-gay men felt ostracized from the gay community because of what they perceived to be its anti-Christian bias and hypersexualization but were still drawn to it and its so-called "worldly perversions." In many ways, the men in this book line up with other African Pentecostals in their beliefs that homosexuality is demonic and morally wrong, though they struggled with being judged and ridiculed for their so-called "sinful" desires. HRM members held stereotypical ideas of the gay male community, viewing it as full of "sexual sinners" who had frequent and dysfunctional nonemotional sexual encounters. Few had been part of the gay community or even at its peripheries before their time in the ministry. Instead, most had fantasized about other men or had what they hoped were discreet sexual encounters. Overall, these men viewed their same-sex desires and their consequences as the biggest failures in their lives and sought to transform themselves through desire work. Even after some HRM ex-members came out, detailed in chapter 5, few were involved extensively in gay and lesbian specific activities or communities, though this changed for some men slowly over time. These men, especially at the beginnings of leaving the ex-gay lifestyle, had trouble letting go of their views of other gay men as overly sexual and the gay community as a place that enabled "deviant" sexualities. It was hard for them to give up their stereotypical views on gay men as hypersexual and lesbians as emotional manipulators.

Negotiating My Identity

This book is based on fieldwork in Cape Town in 2004 and 2005, from 2007 to 2008, and in 2013. My introduction to the ministry through Brian made it much easier for me to do my fieldwork. Brian is a white ex-gay Pentecostal man originally from outside of Los Angeles. His role as an American who broke South African norms allowed me to break these social conventions as a woman. Brian always talked about sex—who he used to have sex with, where, if he was still "like that," if the person in the corner was definitely his type, and so on—and as a fellow American my questions and comments on sex were not seen as strange. Between 2004 and 2007 I lived in San Francisco, which contributed to the idea that I was not easily shocked about anything to do with sex since I had lived in one of the world's "pink capitals."

South African Pentecostal men are not encouraged to spend time alone with women because it could communicate an interest in dating, as well as provide a venue for sexual transgressions. This rule never applied to me because I was an outsider. I spent a great deal of one-on-one time with various Pentecostal men. I also talked about topics that South African Pentecostal women were not supposed to discuss with men. I was "one of the guys" because I was good at sexual innuendo and would discuss sex and sexuality in detail with them. There was, however, a double standard for both sexuality and sexual pasts. As a woman, my past sexual exploits could not be too numerous if I were to remain respectable. I chose to share sexual experiences about long-term relationships because they did not put me in the promiscuous category. The men, however, could have numerous anonymous sexual encounters without the same judgment.

In her work with teenagers at an American high school, C. J. Pascoe writes about establishing a "least gendered identity" where she drew upon "masculine cultural capital" in order to distance herself from normative femininity (Pascoe 2007: 181). She did this because in her work with adolescent boys she sought to be less sexualized by them. Similarly, in my work I thought of myself as embracing a "least sexual identity" in that I did not want my own sexuality to be the focus of how the men in HRM saw and interacted with me. I self-identify as a lesbian, and I knew this would make the men treat me differently because they were wary of lesbians, seeing them as mannish, gender confused, irrational, and incapable of having healthy emotional relationships. HRM believed that men "acted out" sexually and women "acted out" emotionally. Lesbians were seen as dangerous to be in relationships with because they were viewed as inherently dysfunctional and as having more issues to overcome than gay men. I did not seek to lie to the men in the ministry but I did not want to be put into a box as emotionally and spiritually dangerous. If anyone asked me direct questions about my sexuality or sexual past, I answered them, but in general I sought to have a "least sexual identity." At the end of my year of fieldwork I did share with many of the men my own sexual past and identity, which garnered a mixed response. Alwyn, for example, felt betrayed by me and upset that I had not shared my own struggles and been honest when he felt that he had been authentic and vulnerable with me. Michael and Liam were more forgiving and felt relieved that their own struggles made them seem less like "freaks" based on my also being gay. They said that my own subjectivity meant I could understand them better. Liam added that he would not have told the ministry either because they were so judgmental. For me, a "less sexual identity" allowed me to do my fieldwork, though it did make me uncomfortable.

I am not a Pentecostal nor did I present myself as one. I was raised in a mixed religious household with a Jewish mother and a Christian father and presented myself as such. I was raised closer to the Christian side of my family and went to Divinity School, so I was well versed in the Bible and more mainstream Christian rituals, worship, and theologies. Initially I found Pentecostal worship, with its live electronic band music and spiritual embodiment, exotic and overwhelming in comparison to my staid Presbyterian childhood experiences. Over time, I learned to enjoy the music and became more at ease with the more lively and charismatic parts of church and ministry life, like speaking in tongues, being filled with the Holy Spirit, and the focus on the demonic, though the latter did make me uncomfortable at times. No one tried to convert me to Pentecostalism, though those who knew I was not baptized thought I should be in the Church of the Reborn. During the time before my fieldwork I was attending a nondenominational open and affirming church, Glide Memorial Church, in San Francisco, so when Brian and I would have conflicts about submission to his or Pastor Jurie's authority, I deferred to my affiliation there, saying it was my home church and not Church of the Reborn. For example, when I was told to submit, I would say that I did not have to because I was not at my home church, and I let the ministry infer that I may have submitted there. I found that being part Jewish also gave me some room to fall back on when I felt overwhelmed or needed some distance. For example, when I was asked why I was not baptized, I said it was because it would upset my mother, which was true, but I did not mention I did not want to be baptized either.

I was a participant-observer at a number of fieldsites and volunteered in the ministry's office to perform administrative tasks. I did semistructured interviews with thirty-one people, some multiple times, lasting from one to four hours in 2008 and 2013. In 2007 I was frequently at the Church of the Reborn. I spent two or three days a week in HRM's offices in the church building and attended Sunday morning and evening services. Every Wednesday night I participated in a Life Group, a small gathering of church members living in the same neighborhood or with something in common, for example, there were groups for youth and married couples. These two-hour gatherings combined worship, prayer, Bible study, and socializing.

In 2007, I hesitatingly agreed to be an assistant leader for the same "Life Matters for the Family" course I had observed in 2005. I consented only because I was not expected to teach but just to observe for the eight weeks of the class.[15] The leaders held a weekly prayer and spiritual warfare (the belief that there is a constant and persistent war between Satan and God that Christians must also actively participate in through spiritual battles) session, went to class, and finally broke into smaller gender-segregated groups for discussion and prayer. I was assigned to a leader with an abrasive communication style; the six women in our small group all dropped out of the class by the fourth week. I was relieved because I was uncomfortable with the leader, specifically when she told two women their feelings were "wrong" and another that she misread the Bible.

I attended the ministry's annual weekend retreat in 2004 and 2008. Leaders went away together to socialize, pray, talk about the future of the ministry, and discuss the past year. In 2008, I attended a secular sexual addiction conference in Cape Town run by Patrick Carnes, an international expert on sexual addiction from the United States, with HRM leaders. In 2005 and 2007, I attended the ministry's annual fundraising events. The event in 2005 was an informal dinner at an upscale restaurant; in 2007, the fundraiser featured a formal "ball" with dancing and a charity auction. I was also present for a Gay Pride Parade Outreach during Cape Town's 2008 Gay Pride festivities and was the scribe at Strategic Planning meetings, though

I was not allowed to attend board or counseling supervision meetings because they were confidential. Gossip was an important part of my fieldwork since it was very popular in the ministry, although everyone claimed it was wrong and a "tool" of Satan. For example, the content of board meetings, like most other "confidential" matters, was discussed in detail by almost everyone.

I spent my social time with ministry and church members. I attended an evangelical/Pentecostal Singles Ball and a number of Christian weddings with a leader who was a wedding photographer. HRM, church members, and I shared meals and went to the gym, on picnics, out for coffee and wine tasting, and to the movies. My apartment became a hub of social activity; I had afternoon teas and dinners with friends from HRM and the church a few times a week. It was often easy to forget the rampant homophobia of HRM. Sometimes when we were at the movies or drinking tea at my apartment and chatting, I felt like I was studying a group of kind, funny, and quirky men, but then I'd be reminded through homophobic or racist comments that I was studying a group with whom I had key differences. For example, I did not agree with HRM's beliefs and ideas about homosexuality. I did not and do not believe that gay people, including me, are going to hell, have psychological problems, or are doomed to a life of unhappiness unless they change their sexual orientations.

I think that there is value in studying groups we do not agree with, and I situate this book within a longer trajectory of scholars studying groups on the Right, groups of people different from themselves (see for example Bornstein 2005; Blee 2002; Harding 2000; Ginsburg 1989). Other scholars who have studied the ex-gay movement have also disagreed with their rhetoric (Gerber 2012; Erzen 2006). Anthropology has historically studied the disenfranchised, but I was interested in studying a group that could not be rehabilitated into a feminist or social justice project (for a discussion on this, see Mahmood 2005).

I also spent time with ministry members' openly gay friends. I was initially surprised that for his thirtieth birthday Afrikaans HRM leader Alwyn invited people with a range of sexual selves. Even more shocking to me at the time was that almost everyone came to the party. For hours, people chatted, laughed, and drank wine together. One of the first steps in starting the ex-gay process is that one is supposed to stop talking to anyone from "the [gay] lifestyle" and to stay away from gay people and places. Although some of the men in HRM lived like this, I found that the longer they were in the ministry, the more likely they were to have "out" gay friends. The men became very close in the years they knew each other and were frequently unwilling to stop being friends if someone left the ministry. On many occasions, I found myself spending time in a group made up of Pentecostal ex-gay and formerly ex-gay men.

Many people left or were forced out of HRM and the Church of the Reborn during my year of fieldwork, including me. Brian and I had a series of arguments about HRM's choice to do a Pride Outreach in 2008 and to hand out hundreds of business cards advertising an "after-party" website that was actually for an anonymous ex-gay organization, which I write about in chapter 5. When I communicated that I thought lying about the website was wrong, Brian told me to stop questioning his decisions and to "submit" to his authority. After a few rounds of "Bible chicken" and a loud argument in the church offices, I was thanked for my service and told not to come into the office anymore.[16]

This conflict complicated my fieldwork, which ended up being split into two phases. I spent the first seven months largely in the ministry offices and at the church. In the second phase I worked from my apartment and followed people who were present and past ministry members or worked/attended Church of the Reborn. I originally thought that being on the outs with Brian would harm my fieldwork, but it turned out to be very useful. I learned how unhappy people were, and as an official outsider I was viewed as safe for sharing complaints and gossip. I attended services at churches that past HRM leaders and church employees joined, spending my Sundays at a variety of evangelical and Pentecostal churches in and around Cape Town, including the Vineyard and His People.

I was also accepted as a researcher and volunteer because of Pentecostal causality, where otherworldly intervention affects choices, for example, the frequently invoked "God laid it on my heart." Brian believed that God told him to come to South Africa and begin the ministry. I always told people I was an anthropologist doing research and was not a missionary, but I was frequently introduced as a missionary despite my objections. Some of the members and workers at the church believed I had come to South Africa to find a husband. One Church of the Reborn staff member came into the HRM office one morning to tell me that "God had shown her" that I had "flown over the ocean" to find the husband God "ordained" for me. She was disappointed with me when I left single.

The ministry had become much more official since 2004. The first two summers I volunteered in the office without any formality. However, before I could be approved to work with the ministry in 2007, I had to write a religious and sexual biography for the Board. I was also told that I needed to sign three quasi-legal forms. The first was a detailed Release from Liability, where I agreed not to sue the ministry for any physical, emotional, or spiritual trauma, including negligence. The second form was a Leadership Agreement detailing what kind of emotional and sexual conduct were not allowed and the consequences for participating in such activities. The third form detailed the ministry's policy on consequences and official steps that a person who broke the leadership requirements had to go through in order to be reinstated. I also had to agree to have an "accountability partner" to whom I was supposed to report any sexual or moral transgressions, though partner is a misnomer. Partners actually acted more as confessors. My partner was Abigail, a white woman in her sixties who was not ex-gay, though she came from a background of "sexual brokenness" and was married to a pedophile when she was younger. She and I were supposed to meet every month, but we only had one official meeting in the six months I was assigned to her. After my falling-out with Brian about the Pride Parade, I was removed from the "team" and was no longer expected to meet with Abigail. I dreaded what I was going to be asked to disclose in our one meeting; to my relief, the meeting was mostly gossiping.

My physical appearance, including my femininity, was important to my fieldwork. During one of my trips Brian asked me how often I wore skirts in a given week and about my grooming habits. Would I say I wore skirts once a week, a month, or never? Was I in touch with my femininity? How often did I wear makeup? I did not like this line of questioning. It made me angry and it came up at various times from Brian and other leaders. If I had looked very feminine, like the other women at the church, I would have been subject to the same social norms. This would have cut me off from the men in the ministry. However, I still had to be legible as a woman. Physical appearance, especially masculinity and femininity, are linked to recovery and emotional healthiness in the ex-gay movement. If I had veered too much into the androgynous or "butch" categories, I would have been seen as having unacknowledged problems and become less of a peer and more of a counselee or someone in need of "gender mentoring."

I had to regulate not only my gender presentation but also my visible responses. I learned how to keep my expressions neutral and remain silent when sexist, racist, and homophobic comments were made in my presence. Beginning with my first trip to South Africa in 2004, I worked on controlling my facial expressions when what people said, especially white Afrikaans speakers, was shocking. I was not always successful, however; I often rolled my eyes without thinking. My research involved listening to conversations that I often found disturbing, yet I had to keep myself from responding negatively to comments I was sometimes completely unnerved by hearing. I was careful about responding to homophobia because if I had been seen as too gay friendly, I would have been cut off from conversations about homosexuality. I was conflicted about when to speak up. Over time I learned whom I could speak with more freely.

I frustrated many white Christians in Cape Town and on the farms I visited in the Western Cape when I tried to interject that I found certain comments or actions racist. Although I could be fuming, they rarely got upset, usually dismissing my comments as irrelevant, saying I would never understand race in South Africa. I was most disturbed by the overt racism I saw in HRM. White and coloured men frequently put forward racist ideas about coloured and black people. Black men were especially vilified, as the men in the ministry reproduced, as detailed earlier, colonial and apartheid-era stereotypes of black men as oversexed, irresponsible, and leading the country toward economic, political, and moral ruin. A nonwhite researcher may have been exposed to less of this "backstage talk" where whites felt comfortable expressing racist talk amongst themselves, assuming that other in-group members shared their views (Verwey and Quayle 2012: 552). In many ways I was more prepared for homophobia than racism, in that I expected homophobic talk but, naively in many ways, thought that a multi-racial ministry would not lead to so much racism. HRM members and ex-members may disagree with my assessments of them as homophobic, sexist, and racist.

In 2013, I returned to Cape Town after a five-year absence to do follow-up fieldwork, the content of which is detailed in chapter 5. I ended up spending most of my time with now openly gay ex-ministry members. I had little contact with men still working the ex-gay process, who knew I was now supporting the newly out men, something which made me suspect in their eyes.

Outline of the Book

In chapter 1, I look at the reasons behind HRM's success after the ending of apartheid. I discuss how the convergence of a variety of social movements and discourses created the environment for the ministry to flourish in a particular historical circumstance. I pay special attention to twelve-step movements and the Truth and Reconciliation Commission. Chapter 2 examines the intimate work that Pentecostals employed to move closer to God. He

is understood to initiate healing through (re)fathering men who were denied emotional love and "appropriately" gendered parenting in childhood.
In chapter 3, I address how South African Pentecostal men learned how
to protect themselves, their families, their communities, and the nation in
what was explained as a battle between Satan and God. I show how ex-gay
men performed work like prayer, speaking in tongues, deliverance (exorcism), and spiritual warfare to battle personal and corporate sin. In chapter
4 I concentrate on how ministry members worked to achieve heterosexual desire, though they were often unsuccessful. I address the sequential
changes in heterosexual desire work. In chapter 5, I look at the narratives of
newly "out" gay men and their reflections on their time in HRM. I focus on
the ways that they are now seeing and understanding themselves through a
language of "integration" and "wholeness." In the afterword, I return to the
question of failure and self-making.

CULTURAL CONVERGENCES

God started putting me back in touch with my inner self and my emotions.
It was very important to God that I go through this [ex-gay] process. —TRISTAN

I attended part of a Healing Revelation Ministries (HRM) workshop in a
suburban Cape Town Dutch Reformed Church in 2004. Herman, an Afrikaans longtime ministry member, gave his testimony that night to get the
workshop started. Although married with a child and "out of the [gay] lifestyle" for thirteen years, he explained to the rapt second-year Bible school
students that he still needed to see himself as an "addict." Herman explained,
"I will never say I am over it [same-sex attraction]. When I say it, Satan
takes control." Ex-gay Pentecostal work on the self is similar to the labor
that many alcoholics, despite years of sobriety, perform. Some ex-gay men
like Herman even use the language of addiction. After Herman gave his
testimony, he cautioned the students, many who were training to be Christian counselors, not to expect "healing from homosexuality" to be instan-
taneous because "recovery is a long-term process" and "one must work for
it and work to keep it." At the beginnings of the new democratic nation in a
new millennium, the ministry provided ex-gay men with the language and
tools to be "who God made them to be" and to help them in discovering
their "true [heterosexual] selves." Ex-gay men were supposed to be always
working hard on themselves, something they shared in common with other
groups of South African citizens, discussed in detail below. Herman's language and practices of self-work did not take place in a cultural vacuum.

HRM offered one-on-one counseling, as well as support groups, workshops, and classes for church members and leaders. Their classes all offered a form of "freedom" from preconversion problems and pasts: family and adolescent struggles, addictions, pain and anger, and same-sex attraction. All the classes presented natal familial relations and childhood trauma as the root of later dysfunction. Ministry classes discussed the development of codependency and shame because they were seen as the "roots" that explained how many adults ended up in bad relationships and had poor self-esteem. HRM used biblical passages to reinforce psychological theories. Attendees at courses, counselees, and ministry members were taught to see their pasts differently, rereading life stages for key points of crisis and trauma.

Classes ran between eight and twelve weeks. The class format was two one-hour segments. The first hour was a testimony and lesson; this was followed by a second hour of small group discussion and prayer that was divided up by gender, though men sometimes led a women's group due to the small number of women leaders. As an observer at a variety of ministry classes and the small groups that met afterward, I saw how participants were taught to be emotionally vulnerable, a key piece of the ex-gay process. Men were taught that they had to learn to "yield" to God in order to receive His love. HRM leaders said that this was more difficult for men and did not come "naturally" to them like it did with women, whom the ministry saw as "naturally" more emotionally intuitive and open to receiving the love of others and God. Men were encouraged to confess shame publicly, ask God for His forgiveness, cry in front of their small groups, and engage in charismatic worship as ways to "yield." HRM taught that men would be unable to move forward in the ex-gay process without emotional vulnerability because it was receiving God's love that allowed them to learn to be open, which I discuss in detail in the next chapter.

For ex-gay men, classes and workshops, like the one where Herman gave his testimony, were locations to perform their new selves. These selves had a historical and cultural context. This chapter looks at the ways that ex-gay ministry HRM drew on the language and tools of emerging and converging social projects in South Africa at the turn of the millennium in their self-making work. Such projects included American-originated twelve-step movements, particularly AA (Alcoholics Anonymous), and postapartheid political institutions like the South African TRC (Truth and Reconciliation Commission). The rise of movements like AA and the TRC were two convergences that provided HRM cultural legitimacy and a larger framework for their work.

HRM drew on AA and the TRC's existing discourses and practices of self-work, employing the confessional as a way to assist people in forming morally and ethically superior selves and initiating new subjectivities through self-conscious work. Invoking the familiar rhetoric of the TRC and AA made HRM's work to transform sexuality and the way it sought to do so seem less foreign to South Africans. I begin by identifying specific strategies and rhetoric employed by AA and the TRC and the ways they were taken up in HRM's self-making projects. Then I address two other strategies central to HRM's work: sexual addiction meetings and faith-based counseling. I end the chapter by highlighting HRM's ideas about the causes and cures for homosexuality and their understanding of what constituted "success" and how they sought to achieve it.

Twelve-Step Programs and Self-Work

It bears noting that HRM's founder, Brian, disavowed twelve-step ideology completely, claiming it was unchristian. However, I found that despite his position, the ministry was flooded with twelve-step rhetoric and practices. Twelve-step ideas of "codependency," the "inner child," and "dysfunction" had the same definitions in the ministry, though terms were sometimes altered, for example codependency was called "relational idolatry." HRM used the popular discourses of the American recovery movement on self-esteem, self-worth, and learning how to grow. For example, at the end of one HRM leadership training session, everyone was given a list of positive daily affirmations like "I am worthy of love." We were instructed to recite them in front of a mirror twice a day to increase our self-esteem. Despite Brian's negation of twelve-step practices, I think they are essential to understanding the work that HRM asked men to perform in their journeys toward heterosexuality. I detail this history below.

Alcoholics Anonymous (AA) developed a global identity based on discourses of self-control and self-surveillance (Warhol 2002). AA was founded in 1935 in the United States and it marked the beginning of a new kind of self-help culture. The innovation of AA was that individuals with the same addictive behavior became experts on their own disease, which is also present in the ex-gay movement, where leadership and expertise are based on "recovery" from "sinful" same-sex attraction. Accountability and confession to other alcoholics, seeing themselves as powerless over addiction, and constant reliance on God all came together to form a new kind of self in twentieth-century American culture—the alcoholic. Twelve-step discourses and healing methods have traveled globally, including to South Africa; although people who followed them were often unfamiliar with their lineage. These discourses have been popularized to international audiences through talk show hosts like Oprah Winfrey, who provided resources for healing through her choice of experts, audience participation, and the sharing of stories by guests (Illouz 2003; Wilson 2003). HRM drew on self-help culture and shared with twelve-step groups like Alcoholic Anonymous the cultivation and care of the subject, work to move toward becoming an ideal person, and a community to help with self-formation.

Although it claims to be "spiritual," not "religious," AA relies on Christian, specifically Protestant, theologies and social practices. AA and other twelve-step groups use the language of spirituality and a "Higher Power." The word "God" is used in popular slogans like "Let Go and Let God" and in the original twelve steps. Ernest Kurtz writes, "Whether presented as 'serenity' or as attained adult life, the sobriety promised by Alcoholics Anonymous was clearly salvation" (Kurtz 1979: 183). Group members are born-again as self-aware alcoholics who know they have an addiction that needs to be worked on. Twelve-step programs construct subjects who constantly work, evaluate, and correct themselves. They believe that a new and better self emerges through suffering, sharing details of personal failures in a public forum, self-surveillance, and repeated confessionals to get rid of shame. Second-generation twelve-step recovery groups like Co-Dependents Anonymous and Sex Addicts Anonymous popularized ideas about dysfunctional families and explained the roots of addictions in childhood trauma (Denzin and Johnson 1993). HRM's mobilization of self-help and twelve-step ideas was clear in their focus on trauma, sex addiction, and emotional codependency, which were standard parts of most testimonials.

Twelve-step programs are focused on the individual, particularly the self's development, growth, and constant care. This self involves hard work, clear in slogans like "Keep Coming Back . . . It Works If You Work It" and in the Serenity Prayer, which reads, "God grant me the serenity to accept the things I cannot change, the courage to change the things I can, and the wisdom to know the difference." For people in twelve-step programs, changing the self is key to a better life. According to Leslie Irvine, the subjects of twelve-step discourse and the self-help industry are "allegedly entitled to happiness, high self-esteem, and personal satisfaction" (Irvine 1999: 5).

Twelve-step members share a disease that affects their ability to develop a healthy sense of self, or a sense of self at all. The past is negative in these twelve-step groups, and the present becomes a focus of life—the everyday maintenance of recovery and various forms of sobriety means putting oneself under constant surveillance. The group offers recovery and hope for the development of a new, more socially appropriate, and healthy subject who can have intimate and boundary appropriate relationships with others. This subject is an individual who focuses on personal integrity and self-control.

Twelve-step members discursively constitute new subjectivities through the construction, performance, and repetition of testimonials. Nikolas Rose writes, "In the act of speaking, through the obligation to produce words that are true to an inner reality, through the self-examination that precedes and accompanies speech, one becomes a subject for oneself" (Rose 1999 [1989]: 244). Subjectivity is not represented vis-à-vis testimonials but created through them. In his work on voluntary counseling and testing in faith-based organizations in Burkina Faso, Vinh-Kim Nguyen discusses how HIV-positive people are taught a new vocabulary and framework to see and discuss themselves. He writes, "These confessional technologies, ostensibly used to help people 'come out' with their HIV positivity, in effect trained them to talk about their innermost selves in public" (Nguyen 2009: 360). Although confession is often thought of as spontaneous outpouring of one's feelings and desires, it is also a form of learning that, like testimonials, assists in constructing the self. A new, improved self emerges through telling narratives of subjectivity.

Testimonies become more standardized over time, a well-noted phenomenon in twelve-step movements (see for example Carr 2011; Brandes 2002; Warhol 2002; Holland et al. 1998). This standardization often leads to greater connection among group members, as they are able to easily see themselves in other people's scripts (Travis 2009: 130). I also found this process in my research on ex-gay Pentecostal men, whose testimonies of "recovery" to heterosexuality became more uniform the longer they were involved in the ministry. In HRM, testimony was key to self-making. It was a way for ex-gay men to prove their changes in subjectivity and, similarly to other twelve-step movements, a way to be accountable to the community and have them bear witness to their (hopefully) dramatic self-transformation. Edwin, a twenty-four-year-old Afrikaans man, shared his testimonial with me soon after joining the ministry. As a new ministry member, he had not yet been integrated into ministry discourse. He never employed ex-gay terms like "the [gay] lifestyle," "same-sex attraction," or "homosexual tendencies." Instead, he discussed himself repeatedly as "gay," a term frowned upon in HRM because it referred to selfhood, not a behavior or desires. He soon left the ministry and was never socialized into their language and framework.

Over time, men altered their testimonials to integrate ministry ideas into their explanations for same-sex attraction. I often observed that when men first came to the ministry for counseling, they began their testimonials describing their reasons for being there with an explanation of their first sexual experience with a man, the first time they realized they felt sexually attracted to a man, and/or started to watch gay pornography. This later shifted to men beginning their testimonials with childhood pain and trauma, particularly stories about negligent or absent fathers. Men learned how to reframe their selves and their reasons for same-sex attraction to fit into ministry-provided structures. For example, white ministry leader Tristan explained to me, "God started putting me back in touch with my inner self and my emotions. It was very important to God that I go through this [ex-gay] process. I think it was the first thing I sort of realized . . . it's important for God the Father to affirm me in my masculinity as a man, the way my father didn't. I wasn't able to connect with Father God at all until he took me through the process . . . I think the biggest thing is learning to meet my needs through healthy relationships in the church instead of through addictive sexual thoughts or practices. So as I learned to have healthy relationships and healthy friendships, the need to meet my [emotional] needs through sexual contact or fantasies diminished and diminished until they were very little." For Tristan, learning how to see men in a new light was key to his desire work. He was able to replace his same-sex desires and practices with "healthy" thoughts and relationships through work that was facilitated by his deep emotional relationship with God.

The ministry also offered the men tools like "accountability partners," known in twelve-step rhetoric as sponsors. This was one person or a group that ex-gay men were supposed to be in constant communication with about their "struggles." Men were encouraged to spend social time together to embolden a culture of confession. Everyone in the ministry, including me, was expected to have an accountability partner. This person was to be one's main confessor, and one was supposed to get together with them at least once a month to admit sexual thoughts, ask for prayer, and get help in reframing one's desires. Besides this ministry-sanctioned relationship, men also used other ministry members as a way to be accountable on a daily or weekly basis. For example, coloured leader Damon explained to me that when he was stressed or things were going negatively in his life, he would begin to "compulsively masturbate," which would then lead to "cruising" to find another man to engage in sexual activity with. He was able to stop some of this behavior through using the supportive community that HRM provided and its carefully cultivated culture of confession. For Damon that meant that he had three prayer partners that were also involved in the ex-gay process whom he could rely on when he was "struggling." He told me that he would send them text messages when he felt like "acting out," asking them for prayer and encouragement. The ability to be honest about his "struggles" led him to have a decrease in his "sexual falls."

The ministry's focus on accountability was one part of a culture of confession where men learned that they should not only share their sexual thoughts but also share them in intimate detail. HRM employed twelve-step language and methods in its program of change, melding the twelve-step idea that the self can be improved with the Pentecostal belief that all things are possible after becoming born-again. HRM's success and cultural legibility was directly tied to the presence and growth of twelve-step groups and self-help ideology in Cape Town. Though twelve-step groups in South Africa have fewer people attending than in the United States, where the groups have a longer history, their core ideas have been popularized through international media. Ex-gay men who attended twelve-step and HRM meetings were involved in processes of change that they believed initiated a working on the self that led to its transformation and improvement.

The Effects of the Truth and Reconciliation Commission

The Truth and Reconciliation Commission (TRC) was a project of the democratically elected ANC government to heal the nation from the trauma of apartheid.[1] Full amnesty was granted to perpetrators of political violence if they publicly disclosed all the atrocities they had committed during National Party rule. Here, the twelve-step idea that telling the truth in testimonials was a transformative self-improvement exercise is clear. The Commission tried to bring together perpetrators and victims of apartheid so that they would see themselves as new national subjects. Apartheid was argued to have hurt everyone—victims and perpetrators. The psychological idea that trauma is only healed through addressing the past was applied to the nation. Chris Colvin explains, "The ground of the (new, healed) self—of the patient or of the nation—is understood to be constituted out of the mastering of a painful past" (Colvin 2000: 160).

There are three effects of the TRC that are important in order to understand how HRM became culturally legible in the postapartheid period. The first is how the Christian nature of the commission popularly linked trauma recovery with Christian discourse and practice. The TRC was explicitly Christian, with commissioners like Archbishop Desmond Tutu utilizing the theological language of "redemption" (Tutu 1999). Christian rituals like prayers began and ended the proceedings (Herwitz 2003). Christianity is a common language and worldview for many South Africans,[2] so it made sense for the TRC to employ Christian discourses and practices. As noted earlier, Christianity is also key to twelve-step rhetoric and practices.

During public TRC hearings, perpetrators were expected to give detailed testimonials on the atrocities they had committed, often to the families of the people they had harmed. People had to confess the "truths" of their actions to be granted amnesty. Perpetrators of political violence had opportunities to ask for personal and national forgiveness. Victims who had experienced traumas like torture also shared their pain with the nation. The idea was that telling the truth could set one free from the past and allow both perpetrators and victims to become reintegrated into one democratic nation. Detailed confessions and pleas for forgiveness nationalized the healing process and trauma became a recognizable psychological condition.

Second, the popularization of apartheid trauma discourses led to their extension to other groups, such as survivors of rape, domestic violence, and crime. It also brought trauma discourses into popular consciousness. Colvin explains, "Since its early appearance in progressive mental health circles during apartheid, and its debut on the national stage with the TRC, the trauma discourse has since traveled more broadly in popular discourse and practice. It has moved out of the clinic and the TRC hearing, and into community healthcare clinics, police stations, newspaper articles and talk shows, and beyond" (Colvin 2008: 227). This process of extension is similar to what occurred in twelve-step groups, where AA's structure and language were applied to addictions other than alcohol, leading to an explosion of groups dealing with a variety of addictions. HRM's use of trauma discourses and Christian recovery techniques begun by the TRC culturally normalized their work because they employed nationally recognizable strategies.

The third important effect of the TRC was in changing the boundaries of what topics were acceptable to discuss in public. There has been an explosion of sex talk in the country by a variety of actors, including in churches and ministries like HRM. During apartheid, sexual violence had almost no public presence. Since the end of apartheid, discourses about sexuality have come much more out into the open due to the end of censorship, debates over gay rights, high rates of HIV/AIDS, and sexual violence. The TRC was essential to a larger postapartheid opening up of discourses about the secret and the hidden, which extended to the realms of sexuality and public discourse on sex. Deborah Posel believes that in South Africa a "public confessional" developed, where admissions of shame, trauma, and the exploitation of others are reconfigured as necessary to the ultimate redemption of the individual and the nation (Posel 2005a). This narrative of redemption has been extended to sex and sexuality. In particular, HRM claimed to offer redemption from a "sinful" sexual past and the possibility, through confession and hard work, of a new, better future where the confessor was free from the weight and sorrow of whom he or she used to be.

HRM's healing methods gained legitimacy because detailed admissions of painful feelings and past actions became key to self-transformation. For example, ministry members were expected to explore shameful experiences in depth, frequently leading to detailed descriptions of childhood abuse and sexual assault in testimonies. The ministry believed that without a detailed confession of all prior "sinful" activity, especially anything that involved sex, "true" and lasting healing would remain out of reach. To facilitate this process, they had specific worksheets to assist a person in forming an exhaustive sexual history. The individual had to write down and explain behaviors such as masturbation and pornography use, and list the names, ages, and genders of all sexual partners.

Similarly, the ministry's Discipleship Form, given to potential counselees before their first appointment, asked for an in-depth history for the person coming in for "discipleship."[3] Typically, discipleship translated into religious counseling. This is the term the ministry used on documents instead of "counseling" because they were not accredited counselors with professional training. The first question on the six-page questionnaire was about personal trauma, indicating the centrality of the concept to the ministry. It signaled to people filling it out the parameters of how to begin to see themselves in order to "heal" and that they should begin to frame their experiences through this lens. In HRM trauma had a broad definition, encompassing a diverse range of abuses. The concept frequently framed testimonials and came up often in conversation. HRM, along with ex-gay ministries around the world, believed that childhood trauma led to "sexual brokenness," including homosexuality and sex addiction. They claimed that the majority of homosexuals were sexually abused or traumatized as children or young adults. In HRM rhetoric, sexual abuse was a broad category and included incest, sexual assault, rape, sexual activity at a young age, and early exposure to pornography. The ex-gay self was a traumatized self and the ministry was supposed to help men get in touch with this abused self and remake it into a new, improved, and empowered self. The Discipleship Form's choice of terminology showed the ministry's use of the concepts from twelve-step groups and the discourses of pain and healing found in the TRC.

The TRC's use of Christianity and the opening of sexual discourses post-apartheid, combined with the popularization of talk-therapy to heal trauma, situated ministry exercises like listing all sexual partners and activities in detail into larger cultural practices of confession and open discussion of sexual practices. Combined with the influence of twelve-step language and kinds of addiction, the details asked for on the Discipleship Form provided clues to how HRM became culturally legible in the postapartheid context. Below, I look closely at two other confessional-based groups and practices that HRM members drew on in their work to become new selves: sexual addiction meetings and faith-based counseling.

Sexual Addiction

As noted above, South Africans began drastically changing how and where sexual activities and subjectivities were discussed starting at the end of apartheid; sex became more public and sexual discourses proliferated because of the constitutional protection of gay rights and conversations on gender inequity and violence (Burchardt 2015; Posel 2005b). The end of the Immorality Act and censorship allowed South Africans to have more access to media related to sex and sexuality. They were more easily able to acquire pornography and stores like Adult World dotted city landscapes. Citizens became inundated with HIV/AIDS messages and programs that discussed condoms and sexual acts in detail. Being a postapartheid member of society meant that conversations on sex were part and parcel of daily life. The introduction of sexual addiction discourses and meetings was part of a larger national trend.

In 2008, I attended a two-day workshop with all the ministry's counselors that Patrick Carnes, recognized as a world expert on sexual addiction, gave in Cape Town. He explained to us that sex addicts had an intimacy disorder that included out-of-control, self-destructive, and obsessive sexual behavior and thoughts that negatively affected every facet of their lives and relationships (Carnes 1997: 15). People are widely claimed to become sex addicts because of childhood sexual abuse (Henderson 2000; Swisher 1995). According to experts like Carnes, sex addiction was a predominantly male disease. Many experts claim that women are more addicted to relationships and men to sex, reinforcing traditional gendered stereotypes (Covington and Beckett 1988: 46). These stereotypes, which posit women as inherently more relational and emotional, were also present in HRM.

The diagnosis of sex addiction was part of a long history, beginning in the eighteenth and nineteenth centuries, of establishing various forms of sexual expression, for example homosexuality, as medical pathologies (Foucault 1990). New sexual "perversions" became scientific discoveries as sexologists and psychiatrists became the established authorities on sexuality and sexual "dysfunction" (Reay, Attwood, and Gooder 2015). The disease of sexual addiction was "discovered" by experts in the 1970s.[4] Statistics on sex addiction vary widely in the United States, with estimates ranging from as low as 3 percent to 6 percent of the population (Henderson 2000) to up to 12 percent (Carnes 2001). There are no official statistics for South Africa, though the numbers are thought to be comparable.[5] Scientific knowledge and "facts" can never be divorced from the sociocultural world in which they are produced (Fausto-Sterling 1997; Martin 1991). For example, sexual addiction emerged and began to grow as a "disease" in American culture in response to the effects of the sexual revolution and fears about HIV/AIDS and how it is transmitted.

Sex Addicts Anonymous (SAA) was the group that HRM members attended in Cape Town. SAA helped people to stop sexually "acting out." HRM and SAA worked in tandem for ex-gay men who also self-identified as sex addicts. HRM members who attended SAA meetings said it helped them in their "recovery" to be with others struggling with the same problem, sex addiction. Although HRM did discuss sex addiction, it was not its main focus. Like Alcoholics Anonymous, SAA worked on the twelve-step model. This begins with the acknowledgment of the problem, and the addict then "works the steps" to interrupt and eventually cease self-destructive behavior through work on the self, like confession and self-surveillance. Helen Keane notes, "Rather than repressing sexual expression, the discourse of sex addiction encourages individuals to develop a habit of obsessive attention to their sexual desires" (Keane 2002: 142). Participants in sex addiction treatment focus extreme attention on the self and its desires.

A similar process occurs in ex-gay ministries, where the focus on shedding same-sex desire leads men to discuss sex in explicit detail and to spend significant amounts of time and energy tracking and evaluating their sexual desires. Tanya Erzen did fieldwork with a live-in ex-gay ministry near San Francisco. Each week the men had to turn in an "accountability report," where they noted each time they masturbated, attempted to "cruise," visited a video store's adult section, or placed or looked at personal advertisements. While the sheets may have been designed to get men to confess and be accountable for "sinful" behaviors, they also had the unintended effect of expanding the men's possibilities for "falling." Erzen writes, "Frank [the ministry's ex-gay founder] designs the accountability sheets to stem men's addictive behaviors and provide them with structure, but they also have the unintended effects of inciting transgressive behavior. The sheets anticipate any possible form of behavioral transgression an ex-gay man might engage in, and even present men with ideas for off-limits behavior they may not have considered" (Erzen 2006: 169). American ex-gay men learned new ways to "sin" through group sharing and process.

Similarly, HRM members, especially those who had never been "in the [gay] lifestyle," were taught new possibilities for "sexual sin" through attending men-only ex-gay and sexual addiction support group meetings. For example, longtime coloured HRM member Adrian told me that he developed an addiction to gay male internet pornography after hearing about specific websites and their content from other support group members. He told me, "Pornography was not an issue for me when I first came to HRM. Now it's an issue. I mean, damn, it's an issue. And it shouldn't be and I've strayed off again." Adrian was exposed to new kinds of sexual acts and places to view them through listening to the testimonials of other ex-gay men. Jaco, an Afrikaans ministry leader and later counselor, also explained to me that it was not until he joined the ministry that he knew what "gay sex" meant. He became sexually excited in the HRM support group meetings when other men detailed their sexual histories and "falls." This led to a short-term internet pornography addiction, which he said he solved by attending Sex Addicts Anonymous Meetings. The tools that sex addiction and ex-gay groups used to help men discipline their desires often had the unintended effect of teaching men more ways to sexually "act out."

There were a variety of options for men and women in Cape Town who wanted to "recover" from dysfunctional and addictive sexual behaviors and subjectivities when I did my year of research in 2007–2008. In Cape Town and the surrounding suburbs one could attend Sex Addicts Anonymous, Sex and Love Addicts Anonymous, Co-Sex Addicts, HRM, and Salt,[6] a Christian sex addicts recovery program. Accompanying Salt was Pepper,[7] a Christian class and support group for the wives of the male sex addicts who attended Salt. Pepper, which focused on codependency and coaddiction, was exclusively for women. The underlying assumption of these groups was that

Christian women could not be addicted to sex, part of the desexualization of women and oversexualization of men that was also present in HRM. The women in Pepper attended meetings to address their own lives and problems, not just to focus on the addict. This model was similar to Al-Anon, Co-Dependents Anonymous,[8] Co-Sex Addicts, and other twelve-step programs for the friends and families of addicts. Most of the wives in Pepper had husbands with an internet pornography addiction, with accompanying compulsive masturbation.

HRM members who believed themselves to be sex addicts also attended SAA and Salt meetings. The multiplicity of sex addiction meetings in and around the city reinforced Cape Town as a certain kind of place—a place of cultural innovation embracing more "modern" and Western twelve-step ideologies of healing. SAA's popularity serves as an indicator that there were a number of people attending twelve-step programs in Cape Town who embraced new senses of self based on twelve-step groups.[9]

Faith-Based Counseling

At the turn of the millennium, faith-based counseling was another method that many South Africans used to understand disease, recovery, healing, and themselves. It offered a unique mix of discourses and practices for transforming the self, drawing from a variety of sources, including Christianity, psychology, NGOs, HIV/AIDS prevention campaigns, and self-help. HRM was part of the larger growth of faith-based counseling in South Africa. This kind of religious therapy is part of a long history of missionary, public health, and NGO interventions into African gender roles and responsibilities and African sexualities (Comaroff and Comaroff 1996; Vaughan 1991). Since colonialism, and continuing until today, many Christian and secular NGOs have sought to "individualize" Africans, convincing them to separate themselves from sociocultural life, responsibilities, roles, and the so-called baggage of cultural "traditions" (Bornstein 2005; Thomas 2000; Burke 1996). Many of these interventions, similarly to HRM, originated in the West or had a European or American leader like Brian at the helm. These Western organizations have long sought to restructure African ways of relating to their bodies, sex lives, gendered subjectivities, and self-formation (Hodzic 2017; Nguyen 2010).

The TRC brought mental health professionals onto the national stage for the first time and popularly linked psychology with Christianity. During apartheid, therapy was inaccessible to almost all South Africans. Today, professional therapy still remains out of reach for most people because of its cost. Churches have stepped in to fill this void, continuing the work they did during apartheid in providing material, psychological, and spiritual resources to black and coloured South Africans (Tutu 1999; Borer 1998; Balia 1989). Today, many churches provide voluntary HIV counseling and testing. The Church of the Reborn, where HRM had its office, had an AIDS Resource Center and offered testing and pre- and post-test counseling, both through drop-ins and by appointment. Their offices were next to HRM's in the church building and they frequently sent the people they categorized as "sexually broken"—that is, anyone who was gay or whom they suspected to have engaged in homosexual activity—to HRM's office for assistance. An ex-gay HIV-positive HRM leader also started an AIDS support group at the church in 2007.

South Africa's HIV/AIDS epidemic and the government's unwillingness[10] and inability to meet the needs of its citizens brought religious-based organizations to the forefront of medical and psychological care for the disease and its prevention (Burchardt 2009). HRM was one of many faith-based groups that offered counseling and support for sexual decision-making and its physical, emotional, and spiritual effects. Faith-based organizations offered new ways to be informed sexual selves within a context where South Africans are encouraged to know their HIV status, make safe(r) sex decisions, and to transform their sexual subjectivities. Social messages that call for people to "Know Your Status!" and to get tested link sexual awareness to self-knowledge. Sexual awareness also became a way to better know the self spiritually. Charismatic and Pentecostal forms of Christianity in Africa, instead of being agents of sexual repression, have been transformed into faiths where sex is routinely discussed in detail (van Dijk 2015; Burchardt 2013). Churches that use faith to encourage new kinds of sexualized selves are part of a larger trend in many African contexts, where the AIDS pandemic and the rise of Pentecostalism have linked spiritual growth with normative ideals of intimate relationships and new kinds of sexual selves (van de Kamp 2016; van Dijk 2013). (I address this development further in chapter 4.)

Ex-gay Pentecostal South Africans were one group out of many in Africa working to achieve new selves through hard work. A number of these groups were dedicated to transforming sex and sexuality, focusing on the transformation of behaviors to initiate an ideal ethical new self. For example, in Namibia, LGBTI organization the Rainbow Project taught workshop participants how to get in touch with their "real [sexual] selves" through embracing Western-based sexual identity categories and how to construct and recite "coming out" narratives (Lorway 2015: 45). These workshops taught a version of the self that is familiar to other NGOS in the context of HIV/AIDS, where the individual and his or her sexual behaviors are paramount. This is similar to HRM, where ex-gays are taught a standard, though clearly very different, narrative of "coming out" with their sexual desires in a public forum. Like the LGBTI people at the Rainbow Project, the men in HRM also learned that their "real" self was sexual, just in this case heterosexual. Many HIV/AIDS interventions also focus on building a new kind of sexual self who is autonomous. For example, in Uganda, this is an agent who makes his or her own sexual decisions and has an inner self on which she or he does significant work to improve (Parikh 2015). Ex-gay men also strove to be sexual agents with deep interior lives. This normative ideal is no doubt difficult to realize given that sex and sexuality are so intimately linked to relationships with others.

This focus on being a new and better individual subject is key to what Lydia Boyd writes about in her work on born-again Christians in Uganda and the influence of the U.S. President's Emergency Plan for AIDS Relief (PEPFAR) on personhood. She refers to the self that PEPFAR advances in its work to form an abstinent and monogamous African self as "the accountable subject," part of public health interventions that link individualism to sexual freedom (Boyd 2015: 5). This born-again "accountable subject" in Uganda, like the ex-gay men in HRM, focuses on behavioral change to reach a new ethical modern sexual subject-hood. Faith-based counseling mixed a variety of spiritual and medical discourses, rendering it difficult to draw a fine line between religion and psychology.

HRM and Christian counseling reproduced the ideas of trauma put forth by the TRC. Prayer and psychology merged in theory, discourse, and practice. However, who was believed to ultimately perform and maintain the healing was very different. In the TRC, the individual person was responsible for self-transformation, while in faith-based counseling, it was God, Jesus, and the Holy Spirit who performed the transformative work. The focus was always ultimately on the "real work" being done by God and the Holy Spirit on each individual's heart. In this framework, healing came from a willingness to be open to God's unconditional love. He was the one who emotionally healed the person.

In HRM, participants learned how to review their lives and reread situations for moments of crisis and trauma. The trauma that harmed the child could even have occurred while still in the mother's womb. One ex-gay coloured man in his early twenties told me that he thought his "homosexual tendencies" began even before birth. His mother desperately wanted a girl, and he believed her desires impacted his gender identity. In his work on American Charismatic Catholics, Thomas Csordas also found that a belief in prebirth trauma could have long-lasting spiritual effects. He writes, "In the Healing of Memories an individual's entire life is prayed for in stages, from the moment of conception to the present" (Csordas 2002: 5). For the men in HRM, the self was an entity that was impacted by a broad range of life stage development.

Ministry classes asked participants to look for what they called "root memories," which were frequently repressed abusive and humiliating experiences from childhood that were understood to have led to the development of homosexuality. Christ needed to be invited into the memory itself, after it was recalled in a "safe space," to heal these memories and the inner child who experienced them (Payne 1995). The person was supposed to welcome Jesus into the traumatic memory and reimagine the memory with Jesus there, offering comfort and love, picking up the child and holding him or her tenderly in His arms.

For Pentecostals, God can move back and forth in time. He can go into one's past and heal pain. The solution for healing trauma in Christian psychology, which HRM practiced, was the same as the healing from trauma that the TRC process popularized. The "talking cure," combined with realigning the self with knowing that the painful past is over, was the same in both. "Root memories," the repressed traumatic memories discussed above, were the key to healing. Popular Christian author Leanne Payne writes, "In order that his deepest mind and heart might fully participate in this yielding, I asked him to picture with eyes closed Christ on the Cross, dying to take those very sins and sicknesses into Himself" (Payne 1995: 20). God was imagined to lead participants to their "root memories," allow people to re-experience them, and then heal them, allowing them to become new selves.

HRM taught that Christ "healed" the inner child in the "root memory" in order for the adult to move on. In an October 2007 ministry class, Afrikaans HRM leader Coenraad gave his testimony. He shared his own "root memory," only remembered in his late twenties. God "revealed" to him through prayer that his same-sex desires stemmed from a "traumatic experience" with his mother. His parents decided to have him circumcised, which is not the norm in Afrikaner communities. While Coenraad was still healing from the procedure, a few family members came over and asked about how he was doing. His mother suddenly pulled his pants and underwear down in front of the other adults and humiliated him. Coenraad said that God was healing his "trauma" and the resulting same-sex attraction. He encouraged others to be hopeful for their own healing. "God lives outside of time," he shared," and "can heal pains from a long time ago and seal it with a prayer."

Damon, another longtime HRM leader, recounted his own experience with Christian methods of healing during a Christian sex addicts support group he attended with other ex-gay men. A coloured man in his early thirties, he was four years old when family and neighbors began sexually abusing him. This abuse went on throughout his childhood, and Damon attempted suicide multiple times. He believed that Brian, HRM's founder, saved his sanity and life. Damon felt he had made progress through Christian counseling and group process. However, he was not ready for what happened when he was repeatedly pushed by two leaders to describe his childhood abuse in detail to his support group to reconnect with his "root memory." He refused multiple times and was told he needed to remember these painful feelings in order to heal. Damon said he could tell what happened to him matter-of-factly in a detached way, but he did not feel safe remembering the specific details of multiple abusive situations.

One leader instructed Damon to imagine that he was the one of the men who had abused him as a child. The process became too much for him, and he blacked out. He does not remember trying to harm anyone but was told afterward that he almost hit the leader with a chair, which he did smash into pieces. The next day Damon called to apologize, thinking he was going to be asked to leave the support group. The leader told him that he was not angry and that it was obvious that God wanted him to release that pain and anger. Damon told me sadly after he recounted the story, "Jesus still has a lot more work to do in my life." He experienced himself as in need of a lot more emotional and spiritual desire work.

Confession and Self-Making in Healing Revelation Ministries

Most of the men who arrived at HRM for their initial counseling appointment were at the end of their ropes emotionally. They had struggled with same-sex desires for many years and how those desires conflicted with their conservative Christian values and upbringings. These men had watched gay pornography, and many had had furtive anonymous sexual encounters while "cruising" in places like public bathrooms. When they met with Brian, the ministry's white American founder, for their initial appointment, he was for most the first Christian person in a role of authority who did not respond negatively to their same-sex desires. Alwyn, an Afrikaans ministry leader and later counselor himself, explained to me, "You could tell him [Brian] anything, the most disgraceful thing about your past [and] he wouldn't judge. And the majority of the guys came with this incredible shame and no one to speak with. Then they had the opportunity where they could talk to a Christian leader and tell him the most perverse sexual behavior and he didn't freak out . . . so that helped to break the shame." Many ex-gay men told me that when they had shared their sexual desires with their church's pastoral staff in the past they received negative reactions, including being sent for deliverance (exorcism), or postrevelation, being ignored and ostracized, adding to the shame they already felt for not being able to control their sexual feelings and actions. Damon told me that Brian "saved his life" because he was at the point of considering suicide after years of sexual abuse as a child and "struggling" with his same-sex desires. He told me that after he came in for his initial counseling appointment, "My whole life got turned around. And it started—the journey of my healing started. He [Brian] was the one person, the first man I could ever trust. The first one who didn't want anything from me, didn't want to get into my pants but he genuinely loved me. He showed me what a father is supposed to be like." Ex-gay men were taught that although God could instantly heal them of their same-sex desires because He could do anything, He chose not to because he wanted the men to address the emotional trauma, abuse, and pain that caused their desires to emerge. A common refrain was, "God loves you too much to leave you where you're at." Men learned that with hard work on the ex-gay process they could transform their comportment, affects, emotional needs, and eventually sexual desires through a long-term program of emotional, religious, and behavioral change.

Brian not only offered the men a compassionate ear, he also presented them a new interpretive lens in which to frame their desires besides that they were "sinners," were bad Christians, or had weak wills—what many men had been told in the past by other Christians. One of the first things ex-gay men learned at HRM was that their same-sex desires largely resulted from a lack of "appropriately gendered" role models in childhood, specifically a failure to emotionally connect with one's father and to receive a "welcoming" into manhood (Payne 1995). (Other causes were childhood bullying, early exposure to pornography, sexual abuse, childhood trauma, and demonic possession.) HRM claimed that the unmet childhood needs for emotional closeness became sexualized in adolescence, and that men sought out more masculine men to affirm their need for male intimacy. In this framework, boys who were "improperly" socialized into masculinity were said to desire other men because they were actually seeking the male closeness, protection, and nurturing they were denied in childhood by physically and emotionally absent fathers. For ex-gay men, "healing" from homosexuality meant emotionally processing childhood trauma and abandonment in counseling and support groups, learning to see other men as friends, not potential lovers, and viewing women as the only gender appropriate for sexual relationships.

Men learned about confession at the beginning of the ex-gay process. It was a key part of practicing desire work because it trained men to be new kinds of selves, teaching them a new frame with which to view and discuss themselves, similar to what is found in twelve-step movements and the TRC, as described earlier. Men began this with confessing to Brian their sexual thoughts and activities in detail, and he helped them see these thoughts not as innate sexual desires but as the sexualization of unmet emotional needs for intimacy. The men learned that they had to confess to God, to leaders, and to each other in order to facilitate a disposition of honesty and emotional openness. This was often very difficult because they had learned to be secretive about what they felt were "sinful" desires and activities.

"Coming out" narratives were also central to the ex-gay process, though the content of testimonials in gay and ex-gay communities clearly contrasted. LGBTI people frequently view "coming out" as having realized their natural/true selves (Gray 2009: 19). Likewise the ex-gay men in HRM discussed the heterosexual self as the "real self," one that until revealed was hidden under the weight of trauma and abuse. Ex-gay "coming out" narratives were refutations of gayness and refusals to engage with the gay community, who were conceptualized as inherently immoral and hypersexualized. However, HRM did not advocate going back into the closet and hiding the same-sex attracted self from view. Instead, they put forth similar ideas to what are often found in the HIV/AIDS testimonials and NGO discourse on sex and sexuality discussed earlier, where narratives of sexuality were key to self-making. Men were expected to openly acknowledge their attractions and their struggles to overcome them.

Ex-gay men used confession to initiate a new, improved, heterosexual self. Brian led each man through the sinner's prayer, the first step in the creation of a new self that was individual and was supposed to break with the "sins" and moral transgressions of the past. The prayer involved admitting that "I" have been a sinner, "I" want to repent, "I" ask for forgiveness for past "sinful" transgressions, and "I" accept Jesus Christ as "my personal" Lord and Savior. This prayer was the first step in initiating a new subjectivity that was based on being a gendered self in a personal relationship with God, and participating in a new Christian community with a renewed moral outlook and behaviors.

Ex-gay Pentecostal men constantly evaluated themselves to attempt to discern whether their sexual desires and actions were based on their own emotions or if they were demonically influenced. They saw themselves as spiritually weaker than other Christians due to their past traumas. They believed that their desires to have sex with other men had "opened" the "doors" to Satan, and they imagined themselves as being in more danger from spiritual contamination than other Christians. This impacted their senses of self significantly, making them into selves that were always evaluating which part of themselves sought to "sin" and which part was being influenced by demons or Satan. The demonic was a key piece of dangerous, otherworldly embodiment and influence for ex-gay Pentecostal men. For example, a member of the HRM advisory board said in a sermon, "Satan tries to come in and give us something nice and tasty . . . The Devil works very subtly." This is part of what made confession so key to the ex-gay process. Men who formed new, more spiritually aware selves had to always be on alert for demonic contamination and be engaged in "spiritual warfare" to protect themselves from what they talked about as Satan's "plan" to get them to "fall," which I discuss in detail in chapter 3.

Measuring Ex-Gay "Success"

Ex-gay ministries and subjects who tried to achieve born-again heterosexuality were invested in quantifying and judging success. In HRM, "success" relied on the number of engagements, marriages, and Christian families that developed and were sustained by ministry members. However, success was a complicated political designation on both sides of the ex-gay divide (LGBTI activists versus religious conservatives) because it was enmeshed in larger nature/nurture debates about whether homosexuality was a choice or if it was biologically determined. Ex-gay activists wanted to remove the application of civil rights protections from the LGBTI community through the promotion of studies that they said proved that being gay was a choice, not inborn. The debate on ex-gay success is detailed below.

There is little agreement in psychological and religious literature on how many men and women convert, change, and permanently remain ex-gay. The ex-gay movement sought scientific and psychological legitimacy, not relying solely on religious discourses in their quest to prove that homosexuality could be changed. Instead, they utilized statistics and psychological studies in an attempt to engage with organizations like the American Psychiatric Association (APA). Instead of dismissing psychology as worldly and irrelevant to Christians, ex-gay ministries drew from both faith and science. They compared their programs to other addiction treatment programs, which have a recovery rate of around 50 percent. According to ex-gay Mormon writer Jason Park, "Clinical evidence shows that the recovery rate for homosexual problems is even greater than for drug addiction and alcoholism" (Park 2013: 35). Ex-gay studies use vague terms when discussing recovery, such as "functional resolution," "significant therapeutic benefit," and successful "healing" from "overt homosexual problems."[11] Success rates noted in ex-gay publications are sometimes as high as 82 percent (Jones and Yarhouse 2007) and were 30–50 percent in a longitudinal ten-year study (Bieber and Bieber 1979). According to prominent international ex-gay figure Sy Rogers, "clinical findings" of "sustained recovery rate" are between 30 and 60 percent. His program in Singapore at the Church of the Savior claimed a higher than average success rate of 60–65 percent (Rogers 1993). However, many studies documenting changes in sexual behavior and orientation have been critiqued for having small sample sizes, biases, and methodological problems (see for example Drescher and Zucker 2006; Besen 2003).

One major ex-gay study controversy occurred in 2001, when Robert Spitzer gave a paper at the annual APA meetings claiming that reparative therapy could work for "highly motivated" people (Spitzer 2003).[12] Reparative therapy is also known as "conversion therapy." It has many of the same premises that ex-gay ministries do without the explicit religiosity (Nicolosi 1993). In 1973 Spitzer was instrumental in getting the APA to remove homosexuality from the DSM as a mental illness, making his later claims supporting reparative therapy even more controversial (for details on the controversy see Hausman 2001). Spitzer's study was heavily biased because ex-gay ministries and the National Association for Research and Therapy on Homosexuality (NARTH) preselected all his subjects. His interviews also turned out to be one-time forty-five-minute telephone conversations with a preselected sample of long-term ex-gay ministry members. Spitzer recanted his study in 2012 and apologized to the gay community for any harm from his work (Carey 2012).

It was difficult to get statistics on the number of people that the ministry worked with over the years. In 2013, Alwyn said he thought there were around five hundred to six hundred people who had come in for counseling between 1997 and 2010, with 80 percent of people coming in for assistance with same-sex attraction. (Other reasons people came for counseling were extramarital affairs, abuse, gender identity issues, pedophilia, and sexual addiction.) When I attended leadership retreats or leadership classes there were between fifteen and twenty people present who were counselors or small group facilitators and did various other tasks for the ministry like fundraising. This group included both men and women. Classes were held sporadically throughout the year for eight- to ten-week sessions and from twenty to thirty people took classes at a time. These people were Pentecostals from the church where HRM had its offices, as well as other evangelical and Pentecostal churches in the area like His People, the Vineyard, and Joshua Generation. Most of the leadership team had been involved in the ex-gay process for years.

No one in the ministry had reliable or consistent data on "success" rates because the ex-gay process was full of "falls," men leaving the ministry and later returning to "recommit" themselves after a period of "backsliding," and men who left after a few months because they felt the ex-gay process was too slow. Information about HRM's "success rates" varied significantly. Brian, the program's founder and director, told me in 2005 that he felt "despondent" because "almost everyone returned to the [gay] lifestyle"; in 2007, he told the assembled group at a ministry-sponsored fundraiser that he was feeling "hopeful" and was seeing "50 percent and growing success rates." In private conversations, ministry leaders usually provided lower numbers. Alwyn cited the success rate in South Africa at around 30 percent in 2007. He said that over the age of thirty-five there was little hope for permanent change, even for those who are dedicated, because people are "too set in their behavior patterns." He believed he had read the statistics in an American ex-gay publication but was unsure. He did not know of anyone at HRM who had come in for initial counseling after thirty-five. Most counselees started their journey to recovery from same-sex attraction in their twenties. Alwyn said that the motivation to change had to be spiritual. He told me, "You need to be also willing to die to yourself, die to the old person. And, I don't know if all people are willing to keep going through it." Alwyn described those who were most successful as "people of prayer," who combined counseling, daily prayer, accountability, and Christian discipline. Ex-gay Pentecostal success was achieved through simultaneous work on the mind, body, and spirit. However, heterosexuality often remained elusive, and few of the men in South Africa were able to remain heterosexual in the long term, which I discuss in detail in chapter 5.

Conclusion

The emergence of an ex-gay self in Cape Town was part of a cultural shift in focus on an agentive sexualized self in a national context where ideas about trauma, healing, and forming an improved subjectivity were popularized through the intersecting discourses of twelve-step ideas and the effects of the Truth and Reconciliation Commission. This chapter contextualized these tools and self-making processes through addressing what allowed HRM to be culturally relevant and to grow at the beginnings of democracy in South Africa. HRM drew on these cultural convergences so that they could be relevant to South African men. AA and the TRC have in common with HRM a focus on self-consciously working on the self, a commitment to a new way to be an individual, behavioral change to initiate new subjectivities, and a focus on the confessional as a way to form superior selves. Despite standing in opposition to South Africa's constitutional protection of gay individuals, HRM flourished in democratic South Africa because of its utilization and refashioning of a variety of postapartheid discourses and practices.

BUILDING GODLY EMOTIONAL INTIMACY

God loved me while I was giving blow jobs to all those guys; He loved me while I was prancing around as a drag queen, while I was selling my ass to all these guys. He loved me. —ALWYN

Like most ex-gay men, Damon, a coloured longtime ministry leader, tied his same-sex attraction to his lack of a father figure in childhood. He explained to me, "I never had a dad who could give me hugs, and could call me out into manhood and all that . . . I mean I never had sexual intercourse with a guy. I think it's the grossest thing on the earth . . . but I'm very much fascinated with a man's penis. And that is where manlihood [*sic*] [is] . . . Just to hold, to be held by another guy, to feel safe, the security . . . that's stuff that my dad all had to teach me, but he wasn't there. So, now to be able to understand all that, makes it for me much, much better." Ministries like HRM claimed that same-sex attraction stemmed from unmet needs for intimacy, particularly from the physical or emotional absence of fathers. HRM taught that these emotional needs became sexualized in adolescence. (Men were understood in this framework to be "naturally" sexual and women "naturally" emotional.) This "father wounding," discussed in more detail later in this chapter, was said to lead to "sexual acting out" and "sexual brokenness."

Damon said that it was only through HRM that he began to understand why he struggled with same-sex attraction. The ministry, specifically his individual counseling sessions with Brian, provided his first stirrings of hope for "healing into heterosexuality." Damon first attempted to commit suicide at the age of twelve after years of sexual abuse that began when he was a toddler. One day over tea he told me how he used to take the rough mesh bag that onions come in and rub it all over his body, cutting himself until he bled to try to make himself feel clean again. He continued to struggle with depression, anxiety, and suicidal thoughts as he grew older. Damon never had an opportunity to have a trusting and affirming relationship with another man until he met Brian at HRM in his twenties. When Brian turned sixty, Damon's gift to him was to change his last name to Brian's to honor him. Damon told me he decided to do this because Brian "affirmed" his masculinity and "re-fathered" him. His relationship with Brian also helped him see God as a safe figure to love and trust. For Damon, like other ex-gay men discussed in this chapter, intimacy with God, Jesus Christ, the Holy Spirit, and ultimately other people, was only possible through intimate work on the self. This work involved a reconfiguration of the self's boundaries, as men had to learn how to allow some supernatural entities into their bodies, hearts, and spirits, while also being on guard against others like Satan and demons, discussed in the next chapter. This new self was not the stereotype of hegemonic masculinity, where men were expected to stand alone and make autonomous decisions based on intellect and without others' inputs. Instead, this new version of intimate masculinity entailed a deep reliance on God and a lowering of the emotional walls and boundaries ex-gay men learned to build over time to protect themselves from peer and parental rejection.

According to ex-gay belief systems, homosexuality was an intimacy disorder. For ex-gay men the process of establishing and maintaining intimacy with God was hard work. They were taught that without creating a deep bond with God, they would remain disconnected, rigid, and emotionally closed off to friendship relationships with other men and romantic relations with women, the ultimate goal of hard work on the self. Ex-gay men like Damon felt that the attainment of godly intimacy was the key to healing their same-sex attractions. They thought that the ability to form connections with others was only possible after being open to receiving God's love and building a relationship with Him. Ex-gay men had to be taught how to be open to experiencing new types of feelings, particularly to love and vulnerability. This was difficult to do when they often had strained relationships with men who were in positions of moral and spiritual authority like their fathers. Ex-gay men learned intimate skills as part of their desire work. They were educated in how to intimately connect with God: hear His voice, feel His touch, and communicate directly with Him and the Holy Spirit. These habits took time and practice to develop and master.

In this chapter I focus on South African ex-gay views on why some men experience same-sex attraction and why the ex-gay self is believed to develop. I explore in more detail HRM's claim that homosexuality was an intimacy disorder that developed because of emotionally absent and abusive fathers. I then examine the variety of relationships that Pentecostals had with God and the different needs these relationships met for intimacy, particularly the nurturing and protection of God the Father and the care and romantic intimacy of Jesus. HRM members attempted to realize heterosexuality through cultivating intimacy with God and disciplining their minds and bodies to experience God's "will" for their lives. Men then applied these intimate skills to earthly relationships, ideally opening the door to richer emotional landscapes and to relationships with women, detailed in chapter 4.

I illustrate how intimacy is fashioned through a variety of work on the self. Ex-gay Pentecostal men claimed that they moved more fully into godly masculinity after allowing themselves to be vulnerable to God. They saw themselves as leading more fulfilling lives after acknowledging the need for His love and care. They were proud to separate themselves from dominant South African norms of masculinity, where men were closed-off emotionally and disconnected from experiencing and expressing love (see, for example, Morrell, Jewkes, and Lindegger 2012; Morrell and Richter 2004; Walker, Reid, and Cornell 2004).

Homosexuality as an "Intimacy Disorder"

In ex-gay rhetoric, what men sought through same-sex attraction and sexual experiences with other men was the protection and physical nurturance they were denied in childhood. HRM claimed that men were physically attracted to other men because they desired the other's masculinity. In this framework, boys who were disconnected from their fathers were unable to form relationships with other boys in childhood. The child did not know how to act in gender-appropriate ways, which led to peer rejection. The father's inability to nurture was said to lead the child to seek physical and emotional closeness from other boys and men. Boys sexualized this desire for love in adolescence. HRM said that children who were denied unconditional parental love and appropriately gendered role models developed feelings of envy for people of the same gender who seemed to possess all the things the child from the dysfunctional family lacked, leading to what is called "emotional cannibalism," the desire to possess the characteristics of another person.[1] Participants in the ministry told me that the reason cannibals eat people is to get at their essence, so "emotional cannibalism" was an attempt to be like the person one idolized.[2]

As noted in the introduction to this chapter, in ex-gay ministries, fathers were critical to affirming gender and sexual subjectivities. Ex-gay rhetoric claimed that boys who were denied intimacy with their fathers had deep, scarring, "father wounds," and they built emotional walls to protect themselves against being hurt. For the men in HRM, "father wounding" was directly tied to developing same-sex attraction, as they looked for male affirmation, touch, and love from other men to try to obtain what they did not receive as children from their fathers. HRM taught men that they sexually desired other men because they were attempting to get "legitimate" needs for intimacy met in "illegitimate" ways.

In this framework, fathers are responsible for passing masculinity on to boys. Christian self-help writer Leanne Payne writes, "It is the father (or father substitute) who affirms sons and daughters in their sexual identity and therefore—because gender identity is a vital part of personhood itself—as persons" (Payne 1995: 11, italics in original). Men in HRM understood masculinity as something to be "transferred" from father to son. This failure by father figures to "welcome" boys into "the world of men" led to a distorted masculine self. However, there were a number of internal contradictions in Christian understandings of masculinity, where masculinity was understood as an "essence." At the same time, Christian men were instructed how to alter themselves to become appropriately masculine.

HRM said that homosexuality and sexual addictions developed as responses to childhood trauma. Many of the men in the church and ministry, like Damon, grew up in less-than-ideal family situations. The most widely cited reasons for not developing as "natural" heterosexual men were either a child's family structures or school/peer experiences. Men in the ministry like Damon were taunted for being *moffies*, gays or sissies, as children, while men like Adrian, with whom I began this book, were teased for being *meisies*, little girls, not boys.

Afrikaans HRM leader and counselor Jaco said that he had a "large father wound" that initially formed because of his father's response to a "traumatic experience" he had at boarding school, which he started attending at the age of six. Jaco grew up in the Western Cape in a farming community, where his father was a farm manager. His older and younger brothers also went to the same boarding school. When he was twelve he went to his older brother Wouter's room to visit, which was in another section of the hostel where the older boys stayed. As soon as he walked in, Wouter watched and did not intervene as his roommates pulled Jaco's pants down, held him on the floor, and started laughing and mocking his penis for being small. He finally got up, pulled up his underwear and pants and ran back to his own room crying and completely humiliated. That weekend at home he told his parents that he wanted to leave boarding school and never return. When they finally got him to say why, his father laughed at him.

A subsequent meeting with the headmaster of the school found Jaco's mother doing all the talking; his father remained silent. The headmaster convinced Jaco to stay, and the incident was not brought up again in the family. However, Jaco was devastated and felt completely rejected by his father and Wouter.[3] After this boarding school incident at twelve, Jaco said that he felt detached not only from his father, but from all men. He interpreted his father's laughter as proof that he was not good or masculine enough.

Men and women could both have "mother wounds" and "father wounds," though they were said to play out differently. The "father wound" in girls was said to consist of the fear and hatred of men, sometimes leading to lesbianism. The "mother wound" was said to develop in boys and girls when mothers did not fulfill what was said to be their "natural" roles as nurturer, or if they smothered children with too much attention. HRM believed that both "mother wounding" and "father wounding" could lead to homosexuality—women became lesbians because they feared men or because they were looking for a substitute mother figure to nurture them; men became homosexual because they wanted the nurturing from substitute father figures or because they hated women. (It is worth nothing that almost everyone has the potential to be homosexual within these parameters.) In ex-gay discourses, "mother wounds" and "father wounds" could lead to extreme "brokenness" for men and women, and to the failure to be able to be intimate with anyone.

Once they became immersed in the ministry, the men in HRM explained that the origin of their same sex attraction was a lack of emotional closeness with their fathers.[4] In a testimony from an anonymous ex-gay man, the reader is encouraged to rethink what it means when he seeks a hug or nonsexual physical affection from another man. The anonymous author writes, "When you really badly want another man to hug you or hold you close, don't panic and think you may be gay. Check out what you are feeling and what you really need. Don't sell your soul for a moment of closeness with someone who is not there for you" (Anonymous n.d.-a: HRM). Ex-gay men were encouraged to see the desire for masculine affirmation and affection as a normal part of a childhood they were denied, not as sexual lust.

For South African ex-gay Pentecostal men, it was only through repairing masculinity, shedding the "false intimacy" of same-sex attraction, that lasting "healing" from homosexuality was thought to be possible to achieve. They were taught that they wanted to be cared for by other men because they had not been appropriately nurtured emotionally in childhood. Leanne Payne discusses the case of Matthew, whom she counseled to help him shed his "homosexual compulsions." She writes, *"he was looking at the other young man and loving a lost part of himself, a part that he could not recognize and accept"* (Payne 1996 [1981]: 42, italics in original). Ex-gay therapies and ministries taught men how to recognize and love the masculine in themselves and how to seek "appropriate" intimacy with others.

Creating Godly Intimacy

A crucial part of the ex-gay experience was attaining a personal relationship with God. He was understood to love each person individually, beginning even before birth. Many Christians described God as a person with an individual personality, likes and dislikes, and unique ways of expressing love. Tanya Luhrmann found that evangelicals in southern California developed closeness with God in a way similar to how they would do so with another person, by learning about His habits and interests and through spending time alone together (Luhrmann 2012). Ex-gay men had to learn how to form deep intimate relationships through working on themselves. Ideally, one's relationship with God was privileged over all other relationships, even with one's spouse. The South African Pentecostals I worked with at HRM and the Church of the Reborn believed a relationship with God was the only connection in which they were guaranteed not to be emotionally wounded, be second best, or experience rejection. God was said to have a special relationship with each individual, communicating to that person in ways that were significant to his prayer life, values, and even what they understand as beauty.

The South African Pentecostals I knew did not believe that they worshiped a distant, inaccessible, or unfeeling God. On the contrary, God could be deeply hurt by human actions. This belief became clear to me in 2005 when I attended a Sunday morning service at the Church of the Reborn. Pastor Jurie explained during his sermon how "upset" and "confused" God became when humans "live a life contrary to His purpose and potential." God was represented as having intense emotional responses that were associated with each person's life choices. Pastor Jurie asked us repeatedly if we understood how much God loved each and every individual in the congregation, repeating multiple times, "God has you in mind all the time." HRM members spoke frequently about fears of "disappointing" God. They did not fear Him or His anger. Instead, they worried more that their sins hurt God, causing Him to feel sadness and rejection.

Many of these South African Pentecostals said that sin created distance in one's relationship with God, making it harder to connect with Him. These Pentecostals believed that any sexual activities outside of heterosexual monogamous marriage would change the depth of possible intimacy with God. They considered engaging in "sexual sins" as especially egregious because the Holy Spirit inhabited the saved body. Glen, a white ministry leader, explained how masturbation damaged his closeness with God and had prevented him from moving forward in the "healing process."[5] He explained, "It [masturbation] pushes you further away from God. If you really walk under condemnation or judgment about it, instead of walking towards God every time that it happens . . . eventually you'll just give up." Similarly, Jaco confessed to me one day over lunch in 2007 about his pornography use and the consequences it had had for his relationship with God. The more pornography he looked at, the more he compulsively masturbated, the lonelier he felt, and the farther away from him God seemed to be. He lost his closeness to God, which he believed had assisted him in remaining accountable for his behavior. His reasons for not engaging in "sexual sin" decreased without godly intimacy. Men who engaged in "sexual sin" produced a self that was closed off from God. For ex-gay men, the new emerging self was understood to be in danger through engaging in "sexual sin." HRM said that same-sex attraction and engaging in "ungodly" sexual activities stunted emotional "healing." The emerging self was dangerously pliable in these moments, subject to both closeness or distance with God and possible demonic contamination, discussed in more detail in the next chapter.

Religious Learning

Believers in a variety of traditions are taught to discipline themselves to experience intimacy with God. Charles Hirschkind details how Muslim men in Egypt built a shared "moral physiology." He explains, "People's sensory responses are similar . . . to the extent that their capacities for hearing or vision have been shaped within a shared disciplinary context. They possess a specific affective-volitional structure as a result of the practices by which one has been formed as a member of a specific community" (Hirschkind

2001: 629). Instead of viewing the pious religious subject as a "natural" by-product of an experience with God, Hirschkind draws attention to how subjects were taught to mold their bodies and minds to realize spiritual and physical closeness with God. This is also similar to the ways in which women in the Egyptian piety movement disciplined themselves to feel and project pious dispositions (Mahmood 2005).

Evangelicals and Pentecostals in a variety of contexts fashion new selves by processes of religious learning (see for example Haynes 2017 in Zambia; Luhrmann, Nusbaum, and Thisted 2010 in America; O'Neill 2010 in Guatemala; Engelke 2007 in Zimbabwe; Coleman 2006 in Sweden). Anthropologists frequently note how evangelical and Pentecostal Christians use the language of disruption, rupture, and interruption to explain their conversion experiences as immediate and complete changes in subjectivity (see for example Robbins 2007; Meyer 1998; van Dijk 1998). Though converts may articulate salvation as an immediate change, in fact they have to learn how to facilitate and interpret transcendent bodily sensations. For Pentecostals, God's love, connection, and favor are expressed through the body. This means being taught to differentiate what sensations are God or the Holy Spirit, which are merely human, and which are demonic and evil. Converts are encouraged always to prioritize connections with God and pay attention to bodily sensations. Without a bodily experience, the authenticity of God's messages remains uncertain. Pentecostals have to discipline themselves and then practice what godly intimacy entails.

For many Pentecostals in South Africa sensory experiences were crucial for a full and lasting connection with God. Postconversion, they had to master the tools to discern God's love through their bodies—hearing His distinct voice and feeling His divine touch, frequently described as an intense, spreading inner warmth. American evangelical Christians in new paradigm churches like the Vineyard were explicitly taught how to connect with God through prayer and scriptural study. Christians facilitated godly communication through being led to certain passages and hearing God during scriptural study and prayer. Tanya Luhrmann found that "learning [w]as at the heart of the process of having faith" (Luhrmann, Nusbaum, and Thisted 2010: 66). This "skilled learning" involved being taught how to communicate and experience God vis-à-vis their bodies. There was also religious instruction on how to facilitate godly interaction. For example, some American evangelicals were taught how to hear God, learning that He had a distinct voice that spoke inside their heads. These Christians said they heard God's voice as distinctive, "the way they recognized a person's voice on the phone" (Luhrmann, Nusbaum, and Thisted 2010: 70). Similarly, Pentecostals at the International Central Gospel Church in Accra, Ghana were taught how to experience God's divine touch through "ongoing bodily processes that 'tunes' the senses to specific sensory experiences" (491), "training and exercise" (502), and "body posture and timing" (de Witte 2011: 506). For Ghanaian Pentecostals, the body was a vehicle that needed to be properly "tuned" to realize God's love and presence. Ex-gay men had to similarly "tune" themselves.

Different group norms affected the ways piety was expressed and actualized. Simon Coleman studied evangelicals at the Word of Life Bible Center in Uppsala, Sweden. He noted the tension between the idea that all people are saved through the born-again experience and church instructions for how adherents should fit into specific standards of sanctification. Coleman writes, "Divinity is clearly democratized in the sense that it becomes located in the Spirits of all who are born-again. Yet the believer learns to subject the self to an internalized disciplinary apparatus whose form is derived from other members of the group" (Coleman 2006: 174). Similarly in HRM piety and emotional intimacy were learned through a shared disciplinary process.

Pentecostals debated the legitimacy of born-again work like speaking in tongues and being filled with the Spirit in different individuals. They read the body for visible clues of piety. In HRM there was inevitably gossip about whether someone's performance of a new, healed self was genuine or questionable. (I discuss this further in the next chapter.) For example, if an ex-gay Pentecostal man did not shed his effeminate mannerisms, his commitment to healing was questioned. The underlying assumption was that the closer one was to God and the more committed to building a relationship with Him, the more healing He would initiate. Men who had transformed their desires were used as evidence of God's love; they had mastered the tools of intimacy.

Born-again Christians felt, tasted, touched, smelled, and heard God's love in culturally and historically specific ways. Groups trained adherents to discipline themselves into how to experience and connect with God in culturally appropriate manners. In his work on American charismatic Catholics, Thomas Csordas found that Christians described their experiences of close communication with God through visions. He attributed this to the cultural privileging of sight, where the visual was proof that something existed (Csordas 1997). In contrast, Mathew Engelke explained that hearing was the dominant sense for godly communication for Friday Masowe apostolics in contemporary Zimbabwe because they claimed that they were, like all Africans, a "musical people." They further devalued the visual because they did not use the Bible in their faith. Instead of claiming that God spoke to them through the practice of reading holy text, verses sung out during worship were the vehicle for the Holy Spirit. Engelke writes, "Verses are said to effect physical and metaphysical changes in the religious subject . . . Ideally, the louder a verse is, the better. The logic behind this is that volume is a gauge of spiritual presence; the louder one sings, the closer God becomes" (2007: 207). Apostolics used songs to achieve the pious self.

Pentecostals disciplined their bodies to experience God's love. People developed godly intimacy through coaching and through watching how the people around them acted. During my fieldwork, I found that the men in HRM privileged the sense of touch for explaining God and the Holy Spirit's presence. Examples I frequently heard were unexplained warmth in the hands and spreading heat beginning in the chest and spreading outward throughout the body. The presence of the Holy Spirit was also discerned through a floral odor, a light dusting of gold on believers' hands, and the spontaneous outpouring of emotions such as tears and holy laughter. Similarly in Brazil, attendees at Pentecostal martial arts fighting ministries felt that God's intimacy was conveyed through holy laughter and tears. For men tears were seen as "evidence that God was 'working' on them" (Rivers 2016: 225) since they were breaking masculine cultural codes.

Christians developed intimacy with God through spending quiet time with Him through prayer, worship, speaking in tongues, confession, and Bible study. Similarly to other evangelicals and Pentecostals, ex-gay men achieved ideal new selves through maximizing ways to experience God's love, approval, and will for their lives. They created bonds with God using the same process as building earthly relationships, for example spending time together, listening to one another, and creating mutual trust. This was also part of the formation of a new masculinity that entailed openness to love and vulnerability. HRM members spoke about the importance of daily intimacy with God, be it through preset prayer time early in the morning or before bed or reading the Bible every day. They explained how God led them to particular passages to read and then communicated deeper meaning to them through their bodies.

For many South African Pentecostals, simply studying and reading the Bible did not provide enough intimacy with God. White HRM leader and counselor Tristan initially attended a Bible College as a way to "heal" his same-sex attraction. However, he found that the Christian education it provided made God seem far removed and distant. He told me, "It [Bible College] was very much a Word-based thing, it wasn't [a] relationship based thing, so it just made me feel more isolated." He started his personal "healing" when he dropped all the "masks" that he put on to be perceived by others as the perfect Christian who "did all the right things, were [sic] in the right positions, said all the right things. But I still struggled with strong same-sex attractions and fantasies and compulsive masturbation . . . [It] made me feel very, very guilty and I kept people at arm's length because I thought if they get too close to me they're going to see behind the mask." Tristan was frightened of people seeing behind the walls he built to cope with his same-sex attraction. He made progress once he formed a deep bond with God. Only then was he able to start working on changing his same-sex attractions and his ability to form intimate relationships with others.

Pentecostalism is a very embodied faith, and speaking in tongues is a key piece of Pentecostal practice. The practice is found in the book of Acts, where the Holy Spirit descends from heaven in what some describe as "tongues of fire" on the day of Pentecost, leading people to speak in an unfamiliar language of the Spirit. People who spoke in tongues exhibited visible proof of an intimate relationship with God. Before my fieldwork I understood speaking in tongues as spontaneous, so I was initially surprised to learn that it was taught at the Church of the Reborn. One Sunday evening at the end of the day's last service, the senior pastor made two announcements. The first was the usual reminder that anyone needing extra prayer/intercession was invited to the front of the church after the service. The second announcement, which was what surprised me, was that anyone interested in learning how to speak in tongues should come to the right side of the stage to sign up for a seminar. People who have not been filled with the Holy Spirit were talked about as not fully saved because they were missing the experiential part of God's love and salvation that is central to Pentecostalism. Even getting into the Church of the Reborn Choir was dependent on having intimately experienced God. On a handout of "Choir Rules and Regulations," potential choir members were instructed to immediately see the Choir Director for assistance if they had not yet been filled with the Spirit. Similarly, Pentecostals in Bible schools in Ghana were taught how to speak in tongues in a "fake it 'til you make it" philosophy. "The convert is encouraged to 'speak out of faith'—that is imitate glossolalic speech—until the Holy Spirit 'kicks in' and authenticates the copy. Practitioners do not see any contradiction here, since they are not imitating the Spirit, but simply yielding to it, or indexing their desire to speak in tongues through mimicry" (Reinhardt 2014: 323). For these Ghanaian Pentecostals it was the work aspect that was evidence of piety; copying those around them was not seen as inauthentic.

As an unsaved person, I could be in the same room and have, on the surface, the same sensory experiences, hearing the same sermon, holding the same person's hands, and breathing in the same smells, but I could not experience what Pentecostals around me did. For example, during the praise and worship section of a Friday evening service, people who just moments before were chatting and smiling began to cry, shake, and speak in tongues. To me, it looked like they were having an intense emotional experience, but friends later explained how their bodies were responding to feeling the presence of the Holy Spirit. I sang along with others, but I did not feel any different from when I had come in and greeted those around me. The singing went on longer than usual and when the pastor came onto the stage he remarked how heavy the presence of the Holy Spirit was that evening, something he read through how his body felt and from observing the prostrate, kneeling, and moving bodies of those throughout the auditorium. My unsaved body did not share the same sensory experiences with saved people.

I had assumed that all Pentecostals prayed and wished to spontaneously speak in tongues because it signified a deep embodiment of faith. My assumption that tongues were spur-of-the-moment masked how working toward sanctity is a learned process. Seeing speaking in tongues as a "natural" expression of sanctity obfuscates understanding how the embodied sanctified self is constructed and performed. It involved hard work on the interior and exterior at the same time (Mahmood 2005).

Discerning God

Men's decisions to convert to Pentecostalism were sometimes tied to the depth and joy of experiencing God's love for the first time and craving more of it through a personal relationship with Him. Jayden was the ex-gay coloured Church of the Reborn's worship leader and a medical school student. He recounted the day he decided to become born again in high school. His decision to be "saved through the blood of Jesus Christ" was based on the depth of his first experience of God. After a Bible study session, the leader asked whether anyone in the group wanted to accept Jesus into his or her life. Jayden immediately experienced a new feeling of "internal warmth." It was this pleasurable sensation that led him to say the sinner's prayer and dedicate his life to God.

Joshua, a Xhosa man in his midtwenties who worked at the church, shared a similar story of choosing to become saved because of the way his body responded to God. After visiting the Church of the Reborn a few times with a friend and being bored with the services, he was shocked to find that one day his body all of a sudden responded to the Holy Spirit. Joshua was surprised to find his hands being lifted in the air during worship, and his feet tapping to the music. He also cried, which was very out of character for him. His said that his salvation was first experienced in his body and heart, then his mind. He was not able to pinpoint the exact feelings he had after being filled with the Spirit, though he felt distinctly "different" from before.

Many South African Pentecostal men interpreted the experience of not being in control of their bodies as proof of transcendence. In order to deeply experience God's love, they had to break away from unsaved norms of masculinity where men did not express emotions, cry, or lose control. However, a contradiction emerged. On the one hand, Pentecostal men stated that God's love allowed them to move closer to achieving ideal masculine heterosexual selves that were able to feel and express love. On the other hand, they could still fit into secular masculine norms by claiming that any behaviors that could be understood as feminine or decreasing their masculinity, for example, getting emotional, were tied to supernatural experiences.

Dawne Moon explained how American Methodists used emotions as the litmus test for knowing God's "true will." Both the liberal and evangelical Methodists she worked with believed that God enlightened them about His truth on homosexuality through their feelings. Moon explained how both groups understand emotions as a privileged location of godly truth, in comparison to scripture, which was more open to interpretation. American self-help, twelve-step programs, and therapeutic discourses have similarly popularized feelings as a form of truth that is indisputable. Moon writes, "Languages about the individual interventions of the Holy Spirit, about transformations of the heart, cannot directly be challenged to a speaker's face. When a speaker employs such a language of emotion to describe how God has spoken to her, detractors are left with little ground for critique . . . When members addressed debates using a language of emotion, their emotional experiences with God came to be the only evidence suitable for determining what is right" (Moon 2004: 204). Emotional encounters with God trumped other forms of knowledge and pious expression.

Pentecostals in South Africa did not privilege the emotions for "true" knowledge of God's will. Instead, they went to great lengths to delineate between feelings and godly communication. Hendrik, an Afrikaans ex-gay man, said there were significant disparities between being filled with the

Holy Spirit and experiencing human emotions. When I asked him to clarify, he said the Holy Spirit provided a sense of "deep security" that was distinct from human emotion. He said, "You feel loved, and . . . you feel secure. And, so secure that you—you can't explain it. And that makes your heart warm." For Hendrik, the rush of being overwhelmed with God's love was distinct from the everyday affection of family and friends. The affective dimension of his experiences with God stood out for him as fundamentally different from human relationships.

HRM and Church of the Reborn members experienced God's love through unexplained bodily responses and heightened emotions that were not attached to everyday circumstances. Many Christians, including Pentecostals in South Africa and the American Methodists whom Dawne Moon studied, used the language of God touching or laying things on their hearts. HRM's founder Brian instructed the men to listen to God speaking in their hearts when they were in pain or crisis. Many South African Pentecostals used phrases like "God touched my heart" or "He changed my heart." They claimed that they could sense their hearts being literally touched by God, though they also used the heart as a metaphor. They could not explain it clearly when I asked, but they fervently claimed it was a sensation that was unique from all others, and clearly indicated it to be an otherworldly feeling. For South African Pentecostals, including the men in HRM, godly communication was embodied. Men in the ministry were taught that intimacy was a key part of their "healing." They learned what these feelings and sensations should feel like in order to be new selves who experienced God's closeness.

Intimate Roles

God served multiple and overlapping roles for many South African Pentecostals: He was God the Father, Christ the Redeemer, and Jesus, a friend, a confidant, and, for some, a lover, boyfriend, and husband. In this section, I look at the two kinds of intimacy that Pentecostal men employed to move into new masculine selves—the nurturing of God the Father and the romantic care of Jesus. Many people connected to Jesus because he was once a man, rather than Christ in His divinity. One ex-gay man explained that he initially related to Jesus, rather than the divine Christ, because he seemed more familiar and accessible from years of attending church and seeing representations of Him. However, there was overlap, with people referring to Christ or God instead of, or along with, Jesus.

HRM believed that affirmation from God the Father healed wounded or "broken" masculinity. They said that God the Father reparented Christian men who never had the chance to be physically and emotionally close with an earthly father in childhood; God acted as a substitute father for men and provided the unconditional love and guidance they were denied. Men at HRM and the church spoke about God the Father "blessing" their masculinities. Leanne Payne wrote that she often worked with men whom the mental health system had given up on. At the root of their psychological problems was the childhood "trauma" of not being nurtured by fathers. She claimed that developing an intimate relationship with Father God allowed them to cease taking psychiatric medications or needing mental health services. She writes, "God found the unaffirmed little boy within each of them [neurotic and depressed men] and pronounced him a man. He freed them to become the masculine makers He created them to be" (Payne 1995: 45). In this framework, God refathered men who were wounded and abused in childhood.

For men working the ex-gay process, lasting healing was only possible through receiving masculine affirmation from God the Father. Ex-gay Alan Medinger writes, "I know from experience that affirmation from the Lord—the voice that speaks to our hearts, 'Good, my son'—is real and profound in its capacity to encourage us. And this is a confirmation of *who we are*. In fact, Jesus is the only one who knows us totally, so He is the only one who can rightfully affirm us for who we are" (2000: 60, italics in original).[6] Here men who look for masculine affirmation from other men or from women are doomed to failure because it is only God and Jesus who can bestow masculinity. Men's selves can only be transformed through God's blessings and through hard work.

Pentecostal men attained their subjectivities from a relationship with God instead of getting a sense of self from external activities like jobs, drinking, sexual encounters, or sports. The goal of masculine self-work was to learn to embrace and embody the "true masculine." The characteristics of the "true masculine" included being in control, initiating, taking authority, doing, being a godly warrior, and getting one's strength from God, not from the self-reliance of worldly masculinity. Pentecostal men saw themselves as distinctly different in values, behavior, and self-awareness from unsaved men. In general, they talked about themselves as having superior principles and values, less ego, and as treating women better than their non-Christian peers. White Afrikaans ex-gay leader Coenraad spoke about the difference between men who look outward for masculine affirmation, which he believed was always fleeting, and Christian men who look inward to God for a masculine identity. For him a man had to "weigh up with God, and that is why things like integrity and strength and inner character [are important]. 'Cos somebody can tell you that you are a man, but it's only that God can drop that in your spirit." For ex-gay Pentecostal men it was God who affirmed and "blessed" their masculinities.

Ex-gay Pentecostal men who wanted to become men of God embarked on a long route toward healing. They had to learn to view God as a safe Father, in contrast to the fathering they experienced as children. Many ministry members were abused as children by biological fathers or father substitutes. To trust God as a Father was a process that took time. Glen had an extremely abusive, mentally ill father who physically and emotionally terrorized him and his brother. His father once chased the boys outside of the house with a shotgun, threatening to shoot them. He then locked them out of the house and shot the gun into the ceiling, making his frightened children think that he had killed himself. Glen said that before becoming born-again, he still viewed God through his experiences with his biological father—full of condemnation and ready to judge and punish him for making a mistake. As he "grew" in his relationship with God, he began to see Him as full of forgiveness and someone to come to in times of trouble to ask for help. He began to understand forgiveness in new ways as he began to receive the love of God the Father. He said that preconversion he was very angry and always ready to fight to prove himself as a man. "I used to say I only believe in the Old Testament, I don't believe in the New. I'm an Old Covenant person. An eye for an eye, a tooth for a tooth. You mess with me, I'll mess with you. You hurt me, I'm gonna take your family out. Which again, is all just hocus-pocus . . . big words coming from a small, broken heart." Glen's childhood pain and trauma, particularly the rejection from his father, led him to become closed off emotionally and to turn to "sexual sin" like compulsive masturbation to cope. Through HRM, he was taught how to be open to receiving God's love and how to experience a new kind of fathering. These intimate skills allowed Glen to emotionally thrive, even going as far as forgiving his father because it was the "right" and Christian thing to do, though they remained estranged.

As discussed earlier, ex-gay discourses claimed that homosexuality was an intimacy disorder that only God the Father could heal. Men needed to have deep, meaningful, and intimate relationships with God to remain ex-gay. In another anonymous testimony, an ex-gay man explained how his view of God dramatically changed during his "healing" process. As a child he saw God "as a distant, strict old man, ready to strike with lightning"

(Anonymous n.d.-b: HRM). After his born-again experience he began to see God's "true character" as a loving Father. This man explained that in his "journey" with God he began to reimagine Him as wanting what was best for him and his life. He believed that God helped him to tear down the "walls" he built against intimacy. "I have begun to turn away from the false ways of obtaining intimacy [through homosexual activities]. As each day passes I am discovering Father God's true intimacy. This reality has created a great desire in me to pursue an even deeper and more alive intimacy with the One who created me" (Anonymous n.d.-b: HRM). For this anonymous writer, being in an open and intimate relationship with God led him to desire more of this closeness with Him and with other human beings in non-sexual ways. His selfhood was significantly transformed through his deep bond with God.

HRM leader and counselor Tristan believed God purposely took him through a long and difficult process to get him to heal. Like Damon, he said that as Father God "affirmed" his masculinity in ways his father had never done, he started to sexually desire men less and less. His emotional closeness with God provided him with the confidence and emotional tools to build healthy nonsexual relationships with other men. "And from it [same-sex attraction] being a daily struggle that took up most of my day, now it is something that only happens once or twice a year . . . then I have to ask myself, 'Why am I needy? What's the underlying need?' . . . Sometimes I almost think God allowed me to be tested once or twice a year so I don't forget." Tristan's ability to form intimate relationships, first with God and then with other people, led to a decrease in his same-sex attractions over time. His desires and his selfhood were transformed through work on the intimate.

Many contemporary evangelicals and Pentecostals experienced intimacy with God through His care for all their concerns, no matter how small. He listened and would act to prove his individual love for each person. He worked in each person's life in a special way. God's love was expressed through emotional support, physical comfort, material gifts, and the removal of life's obstacles. Afrikaans HRM leader Alwyn shared the following story. He wanted an English-language Bible that was priced too high for his budget; however, when he went to the store there was the exact Bible he wanted, and it cost the exact amount of rand he could spend, which was a "miracle" for him. Similarly, Marie Griffith discussed an American middle-aged charismatic Sunday school teacher who struggled for years with how to attractively style her thin hair. One day, the teacher decided to pray to God for assistance, even though she thought it would be insignificant to Him.

However, her prayer was answered when she was able to put in rollers and bobby pins for the first time in her life without difficulty and looked better than ever before. She concluded that God heard her prayer; she learned that He hears and responds to "nitpicking problems in my life. I know now that He cares about everything . . . even the way a Sunday school teacher wants to look" (Griffith 1997: 135). God and Jesus were believed to care about each individual person's struggles and concerns, evident in the care and attention to one's personal problems and daily life.

Holy Romance

Some evangelicals and Pentecostals experienced God and Jesus romantically. In this framework, Jesus was the perfect twenty-first-century man, similar to the masculinity ex-gay men hoped to embody, where men are in charge and also capable of expressing feelings without losing masculine status. As the ideal modern man, Jesus was not effeminate; instead He had deep emotions that He wished to express. He was not a "wimp" who preached "turning the other cheek" (Matthew 5:39) but assertive and righteous, throwing the money changers out of the Temple (Matthew 21:12). He was the attractive muscular carpenter who performed miracles in an assertive manner, not the suffering man on the cross. Marie Griffith explains that American evangelical women in the Christian women's organization Aglow saw God as superior to other men. She writes, "Whether they experience him as husband or father, Aglow women view God as the ideal man, one who makes them feel respected and valued as women and who will not abuse them or take advantage of them the way earthly men do" (Griffith 1997: 131). Similarly, growing up as a fundamentalist Christian in the 1970s, writer Susan Campbell imagined the Jesus she "flirted" back and forth with as "a boyfriend who drives a muscle car—say, a charger—and has tattoos. He's as gentle as a kitten most of the time, but you wouldn't want to cross him" (Campbell 2009: 11–12). For these women, Jesus was an ideal man, both assertive and compassionate.

Some saved women and men experienced Jesus as a romantic lover who wooed them.[7] Even if they were in healthy Christian relationships, only God was said to be able to meet spiritual needs and provide a level of romance that transcended the earthly. Marie Griffith writes that some evangelical women described God as a "Knight in shining armor, your first, honeymoon-passionate love" (Griffith 1997: 222). Jennifer Hirsch and Holly Wardlow explain that romantic love is part of the acquisition of a modern identity that is based on unique individuals falling in love outside the confines of kinship relations and expectations. Romantic intimacy provided a way to become a modern subject who knew him- or herself in new ways (Hirsch and Wardlow 2006: 14–15). Ex-gay men also sought love as a way to achieve a new sense of self.

Jesus's role as boyfriend is part of a longer history in which Christ is seen as the bridegroom and the church and people as His bride. This relationship has a lengthy history in Catholic monasticism and parts of Protestantism. Rebecca Lester studied an active order of Siervas nuns in Puebla de los Angeles, Mexico, in the mid-1990s. She focused on the experience of postulants who had just entered the order. Lester writes, "This [novice stage] is said to be a time of active 'courting' between the novice and Christ, during which she must decide if she wishes to become His bride forever. For this reason, the novices are often referred to as 'novias' [girlfriends], the sweethearts or brides-to-be of Christ" (Lester 2005: 34). The church hierarchy also used the language of romance and courting. The prioress of the order, Mother Veronica, recommended to the postulants to see Jesus as one would a boyfriend. She told the postulants, "'Think about this as if you were thinking about a boyfriend,' she suggested, eliciting giggles from the postulants. 'It's like when you have a boyfriend and you're going to have a date with him. This is how you should think about the Lord. Think to yourself that you're going to enter His house, and He's there waiting for you and you're going to talk intimately with Him'" (Lester 2005: 201). The language used by the postulants and the church hierarchy was one of romantic love, where the women chose otherworldly male companions to fulfill their spiritual and emotional needs. Women's spiritual marriages were understood as full of romance. Though the sisters may never have earthly lovers, they shared a similar language of romantic intimacy with some Protestant evangelical women and men.

Christian men can be feminine in relationship to God because their submission to God does not diminish their earthly masculinity. Even so, many authors of holy romance literature note that falling in love with Jesus can be an easier process for women because they believe that God created women as more relational, interpersonal, and interested in romance (Brestin and Troccoli 2001; McCray 1997). Christian masculinity "experts" John Eldredge and Brent Curtis note that the use of bridal language can be difficult for some men to embrace, but that men also need to be pursued and wooed by God. They write, "As men and women, we want to be chosen, for different reasons, but we both want to be chosen to be welcomed into the heart of things, invited into the Drama to live for our heart. We both want love, the adventure of intimacy, and this is what God's pursuit means for men and for women" (Curtis and Eldredge 2001: 97). As heterosexual men they guard against ideas of homosexuality by claiming the role of the spiritual feminine in a romance with Jesus, which they believe does not undermine their earthly masculinity.

To see Jesus as romantic, one must use one's senses to experience how He woos. In their best-selling Christian book *Captivating: Unveiling the Mystery of a Woman's Soul* (popular in HRM), married couple John and Stasi Eldredge write, "God's version of flowers and chocolates and candlelight dinners comes in the form of sunsets and falling stars; moonlight on lakes and cricket symphonies; warm wind, swaying trees, lush gardens, and fierce devotion" (Eldredge and Eldredge 2005a: 130). Like the true romantic, God tailors His courtship to the individual. John writes that God wooed him by showing him an out-of-season humpback whale close to the shore during time John took to be alone with God. This is explained as a "kiss" from God, a gift that He gives to John as His lover. Stasi expressed frustration, wanting to experience a similar "kiss" that was unique from God to her. Asking for her own whale sighting, she asked God if He loved her as much as John. She explains that his answer was almost immediate; a gift of hundreds of starfish on an abandoned beach for her eyes only. She writes, "God didn't just love me. He LOOOOVED me! Intimately, personally, completely" (Eldredge and Eldredge 2005b: 118, capitals in original). Both men and women are the beloved in this context.

However, not all Christians were comfortable with the "in love" language used in holy romance literature and music. Some felt that it bordered on being "gay" and misrepresented the relationship between Jesus and humanity. For example, theologian and cultural critic John Stackhouse explained that he used the phrase "in love" for one person only in his life—his wife. He wrote on his blog that his main opposition is that "it gives me the homo-erotic creeps to declare that I'm 'in love' with another man" (Stackhouse 2007). It is precisely the humanity of Jesus, His time on earth as a man, that made Stackhouse uncomfortable. Similarly, Christian blogger Dan Edelen felt that he was one of many men who struggled with the image of Jesus as a figure to fall "in love" with, writing that while it may be fine for women to use this language, it made him feel "gay." He also felt that raising Jesus up as a lover does a disservice to Christian men, who can never meet the same standards of perfection as Jesus (Edelen 2007).

Some evangelical and Pentecostal women also critiqued holy romance literature and practices. For example, in *Christianity Today*, commentator Agnieszka Tennant expressed her discomfort with the way that bridal imagery is interpreted. She discussed women who have "date nights" with Jesus, citing the example of one woman who sets the table for two, with one place setting for herself and one for Jesus. Tennant also discussed "prayer, praise, and pampering retreats," where women went for makeovers to look their best for their Prince, Jesus Christ. She believed that holy romance takes too much biblical license, "giving one's relationship with God an air of irreverent chumminess. Somehow, the scenario in which 'his princess' shaves her legs for a date with Jesus seems to leave little room for fear of God" (Tennant 2006).

Despite this, at the Church of the Reborn and other evangelical and Pentecostal churches I attended in Cape Town, like the Vineyard and His People, both women and men sang popular worship music that celebrated being "in love" with God and Jesus. The song "Better Than Life," which I sang many times, included the lyrics

> You hold me in your arms
> And Never let me Go
> You, oh, Lord, make the sunshine
> And the moonlight in the night sky
> You gave me breath and all your love
> I gave my heart to You because I can't stop falling in love with You
> I'll never stop falling in love with You.
>
> (Sampson 2003)

Two of the male worship team leaders in 2007–2008 "struggled" with same-sex desire yet seemed to have no problem singing publicly about the idea of falling in love with God.

For some ex-gay men, Jesus was reconfigured as a divine lover or boyfriend with whom they "fall in love." My first exposure to the romantic Jesus was in an Exodus International newsletter, where a white ex-gay American man shared his healing path with the reader. He writes, "Through all of it I am learning that Jesus alone is 'the one,' my best friend, my always-faithful lover, and He'll take care of all my needs no matter what" (Ensley 2005: 2). I was initially shocked to read this because it seemed counterproductive to try to shed same-sex desires through having an otherworldly boyfriend. I was further surprised when a pastor from another Cape Town Assemblies of God Church visited Church of the Reborn in September 2007. He told the congregation they needed to "flirt with God" and that "Jesus wants to woo you." During this sermon I sat next to HRM leaders who nodded in agreement and provided vocal "Amens" to the visiting pastor.

Some ex-gay South African men understood Jesus through contemporary ideas of Christian romance and intimacy, using the language of being "in love" and reinscribing Jesus as the ideal Pentecostal boyfriend—faithful, emotional, caring, strong, and romantic. They believed that to be "real" heterosexual men they first had to be the feminine partners to the perfect man, Jesus. Without this relationship they did not believe that lasting "healing" from homosexuality was possible. Brian instructed ministry members that the "only way" to obtain long-lasting healing was by "falling in love with Jesus." However, when one or two men expressed confusion about how to implement this kind of relationship, Brian told them to pray about it and spend more time with God. In practice, "falling in love" with Jesus remained cloudy for some men, while a few others claimed it was crucial to their healing.

Alwyn was an ex-gay leader who was "in the [gay] lifestyle" for years before joining HRM. He was also a gay prostitute for a short time to pay his bills while in university. However, this did not last long: Alwyn said that he knew it was wrong, that it was scary, and that God intervened to get him to stop. He was the leader in the ministry with the most "sinful" past, which he delighted in narrating in his testimonial to titillated Christian audiences who were usually both visibly attracted to these narratives for their explicit sexual content and simultaneously shocked by all the "sins" that were being narrated. After he decided to recommit his life to God, he said that Jesus took on a new role in his life, that of the romantic man whom he knew would never hurt him, unlike the men in his past. As he read the Bible from cover to cover and spent time with Jesus, Alwyn said he began to feel a new level of acceptance and comfort. He told me, "God loved me while I was giving blow jobs to all those guys; He loved me while I was prancing around as a drag queen, while I was selling my ass to all these guys. He loved me. [God] says, 'I ravished His heart.'" God was able to see beyond Alwyn's "sinful" activities to his lovable interior.

Alwyn felt "pampered" in this self-declared "honeymoon period" with Jesus. I asked him to explain how being "in love" with Jesus or God was different from "loving" because I was initially surprised that ex-gay Pentecostal men would be comfortable using these terms. He said being "in love" does not have to be associated with the sexual, asking me whether I associated sex and romance. (To which I answered, "Yes.") He clarified that the association of romance with sex is part of the "perversions of the worldly." Alwyn categorized his relationship with Jesus as "a love affair," saying that Jesus saw him as His bride, though noted this was on a spiritual level.

For some ex-gay Pentecostal men like Alwyn, Jesus modeled romantic behavior. Men attempted to apply these lessons to women later in their healing journeys, taking on the role of the romancer. The explanations by ex-gay men in South Africa of Jesus as a boyfriend were ambiguous. Alwyn's relationship with Jesus was not identical to those of evangelical women's. His new sense of self as a heterosexual was cultivated through an alternate type of same-sex relationship with Jesus. Ex-gay men were, ideally, after this experience of being the object of romance, supposed to move into the position of romancer. When Alwyn began a relationship with an ex-gay woman, he applied his romantic skills to his relationship with her. He moved from being wooed by Jesus to attempting to romance Marina. Although he used the tools he learned from his relationship with Jesus, this heterosexual relationship was ultimately unsuccessful. Marina and Alwyn both had trouble becoming sexually attracted to one another, which I discuss in detail in chapter 4.

Conclusion

Ex-gay Pentecostal men believed homosexuality was an "intimacy disorder" that resulted from poor parenting, especially from fathers, in childhood. HRM taught that same-sex attraction was an attempt to get "legitimate" needs for emotional and physical closeness met in "illegitimate" ways. South African ex-gay Pentecostal men thought they uncovered their "true masculinity" through forming and maintaining close emotional bonds with God, who refathered them and "healed" them from childhood trauma and abuse. The more open they were to receiving God's love and acceptance, the more progress they felt they would make in processing and recovering from their painful pasts. Ideally, the closer they were to God, the more likely they were to go to Him with their worries and fears, and the less likely they were to seek out same-sex sexual encounters to cope emotionally. To reach their goal of heterosexual masculinity, the men in HRM worked on new ways to build their capacities for emotional intimacy. These men built a close relationship with God through intimate work that disciplined the body and spirit into maximizing the possibilities for connection and communication with Him. These practices included Bible study, prayer, confession, and speaking in tongues. For ex-gay men, new selves were only made possible through hard desire work. Men's intimacy with God also led to improved relationships with other people because men were better able to identify and discuss their feelings. In the next chapter, I focus on spiritual warfare, the counterbalance to intimacy.

BECOMING SPIRITUAL WARRIORS
Learning How to Fight Demonic Sexual Desires

That was wow. That's an amazing lie [thinking he was born in the wrong body and should have a sex change]. It just goes to show you, how, [stuttering] how, the Enemy can plant stuff in your head or . . . make suggestions and you totally buy them. I mean wow. —ADRIAN on what Satan can do

Too much is made of love . . . The Bible isn't full of wimpy stories. —LIAM

Matthew, a white ex-gay man from Britain, came to visit Afrikaans ministry leaders Jaco and Coenraad in Cape Town in 2008. The three had attended an international ex-gay conference in London in 2007 and had deeply and spiritually connected with each other. Before the visit, Jaco and Coenraad were excited about Matthew's impending arrival. However, once Matthew arrived in Cape Town, things began to go poorly. On the surface, the visit appeared enjoyable for everyone, and Matthew spent time with various members of HRM's leadership team, going sightseeing, wine tasting, and to the beach. However, after spending some intimate spiritual time with Matthew, Coenraad and Alwyn, another HRM ministry leader, both thought that he was clearly under some sort of demonic influence or compulsion. Both claimed that they were being suddenly plagued by homosexual sexual thoughts and dreams after laying hands on Matthew during spiritual intercession (prayer for one's needs or the needs of others). The men did not feel they were subject to a full-on possession but that they were being "triggered" and irritated by sexual demons. Alwyn explained to me how this was possible, saying that, "an evil spirit can be . . . biting at you, gnawing at you."

Alwyn and Coenraad felt that their sexual sobriety was in danger from Matthew's demonic influence. They worried that he would spiritually contaminate them and initiate a demonically influenced "sexual fall." In this framework, Matthew's selfhood was spiritually and morally dangerous to others. Ex-gay men claimed that demons were able to affect what they thought about (here gay sex), their sexual desires, and the sexual choices they made. Demons could still attack saved selves and sought to get people to "sin" in ways that preyed on their weaknesses. For ex-gay men, these weaknesses were sexual. The Pentecostals I knew believed that a person could be saved and still be under demonic influence because it was difficult to "close" all doors to sin while living in a "fallen world."

In HRM ex-gay men learned a new way of conceptualizing the self. They were taught that the self was porous and intersubjective and easily affected by otherworldly beings, both positively (as detailed in the last chapter) and negatively (as I discuss in this chapter). They were told that they needed to rely on God and the Holy Spirit but that they were also surrounded by dangerous supernatural creatures like Satan and his demons, who worked specifically on people's weaknesses. HRM taught ex-gay men that, because of their same-sex desires, they were more spiritually vulnerable to sexually induced demonic thoughts, and that they needed to be always on guard and accountable to themselves, other men, God, and their girlfriends and wives. Demons were believed to be able to infiltrate their thoughts and bodies to suggest homosexual desires and induce "sexual falls."

HRM claimed that most men who "suffered" from same-sex desire were either sexually abused or had experienced childhood trauma. According to HRM, these experiences "opened doors" to demonic forces, allowing demons to repeatedly enter into the men's selves over time. Men who thought that they were demonically influenced or possessed were locked into a self-perpetuating cycle. They were always fighting off demonic influence through spiritual warfare, but demonic influence could still cause them to "act out" and "sin." (Spiritual warfare is the belief that there is a war on earth being fought between God and his supporters and Satan and his demons, and God expects Christians to actively fight in this war as part of their faith.) Men who engaged in "sin" allowed more demonic influence into the self and the cycle continued. Ex-gay men sometimes understood themselves as agents who could fight demons and successfully battle against what they saw as Satan's influence on their sexual desires. At other times, they viewed their desires as the result of a difficult-to-fight satanic plot that was targeting each and every man individually.

The demonic was an attractive framework for ex-gay men because they could both be agents who battled Satan, part of what it meant to be an ideal Pentecostal man, and also be victims of nefarious demonic plots to get them to "sexually sin." The blame for "sexual falls" could be placed on a third party, taking away men's culpability. However, blaming "falls" on the demonic was also potentially problematic. People who focused too much on demonic causes for their behaviors were thought to be avoiding taking responsibility for their actions (see Lettie's story later in this chapter for a discussion of this). Ex-gay men who blamed Satan too much for their actions were suspect for being spiritually lazy and not working hard enough on themselves and their "healing." Men learned to be self-disciplining and how to use ministry-provided tools, discussed in detail below, in order to "fight" what they understood as a constant demonic threat to their ability to actualize heterosexual selves. Sexual self-control was key to masculine self-making for the men in HRM. They, like Pentecostal men in Zambia (van Klinken 2011), Tanzania (Lindhardt 2015), and Benin (Quiroz 2016) saw the ability to be sexually and morally in control of themselves as key to what it meant to be a saved and sanctified Pentecostal man. For the men in HRM, battling the demonic and "sexual sin" were key pieces of self-control work.

In HRM, spiritual warfare had a key place in daily life, desire work, and self-making. These practices required Christians to fight in the battle against evil and Satan through binding (tying up demons to counteract their power) and casting out demons. Spiritual warfare practices include targeted prayers against demonic influences and the casting out of demons from people and places. It was heightened for ex-gay Pentecostal men because they believed that their same-sex attractions had a demonic component. In this chapter I look at how men confronted their demonic desires and how important spiritual warfare was to conquering same-sex attraction. This warfare was personal, ongoing, and embodied. Men were taught a new frame to interpret their desires and new strategies for combatting them. They learned to see themselves in a different way that prioritized how others, both human and supernatural, could affect them. Men needed to recognize and overcome demonic influences to construct and maintain the ex-gay self.

Below, I outline the process of ex-gay self-making and the formation of new (inter)subjectivities. I then use ethnographic data to examine the strong role of the demonic in Pentecostal life and the ways that different actors sought to diagnose demonic possession, often disagreeing about its presence. I go on to look at how Pentecostals understand demonically possessed bodies as different from saved bodies and the ways that they identify demonic manifestation and possession in themselves and others. (Demonic manifesting is the term used when the demon makes itself known.) I move on to examining "demonic sexual desires" and the spiritual warfare tools HRM provided ministry members to rid themselves of demonic influence, including HRM-supplied prayers and spiritual mapping.

Intersubjective Self-Making

In many African Pentecostal churches and ministries, "falls" lead to public shaming and ostracizing (Parsitau 2009; Garner 2000). This was not the case in HRM, where ex-gay men were expected to "backslide" because the ministry believed it was difficult to rid the self of demonic influence and that new behaviors took time to be internalized. This general attitude to "sin," where the blame is not put wholly on the person who "fell," is unique for many Pentecostal churches, where a variety of "sins" like out-of-wedlock pregnancy, sexual relationships outside of marriage, and a host of other "sexual sins" can lead to marginalization, dismissal from church duties, ostracizing, and excommunication. In HRM, men were taught that they would have periodic "sexual falls" as part of their work on the self. Ex-gay men had to learn how to be emotionally vulnerable and open and to share with their counselors, "accountability partners," support groups, and God when they felt "tempted." HRM provided the tools to combat the feared spiritual consequences of "sexual sin," to address anxieties and fears, and to allow men to become more in control of themselves and their desires. Ex-gay men were encouraged to always confess their "falls" and then recommit themselves to God and the ex-gay process.

The ex-gay process was part of a larger focus on work on the self in Pentecostalism. Pentecostalism is often represented as a complete break with the old "sinful" self, relationships, and priorities. Despite this narrative arc about the new saved self, Pentecostals still struggled to remain spiritually pure and live righteous lives on a daily basis (Engelke 2010; van Dijk 2001). Although most Pentecostals described their salvation as a distinct rupture, conversion was actually a long process that involved everyday forms of work such as prayer, attending church and Bible study, connecting with God, and deliverance. (Deliverance is the process of cleansing a person of demons and satanic influence and reconnecting him or her with God and the Holy Spirit.) Ruth Marshall writes, "Becoming Born-Again is an event of rupture but *being* Born-Again is an ongoing existential project, not a state acquired once and for all, a process that is never fully achieved and always runs the risk of being compromised" (Marshall 2009: 131, italics in original). My research revealed that becoming heterosexual was also a process that was never complete. Men's desires and sexual activities affected the possibilities for their salvation and the actualization of the saved self.

The born-again self is never just a separate, isolated, self-contained entity. Katrien Pype writes, "Given the constant intervention of otherworldly spirits in the lives of Christians, it is difficult to accept the image of the self-governing subject in this context" (Pype 2012: 168). Instead, Pentecostals conceive of the self as intersubjective—both individual and "dividual." Girish Daswani explains, "I understand the process of maintaining 'individuality' as an expression of distancing oneself from the control and moral expectations of certain significant others; and I view 'dividuality' as the close proximity and the expected as well as the unexpected pull of others—human and nonhuman—in one's life, where persons are seen to be composed of relationships and substances" (Daswani 2015: 108). The Pentecostal self is both individual and dividual because it is impacted by and can impact a variety of otherworldly beings, the most commonly discussed being God, Jesus Christ, the Holy Spirit, Satan, witches, and demons. South African ex-gay men believed that they were constantly and consistently under a barrage of specific attacks against their sexualities and sexual self-making. Their experiences as dividual selves were extreme, even in a Pentecostal framework where Satan is understood to develop targeted assaults against a person's weaknesses. They felt under attack and needed to be on emotional and spiritual guard. Ex-gay Pentecostal men constantly evaluated themselves to attempt to discern whether their sexual desires and actions were based on their own emotions or whether they were demonically influenced. Their senses of self were dividual, relational, and malleable.

Demons in Pentecostal Life

Demons appear throughout the Bible and Christian history. Jesus and his disciples cast out demons at various places in the New Testament. In Matthew 8:16, Jesus "drove out the spirits with a word," and in Mark 1:23–27, Jesus rebuked and silenced an "unclean spirit" to the amazement of the crowd (Amplified Bible 1987). Early monastic texts are full of battles between monks in their quest for ascetic purity and dangerous otherworldly beings (Brakke 2006). Contemporary Pentecostals claim to continue the battle against evil through spiritual warfare practices.

Satan and demons are prominent figures in African Pentecostal lives (see, for example, Anderson 2014; Haustein 2011; Asamoah-Gyadu 2007; Meyer 1995). Satan is also known as the Enemy, the Great Deceiver, and the Beast. He has demons that "manifest" on earth and take control of human bodies. Pentecostals claim that Satan attempts to muddle their thoughts by sending them "sinful" ideas and desires to get them to "fall" (Lindhardt 2010). They have to learn how to close themselves to Satanic influences and work to keep demons at bay. Van de Kamp (2011) describes how Pentecostal women in Mozambique are taught to seal off their bodies from demonic interference through embracing the indwelling of the Holy Spirit and fighting Satan in spiritual shields. She writes, "Converts need to be attentive and ready soldiers, continuously dressed in their spiritual armor. They are thus always in a war situation and need a strong and determined attitude" (van de Kamp 2011: 527). Pentecostals must be always ready to battle Satan and demonic interference in daily life and to perform rituals and spiritual warfare practices to combat demonic effects. African churches provide followers with the language and tools to fight Satan. For example, in Durban, believers who belong to the Universal Church of the Kingdom of God claim that exorcisms are a vital part of spiritual life. However, these practices also make Christians spiritually weak and more inclined to further demonic interferences. To counter this, sanctified and ritually protected objects, holy water, and holy oil are provided to followers as demonic blockers and are worn on the body (Van Wyk 2014: 43).

For Pentecostals heaven and hell are actual places, with some Christians claiming to have visited one or the other with God's guidance (see for example Wiese 2006; Thomas 2003; Baxter and Lowery 1998). The Holy Spirit, Jesus, angels, demons, ancestors, and witches are agents with real power in human life, not the metaphors or literary devices of more mainstream Christianity. In Pentecostalism, Satan's hand is seen in misfortune, accidents, bodily pains, disease, financial problems, and hosts of other difficulties, problems that are also tied to witchcraft or the withdrawal of the ancestors' protection. Pentecostals see the ancestors and *sangomas* (traditional healers) as demonic witches who work for Satan. Indigenous religious beliefs, healers, places, spirits, and the ancestors are reinscribed as demonic. For example, marine spirits like Mami Wata are believed to be demons that lead people to make immoral sexual choices (Anderson 2014).

African Pentecostalism abounds with examples of the syncretism of Christianity with African ancestral beliefs. However, among the white and coloured clients of HRM, Western beliefs about demons and Satan predominated. Paul Gifford explains, "These two strands—the African and the

Western—reinforce one another, even feed off one another, and in certain circles tend to coalesce" (2001: 70). The demonic discourses discussed in this chapter are in no way coherent and do not constitute an ordered system. Although South African Pentecostals may have claimed that demonic possession was easy to understand, there were a variety of interpretations for what was and was not demonic. This is discussed in detail below.

South African Pentecostals said that they could recognize the demonic through bodily sensations and feelings. In this framework, demonic influence and bondage could be spread through touch. Therefore, people who laid hands on someone else could be in spiritual danger. Alwyn's solution to the problem of possible spiritual contamination was to go through a process of spiritual warfare to cleanse himself. His weapon of choice was to speak in tongues. He noted that when he spoke in tongues, he felt any "bondage" being released and the indwelling of the Holy Spirit through changes in his body. He explained, "The moment I switch to tongues, I'm being stirred from the inside. It's like all of a sudden I'm breathing, I'm just breathing so much deeper and more. And I feel—it might sound weird—but I feel my hands, my palms of my hand. It feels like it's burning. And I start feeling like I'm warm. And I'll just like keep going. And then it just flows and flows. And then afterwards, I feel so strengthened. Excuse me, I feel like, bring it on, bring it on. And for me, it's . . . refreshing." For Alwyn, the release from any demonic interference was embodied. He felt renewed and closer to God and the Holy Spirit after participation in spiritual warfare activities like speaking in tongues. He went through a similar process after he interceded spiritually for someone. After he laid hands on someone else, he "washed" himself spiritually by praying, speaking in tongues, and casting away any "spirits of lust" that could have become attached to him. Spiritual warfare made Alwyn feel authoritative and empowered. He felt that these practices allowed him to possess a godly masculinity.

Men like Alwyn sought to be spiritual warriors who not only protected themselves but also acted proactively in a global war against Satan. The ex-gay men in HRM used Jesus as their masculine ideal and saw him as the original spiritual warrior. They discussed Him as a vigorous, physically strong man who stood up for his beliefs, not as a helpless victim or a dying, weakened body on the Cross. HRM members highlighted the biblical examples of Jesus bodily forcing the moneychangers out of the temple (Mark 11, Matthew 21, Luke 19, John 2) and the feat of his forty days in the desert (Luke 4, Mark 1, Matthew 4). The men in HRM spoke about a Jesus Christ who took charge, fought for his beliefs, and was a spiritual warrior, not the prince of peace. White HRM leader Liam told me, "You know Christ wasn't a wimp. He was outspoken, he had opinions, he was clever. He was learned and intellectual and he took people on if they needed to be attended to. Too much is made of love ... The Bible isn't full of wimpy stories." For Liam, Jesus Christ was the kind of masculine man he aspired to be. Men like Alwyn and Liam wanted to be spiritual warriors and drew on biblical ideals in their behaviors and self-constructions.

Demonic Discernment

For born-again Christians, discernment refers to a process of actively listening to God to try to understand what decision He wants a person to make. It is a process of prayer that can include fasting and spiritual warfare to help remove spiritual blockages. South African Pentecostals used discernment to judge whether someone was manifesting demons or the Holy Spirit or incorrectly claiming religious causation. Other interpretive frameworks included mental illness,[1] irresponsible behavior, or spiritual immaturity. For Pentecostals, discernment was a key process because of the dividual self, where otherworldly others could drastically affect a person's thoughts, feelings, and behaviors. They had to be permeable in order to be open to the Holy Spirit and God. However, this also exposed them to possible demonic import, manifestations, and possession. Despite conversion, many Pentecostals continued to experience demonic interference and thus needed discernment to diagnose what was happening to them. Pentecostals had to continue to address prior kinship ties and the pulls of "traditional" spirits. For example, Ghanaian Pentecostals had to engage in discernment to diagnose whether they were filled with the Holy Spirit or "competing spirits who, by default, continue to be in a relationship with them after they become born-again" (Daswani 2011: 275). For the men in HRM, the born-again experience did not lead to the end of "competing spirits" because of the belief that same-sex sexual desires could have a demonic origin, often from childhood trauma, and because their participation in "sexual sin" was understood to invite more demons into their bodies.

David was a spiritual counselor at the Church of the Reborn who was never quick to blame the demonic, always looking first for human responsibility.[2] He also took HRM classes. South African Pentecostals believed that "divine protection" was always available for Christians and that spiritual warfare was an important part of Pentecostal life. However, David also thought that with "spiritual maturity" should come greater wisdom to see that salvation was no guarantee of better fortune because Christians still lived in a "fallen" world. David felt that many Pentecostals, especially the newly saved, did not take into account that being born again did not stop bad things and accidents from happening to them. They might point to the demonic when salvation did not immediately lead to a better life. He found that new Christians often wanted answers from God quickly and did not take the time to listen to and discern His will. David also thought that people who had been saved for longer periods of time could get "lazy" about spending necessary time with God. Instead, they became too focused on blaming outward causes for problems and pointed too quickly to the demonic. He told me, "I think sometimes when people are unsure, it's like, let me just do deliverance . . . just in case. It's almost like, let me shoot in the bush. I never know, there might be . . . something in there." For some Pentecostals deliverance was a catch-all tool.

I begin with David's ideas to situate a significant incident that affected both HRM and the Church of the Reborn. I focus specifically on the upheaval caused by one female ministry member whose erratic behavior caused different interpretations by various leaders—some wanted to send her for deliverance, others thought she needed psychiatric medication, and still others believed that she was angry and giving a spiritual cause to excuse what they saw as her inappropriate actions. This example also demonstrates the point raised earlier about demonic discernment being ambiguous and contradictory. Although Pentecostals frequently claimed that demonic possession was clear-cut and easy to see, the story below illustrates the ways that a diagnosis of spiritual possession depends greatly on context and the subjectivity of the person.

Lettie was a coloured Pentecostal ex-lesbian. She had been involved in HRM for about a year when I met her in 2007. We also attended the same Life Group. Lettie was on the far end of charismatic: always the first one to speak in tongues, throw her hands in the air during worship, blame Satan, or celebrate the Holy Spirit. She had a reputation as being emotionally needy, and I was told that she did not know appropriate interpersonal boundaries because of her dysfunctional and emotionally enmeshed lesbian past. I was warned by male ministry leaders to be wary of her or to stay away from her altogether. South African Pentecostals believed that proximity to a possessed person could spiritually contaminate others; knowing who is possessed allowed them to protect themselves and warn others. The men in HRM saw it as their duty to protect women from physical and spiritual dangers. Alwyn warned the women in HRM, including me, to stay away from

Lettie since she was "spiritually dangerous." He worried we would become spiritually contaminated from close proximity to her; he thought that as women we would be susceptible to emotional manipulation and same-sex contagion. The men at the church and HRM did not feel the same vulnerability to Lettie's demons because she was a woman and they were not sexually involved with her.

Lettie was most often found in the company of Afrikaans women who were present or past ministry members, two of whom were also Pentecostal ex-lesbians who were rumored to be in some sort of inappropriate and non-ministry-sanctioned relationship. Lettie was involved in a small and spiritually intense women's group with these women. They held "girls' prayer nights," where they worshipped, prayed for each other, and worked on personal "breakthroughs." Lettie's progressively strange behavior, which I detail below, became increasingly oppressive to the other women in the prayer group. Elisbe, another Afrikaans ministry leader who was part of the group, felt that Lettie did not leave room for others to share, connect with God, or get their own spiritual needs met. Lettie spiritually overtook and manipulated the prayer group.

At the same time, Lettie's actions became difficult to understand in a number of church and HRM settings. In September she sent an email to a male HRM leader that was widely perceived to be inappropriate, aggressive, and sexually harassing. In it, she typed out the words to a love song, which included lyrics about "always doing what my man asks." For HRM leaders, the most upsetting part of Lettie's email was the part of the message that read that when the recipient "affirmed her femininity" and "raised her up spiritually," his words "penetrate her all the way down into her G-spot." The leaders, who had an emergency meeting to discuss what to do about the situation, were distressed that Lettie was acting masculine in being sexually aggressive. I first learned about the situation through ministry gossip. I was told "confidentially" about the situation and instructed not to discuss it with anyone else. However, in typical HRM fashion, everyone soon knew the whole story and analyzed it openly. Ministry members debated about what could have caused Lettie's actions and how to help her.

Around the same time, a Church of the Reborn administrator received a frantic phone call from Lettie's employer. She had not shown up to work in two days, and the church was listed as her emergency contact. Church employees attempted to get in touch with her through text messages and repeated phone calls, but she never replied. Lettie's prayer group got worried and drove the half hour to her flat when she did not respond to their attempts to see if she was hurt or in trouble. The women rang the doorbell and banged on doors. Suddenly, Lettie opened her back door, clutching her Bible. Yelling, she informed them that God had told her to pray alone for two days. At the top of her lungs, she told the astonished women that they had no faith in God and no right to come and bother her. Later, Elisbe said that Lettie was ranting, and when she looked her in the eyes, "Lettie wasn't there." This was later used as part of the argument for demonic possession. The women left in tears and kept saying that they were worried but did not want to invade her privacy. Although I did not hear this articulated explicitly, it is possible that they also left because they were fearful of Lettie's behavior and worried that she was under demonic influence that could have affected them negatively.

When Lettie returned to church and ministry events after an absence, her behavior remained erratic. At Life Group one evening, she rudely and repeatedly tried to interrupt the speaker's testimony. Originally from East Africa, the black male guest speaker shared his conversion experience in detail. At the time he had become born-again he was considering converting to either Christianity or Islam. He narrated for us how one night a local witchdoctor sent a bewitched cat over to his house. Fearful, he called out the name of Allah and nothing happened. He then called out the name of Jesus Christ and the cat went away. He became a Christian immediately, saying the "Sinner's Prayer" and giving his life to Jesus Christ. As he attempted to share in English, which was not his first or second language, Lettie stood up behind him, waving her arms and saying in a loud whisper to the leaders that they needed to silence the speaker because even mentioning Satan invited demons into a space. We were all in danger, she warned, from the speaker's storytelling. After she left, her behavior was dissected and discussed as inappropriate and rude.

Church and ministry members argued over Lettie's ongoing behavior. Some claimed that she was demonically possessed and was in need of deliverance. Lettie herself believed she was under a form of spiritual bondage and used this to explain her actions. On her own initiative, she went for deliverance and explained her behavior as demonic manifestations, not as the results of any choices she made. She never apologized to anyone for any of her actions, further upsetting ministry and church members. Others believed that Lettie was emotionally "acting out" due to an undiagnosed mental illness like bipolar disorder. Those who thought she was demon possessed tended to agree that she also needed intense Christian counseling. Once a person began to manifest demons, other Christians feared that although the original demons were cast out, a personal problem or vulnerability could make demonic influence easily possible again.

Still others said that Lettie claimed possession to get around taking responsibility for her misconduct. David believed that Lettie was manipulative and when her bad behavior did not get the results she wanted, she "over-spiritualized" it to avoid responsibility, blaming it on some demonic force. Pentecostals use the term "over-spiritualizing," largely in a negative way, to explain instances when people blame everything on the supernatural. When David and I discussed the various disruptions Lettie caused in the church and ministry, especially her refusal to apologize, he told me sarcastically, while rolling his eyes, "I'm sure God told her to do it." He was angry that she was being spiritually and personally immature.

Four white ministry members, three Afrikaans individuals, and Brian, who is also white, told me separately that some of Lettie's behavior could be understood culturally. They said that coloured churches have different behavioral and social norms. However, David, who is coloured, thought she was completely out of line and her behavior could not be blamed on a different cultural context. Lettie continued to attend the Church of the Reborn, but she quit HRM and our weekly Life Group. The root of her behavior remained unclear and debated. For HRM members, discernment was an important tool but not one that necessarily erased ambiguities. Demonic discernment was more complicated than people explained it to be and was affected and altered by the subjectivity of the person under discussion. Lettie's past as an ex-lesbian and her coloured identity changed how others interpreted her actions. HRM leaders used so-called cultural explanations and ministry-normative sexuality-based stereotypes to claim that lesbians were more emotionally needy and emotionally unstable. Lettie's actions were diagnosed differently than a white ex-gay man's or a heterosexual woman's would have been.

Demonic Bodies

HRM members were predisposed to view Lettie as possessed because of her lesbian past. Many born-again Christians believe that the "broken" are more liable to be spiritually attacked. Thomas Csordas explains that demons are believed to "prey on the vulnerability self-created by sin" (Csordas 1997: 193). For these Christians, demonic possession and manifestation are linked to bodies that surpass normal human capabilities. South African Pentecostals said that demons could possess a person, but not always manifest. The possessed person often said that he or she did not remember manifesting, which is brought on by emotional or spiritual stress. He would remember feeling "funny" before the manifestation and there was often memory loss. Vomiting, thrashing about, and other bodily changes could occur, such as eyes rolling back in the head, a deep voice coming from the person, or sudden physical strength. Damon said that in one of his deliverance sessions, as soon as he started manifesting, he began to swear in a "weird voice." His body convulsed, and he screamed and fought off those trying to assist him. Although he was skinny and sickly at the time, it took six men to hold him down. It was not until he saw something come out of him and run into the bushes that he calmed down.

Pentecostals said that the demonic body was able to transcend natural boundaries. Joshua, a Xhosa man, worked at the Church of the Reborn and was a *sangoma* (traditional healer) before his conversion. He told me that during his training he had to spend time alone with the ancestors in a sacred forest, river, and ocean. He said that he was able to stay under water for days at a time without coming up for air, eating, or sleeping. It was during this time that the ancestors taught him how to heal others and showed him which herbs he needed to recognize to make *muthi* (medicine). Joshua, like other Pentecostals, believed indigenous African religions were demonic. He viewed his time as a *sangoma* negatively. Pentecostals did not doubt the truth of Joshua's time spent underwater. They believed that he literally spent the time underwater without a breathing apparatus. For Pentecostals, demons were able to bypass normal human limitations.

Bianca, the white wife of an HRM leader, told me that she only knew the depth of a friend's demonic possession once the friend was healed. The friend came from an "occult background" and was previously a self-identified witch. She was often physically ill from her possession and her illnesses got worse the more she fought off Satan. Bianca said that her friend would wake up at night being strangled by demons. Pentecostals believe that deliverance can be a one-time occurrence or be done multiple times over a period of years. For Bianca's friend the process took years, during which time her eye color began to change. Before her deliverance, her friend's eyes were gray, and one day Bianca noticed they were a brilliant green. Bianca was shocked and believed the change in her friend's eye color served as outer visible proof of inner healing. Pentecostals read bodies for evidence of possession, manifestation, and healing.

I was told repeatedly that people often resemble animals when manifesting demons. Carla, a white Pentecostal woman in her early sixties, had been saved twenty years earlier in England. British by birth, she originally came to South Africa after answering a missionary "call" from God in her mid-fifties. Carla was married twice before and she joked that she should never be allowed to do marriage counseling since she advocated divorce, even for Christians. She believed in deliverance and said that she had seen demons manifesting numerous times, both in England and South Africa. One day over tea she told me how her second husband was "definitely demon possessed" and recounted how his face transformed when he was manifesting. She said he would resemble a goat, an animal historically associated with Satan; she would watch as nubby horns formed on his skull above his eyebrows. His eyes also morphed and moved closer together, turning yellow, and the smell of sulfur came off his breath.

Carla also recounted witnessing how a possessed man in Jersey, England, started to resemble a snake at a church deliverance session. He writhed on the ground, arms and shoulders turned inward, contorting his torso to resemble a snake's body. His hands were clenched and his fingers locked, pulled in close to his sides. Even his eyes became red and looked tiny. Carla also believed that one of our mutual friends was demonically possessed. Liam was an HRM leader who had a few physical tics and nervous habits. He was a bit socially awkward and a self-confessed obsessive compulsive. Carla explained his tics as one of the ways she knew he was manifesting. She compared him to a dog with fleas, the demons pushing his buttons and making him twitch and "act out."

HRM members claimed that challenging evil led to increased demonic activity. For example, after their Gay Pride Outreach in March 2008, members believed that Satan was "on the war path against us." HRM members sent emails back and forth with a growing list of events that they believed could only have come from "the Enemy," including visa problems that almost led to the American founder's deportation, a falling skylight that barely missed another's head, and a series of financial problems and sexual struggles for various other leaders. One email I received read, "Thank you for your continued faithful prayers . . . It's not over . . . In fact the battle has just begun again! The Enemy might have had the first shot but we are on the offensive with the sword in hand!!!" HRM members understood their misfortunes through the lens of the demonic.

HRM provided tools for ex-gay men to combat the feared spiritual consequences of "sexual sin," to combat anxieties, and to allow them to feel more
in control of the self. They taught ex-gay men that they could fight demonic
interference and possession by using ministry-provided spiritual warfare
tools such as specific prayers and spiritual mapping, discussed below. These
spiritual warfare prayers, one on breaking "soul-ties" and the other on pornography use, were a key part of the ex-gay process because the men in the
ministry had periodic and, as detailed earlier, expected "sexual falls." Men
needed to immediately confess to other ministry members or God and perform these prayers in order to fight demonic contamination and close the
"doors" to Satan they believed they had "opened" through "sinful" sexual
activity. HRM taught spiritual warfare prayers to ex-gay men as part of their
focus on both ridding the self of demons and reclaiming parts of the self
that they saw as lost through "sexual sin." Ex-gay men had to perform spiritual recovery work. The ministry's ideas about the self being relational and
porous are evident in these spiritual warfare prayers and their stated effects.

Ex-gay men in the ministry understood themselves to be extremely spiritually vulnerable because of their same-sex desires. They felt that they were
more sensitive to demonic intervention around sex than others because
they had "opened" doors sexually to Satan in the past either through their
own sexual decision-making or because they were abused as children. This
language of "open" and "closed" doors was a common one in the ministry.
Masturbation, pornography use, nonmarital heterosexual sex, and same-
sex sexual encounters were all said to "open the doors" to demons. It was
only through prayer, especially evoking the blood of Christ for protection,
spiritual cleansing, spiritual warfare, and the breaking of "soul-ties" that
these doors could be shut. When I asked Afrikaans ministry leader Coenraad what an "open door" meant, he told me, "When I say 'open a door' it's
an area in your life that you make sensitive to oppression. It's maybe like
somebody ripping off part of your skin, so that bit is sensitive for infection.
And then he [Satan] would go and throw stuff on that open wound to make
it infected . . . A spirit of lust can sort of, what's the word, pester or inflict
or whatever, come and irritate somebody that's struggling with sexuality."
These "opened doors" were what allowed saved people still to experience
demonic interference.

Pentecostals around the world believe that Satan tries to make saved
individuals "sin" by planting sexual desires outside of "God's ways." For

many evangelical and Pentecostal Christians, the body is a battleground between Satan and the Holy Spirit (DeRogatis 2015). These Christians think that Satan employs demons to do his bidding. In her book *When Godly People Do Ungodly Things: Arming Yourself in the Age of Seduction*, Christian writer Beth Moore writes that Satan targeted born-again believers. She writes, "Since the Spirit of Christ now dwells in the temple of believers' bodies, getting a Christian engaged in 'sexual sin' is the closest Satan can come to personally assaulting Christ" (Moore 2002: 24). Pentecostals view themselves as especially vulnerable to demonic attacks because of the focus in the faith on spiritual warfare. For the men in HRM, anxieties about Satan coming after them to get them to "sexually sin" loomed large in their daily lives. Like many evangelical, charismatic, and Pentecostal Christians, HRM members believed that Satan took advantage of vulnerabilities and fears to keep people from leading blessed and happy lives. For example, ex-gay coloured ministry member Adrian thought that Satan used his gender identity confusion and same-sex desire to keep him in "spiritual bondage." When I asked him about his wish to have a sex change and live as a woman (Adrian had gone as far as meeting with a psychologist to discuss the possibility of a sex change operation), he told me that the power of his longing to change his gender was proof of the power of the devil. He said, "That was wow. That's an amazing lie [thinking he was born in the wrong body]. It just goes to show you, how, [stuttering] how, the Enemy can plant stuff in your head or . . . make suggestions and you totally buy them. I mean wow." Adrian believed that Satan had sought to get him to transform himself into a woman by preying on his feelings of masculine inadequacy and the childhood trauma of being teased for being effeminate and too much like a girl.

HRM is one of many religious groups in Africa that performs deliverance and engages in spiritual warfare to "cure" people of their same-sex attractions. Nelson Muparamoto details a Pentecostal exorcism of gay men in contemporary Zimbabwe. In this case, a church prophet linked gayness and effeminate affect to possession by a demonic marine spirit, in particular, a mermaid. The prophet claimed that two gay men needed deliverance to be "cured" of their desires and self-presentations. He made each man drink a special tea, then proceeded, with help, to hold them down on the ground and poke them in the stomachs with a ritual staff until they vomited, which was interpreted as evidence that the spirit of the mermaid had left their bodies (Muparamoto 2016: 151). I bring this up so that HRM's beliefs and spiritual warfare practices are not understood as aberrations in Pentecostal life. They share with many other African Pentecostals not only beliefs about homosexuality, "sexual sin," and demons but also practices in how to rid them from the body, a process that could sometimes take repeated efforts and years.

HRM claimed that "sexual sin" was especially damaging because it led to shame, damaged interpersonal relations, broken families, and people leaving the church, which was understood to be a key piece of Satan's plan to "take over" the earth. They believed that Satan wanted more "sin" to occur, and that he used sex as one of his key areas of intervention in saved people's lives. HRM members thought that Satan worked specifically around a person's weaknesses to craft a personal program to influence "sinful" behavior in each believer. Similarly, American Christian masculinity "expert" John Eldredge warned saved men that Satan would subtly offer a "tailor-made" formula to get them to commit "sexual sins." He writes, "You'll see a beautiful woman and something in you will say, *You want her.* That's the Evil One appealing to the traitor within. If the traitor says, *Yes, I do*, then the lust really begins to take hold. Let that go on for years and you've given him a stronghold" (Eldredge 2001: 163, italics in original). Satan was seen to strive to get men to "sexually sin" because God had made them more inherently sexual than women.

Ex-gay men's sexual choices were thought to have allowed or "welcomed" demons to become entrenched in the self, making deliverance a process that took time. White ministry leader Tristan told me that when he first married his wife, Bianca, she had to "deliver him" a number of times, sometimes when they were lying in bed at night before going to sleep. He said, "I was very full of demons; my deliverance was over a couple of years." Men who went for deliverance one time only were usually disappointed that it did not instantly cure them of their same-sex attraction. The reason for this was precisely because demons had become part of the self.

HRM believed that demons were transferred from spiritually contaminated people through touch or close proximity. They said that sexual violence was one of the main ways demons entered unprotected people. Proponents of these ideas claimed that children were especially spiritually vulnerable because of their innocence. They argued that child abuse originally "opened doors" to demons. These openings were said to have direct effects on the formation of the self because demons became a part of the formation of the person. These Pentecostals believed that because of a child's spiritual vulnerability and weakness, demons could easily enter a child and remain undetected for years. This affected how some Pentecostals interacted with gay people. For example, Afrikaans Pentecostal parents Faan and Liesl decided to forgo a prearranged dinner date when they found out that a gay couple were also going to be spending time at their babysitter's flat during the same night and would potentially have contact with their child. They believed that a touch from a homosexual or even close proximity could spiritually harm their child, maybe permanently.

South African Pentecostals claimed that demonic possession at a young age would alter the developing person's subjectivity because the demon became part of the person's sense of self. Tristan explained, "Demons have certain traits and the person they live in takes on the traits of the demon." Pentecostals thought that deliverance could cause deep emotional pain for the person with demonic contamination or possession. Carla told me that a demon becomes like a "friend" that "tells you nice things and it encouraged you to do things that you like to do. And then it pours shame on you and you do it . . . If you're penetrated as a little girl or a little boy, or if you've been fiddled with, those demons, they go Woo! There's a scar and they just attach themselves. You'll find a lot of gay people have been molested and that's where the demons enter. That's when the demons take authority. Takes hold, when they're children . . . it's a part of your being and when it comes out you feel like you've been ripped apart." Demons became part of the developing self. Furthermore, this Pentecostal belief system stated that even after a demon was exorcised, there could be lingering effects. According to this logic, people possessed as children formed unhealthy thought and behavior patterns while under demonic influence. The newly delivered person had to relearn ethics and "proper" ways of being in the world. This was one of the reasons HRM believed that in addition to confession and deliverance, loving Christian counseling and accountability structures were necessary to long-lasting "healing."

The Pentecostals I worked with believed that sex could spiritually injure a person because it "opened doors" to demons, regardless if someone was saved. Each time a person had "ungodly sex," he or she "lost" a part of the spiritual self to a sexual partner. In HRM, these were referred to as "soul-ties." They were positive in heterosexual marriage because they built a strong bond; but were negative when a person had sex outside the confines of "godly sex." HRM members shared with many other Pentecostals and evangelicals around the world similar ideas about the spiritual consequences of sex. Some American evangelicals believe that STDs stands for "sexually transmitted demons." They claim that demons are transmitted through body fluids and can become part of DNA (DeRogatis 2015: 87).

Other Pentecostals in Kinshasa believed that bodily fluids like saliva, blood, and semen passed demons between people, leading to the "exchange of spirits through sex" (Pype 2012: 266). African American Pentecostal prophetess Juanita Bynum[3] taught that "unsaved" sex led to "spiritual bondage." She shared with South African Pentecostals the idea that sex could lead to serious spiritual losses. Bynum thought that women bore the brunt of this because semen carried with it the spirit of the sexual partner and all his past sexual partners, depositing numerous "spiritual ties" through bodily fluids (2000). Bynum differed from HRM in believing that while men can be in spiritual bondage, women's bodies and their God-given divine nature as "receivers" left them especially spiritually vulnerable.[4] Similarly, Ty Adams, an African American ex-lesbian Pentecostal evangelist, explained, "Sexual intercourse seals a man and a woman regardless if they are married or not. When you have sex outside of marriage, contrary to God's way, AN UNHOLY SPIRIT SEALS you in that man or woman" (Adams 2006: 23, capitals in original). Bynum and Adams shared with HRM, and a number of other Pentecostal groups around the world, the idea that sexual activities had spiritual consequences and led to the loss of the self.

Within Pentecostal discourse, "idolatry" is the offense of making something or someone else more important than God. For some Zimbabwean women, idolatry was linked to an overactive sexual imagination and sexual appetite, any participation in masturbation, and the use of sex toys (Mate 2002: 558). In HRM, same-sex sexual relations and homosexuality were viewed as "idolatry." The ministry claimed that homosexual desires constituted worshiping another person, leaving less room to adore and connect with God. In this framework, a person's sense of self was harmed through idolatry because the idolater was willing to twist himself emotionally to fulfill whatever need the person being idolized desired. This also led to losing a part of the self. HRM had a spiritual warfare prayer to break "soul-ties" that involved the renunciation of every sexual encounter in a person's life, including molestation and sexual assault. The person engaging in "sexual sin" was expected to renounce each person individually as an idol. This meant making an exhaustive list of prior sexual experiences and telling an accountability partner or counselor about each one in detail. The prayer allowed the person doing it to "reclaim" every piece of the self that had been left behind through "ungodly" sexual activity. It actively sought to make the person spiritually whole. Here it is evident that the ex-gay Pentecostal self is both an individual who acts on his own behalf and a dividual who is affected by otherworldly beings and substances. This prayer to break "soul-ties" illustrates both the agency of the person reclaiming the self and that this self is permeable.

For men like Alwyn, making the list was difficult, as he claimed to have had more than seven hundred sexual partners. When he did the prayer with Brian, he had to speak each name aloud to renounce that person and break the "soul-tie," a time-consuming and emotionally draining process. This prayer "called back" any part of the self that had been given away through "unnatural sex" and released from the confessor any part of past sexual partners he or she could be carrying around. After the tie was broken in the name of Jesus, the prayer asked for God to cleanse the person and wash away, through the blood of Christ, any "ungodly" feelings, attachments, and memories. Men petitioned God to "fill" the empty spaces recently vacated by "sexual sin" that were now "open" post healing. HRM believed men to be whole again once these dispersed pieces were brought back together.

Damon also performed the prayer to break soul-ties and narrated for me what the prayer did to his sense of self. Damon told me, "You just renounce everything you've done with guys . . . I had this bucket. And a lot of stuff just came out of me, [that] I thought would never be inside of me. And I mean there's definitely areas where I could feel stuff leaving me . . . throwing up, vomiting, and screaming and shouting and fighting and all that." He was shocked at the number of demons he said he felt leaving him. He felt spiritually "lighter" afterward, although he still struggled with masturbation and "sexual falls." Damon felt that his Christian selfhood was redeemed and renewed postdeliverance through the use of this ministry-supplied spiritual warfare prayer.

HRM claimed that pornography use also created "soul-ties." All the men in the ministry struggled with pornography use and accompanying masturbation, seen as committing the "sins" of "lust" and "idolatry." The ministry encouraged the men to use a specific prayer it had developed that dealt with pornography use. When a person recited it, he confessed to God that he had looked at sexual images that led him to masturbate, had raised these images up as "idols," and had committed "idolatry." This prayer was almost identical to the prayer on breaking "soul-ties" but with the addition of masturbation as a "sexual sin."

One ministry member who used the spiritual warfare prayer on pornography use on a regular basis was Hendrik, an Afrikaans man who was forty years old in 2008. He frequently struggled with the desire to look at pornography, especially at the end of the week when he felt stressed. After work Hendrik would ride his motorcycle to the video store and often come home with an R- or X-rated DVD. He told me this prayer against pornography worked well because it gave him a formula to confess his "sexual sins" to God and a framework for how to perform the confession. The prayer helped him work through what he needed to do to receive "healing." Hendrik found the prayer a good vehicle to bring his whole person to God—feelings, mind, spirit, and body—to help get rid of sexual images and to try to erase the demonic "footprints" that he felt masturbation left in his life. He saw the images he looked at in pornography as having "served a false god" and said that unless he asked God to erase the images from his mind, he would continue to focus on them and make the men in the images into "idols." Until he performed the prayer, confessed, and repented, he believed that demonic "doors" remained "open," leading to further Satanic influences and possible "sexual sin."

Hendrik said that he felt powerless in the face of his sexual desires without the HRM-supplied tools of spiritual warfare. He detailed for me an experience of how good he felt after confessing and asking for God's forgiveness after looking at pornography and masturbating. He told me, "I got up from my bed, went to the kitchen to go and make coffee, and by the time I was in the kitchen I was so overwhelmed by the same feeling again of God's love. So, I started praising God for His forgiveness. And, the moment I started doing that I was totally overtaken by the Holy Spirit. And I was so impressed with God that He would so quickly forgive." For men like Hendrik, parts of the self were contaminated or lost through "sexual sin." HRM spiritual warfare prayers were ways to reclaim the self. Hendrik felt full of God's love and grace but these prayers did not protect him from his desire to watch pornography. For him, the root of that problem was much more complicated. He was trapped in a situation where he was both an agent of his own salvation and a victim of Satan's "plot" to get him to sin. Hendrik was caught up in a self-perpetuating cycle where he was supposed to fight off the demonic but also was expected to have the demonic affect and alter his sense of self.

Spiritual Mapping

The men in HRM used another spiritual warfare tool in self-work, that of spiritual mapping. Pentecostals throughout the world claim it is their duty to locate "demonic places" and engage in spiritual warfare to reclaim these locations for God, a practice known as spiritual mapping (Robbins 2012; Asamoah-Gyadu 2007; van Dijk 2007). This practice originated in the late 1980s and early 1990s in North American evangelical life; it is usually traced to the writings of theologian C. Peter Wagner and to the conservative evangelical Fuller Theological Seminary in Pasadena, California (Holvast 2009). Spiritual mapping was widely disseminated by the mid-1990s and early 2000s. Pentecostals believe that land can be cursed, and the actions of ancestors in a family and place can lead to long-term "spiritual curses." They cite Numbers 14:18 frequently in these discussions: "The Lord is long-suffering and slow to anger, and abundant in mercy and loving-kindness, forgiving iniquity and transgression; but He will by no means clear the guilty, visiting the iniquity of the fathers upon the children, upon the third and fourth generation" (Amplified Bible 1987). For these Pentecostals, "sin" and its consequences are passed down through spiritual inheritances, and these affect self-making and maintenance. For example, in Haiti, many Pentecostals believed that the 2010 earthquake and the nation's economic and political problems were "evidence, proof, and result of deep demonic entrenchment" (McAlister 2014: 191). These Haitian Pentecostals linked this "entrenchment" to the effects of enslavement, slave rebellion, and African indigenous religions, claiming that Haiti had been "given to Satan" (McAlister 2014: 193).

In Cape Town, Pentecostals viewed the proliferation of pornography shops, bathhouses, gay bars, and the gay-identified neighborhoods of Sea Point (where HRM was located) and Green Point as visual proof of Cape Town's "sinfulness." In the Pentecostal imagination, Cape Town was in spiritual bondage, possessed by the "spirit of homosexuality." Spiritually polluted places were said to lead to possessed bodies, and the spirit of a place could have dire effects on Christian bodies and sexual choices.[5] HRM members believed that living in Cape Town influenced their sexual desires and actions. They read the landscape for seen and unseen signs of satanic influence.

Spiritual mappers read landscapes for "principalities and powers" in which Satan "rules" part of the human world and is always seeking over-powering influence (Ephesians 6:12). These Pentecostals maintain that "territorial spirits" are present in places with a wide variety of "social scourges" such as crime, drugs, gangs, non-Christian healers and faiths, and the absence of church growth and successful evangelism (Lampman 1999). Problems that many non-Christians would view as secular matters—for example, the efficacy of city services—become Pentecostalized and serve as evidence for the necessity of spiritual mapping. For example, Kevin O'Neill writes about neo-Pentecostals in Guatemala City who believe that demons are inhabiting and destroying the city through political corruption and gang violence (2010: 95).

Mappers investigate the historical, cultural, anthropological, economic, and political history of an area. This history can include war, conquest, genocide, and political violence; places that are considered "worldly" and understood to "encourage sin," such as escort agencies and areas where prostitutes work, gambling and sex shops, gay clubs, and race tracks; all non-Christian religions and where they meet for worship; and places marked as "occult," a broad term Pentecostals use to indicate a diversity of groups and practices, such as the Freemasons, indigenous religious traditions and healers (who are seen as witches), and meditation, martial art, and yoga centers (Kanaan Ministries n.d.; van der Meer 2010). Various Pentecostals expressed to me the idea that a place's "spiritual history" influenced subsequent generations. HRM used the language of "generational inequity," "the sins of the fathers," and "ancestral curses" to express the idea that sin was passed down through the generations unless specifically broken through the born-again experience and spiritual warfare. HRM coloured member Jayden was unsure whether there was something called "the gay spirit," but he did see that he was not the only one struggling with same-sex attraction. He had openly gay and closeted family members on both sides of his family. He wondered whether this was caused by an ancestral curse that continued to have drastic effects on his family lineage.

The first time I heard that there was some sort of "spiritual covering" over Cape Town was during my second trip to South Africa in 2005. I was tired after a long day of fieldwork and went into the hostel where I was staying, ready to fall into bed. I entered the TV room on the first floor to find Ivan, an openly gay Afrikaans man in his early thirties who worked and lived there, watching television. I said hello and began to walk past him to go upstairs. He stopped me and asked me as a "good person" what I would think of what he did that evening. He yanked up his black T-shirt, which he was wearing with leather pants and thick-soled construction type boots, and told me to look at his chest. His T-shirt was covering a metal studded harness and he told me that he had spent the night at a leather bar, having sex with eight different men in public. "Anything goes here," he said, "anything goes in Cape Town."

Ivan explained that being in the city itself made him sexually "act out." He was clear that he was not the only one who felt this way and told me more than once that he was "not crazy." Ivan, who previously lived in Hermanus, said that when he drove into Cape Town he knew when he crossed over into the city limits because he felt a kind of evil presence. When I mentioned this interaction the next morning at church to a ministry member he said that he had also heard the same thing from other people about Cape Town—there was a palpable haze of evil over the city that people could sense and feel. Some conservative Christians claimed that Cape Town's "spiritual covering" also led to more childhood sexual abuse and pedophilia. In their book *The Pink Agenda: Sexual Revolution in South Africa and the Ruin of the Family*, Christian authors Christine McCafferty and Peter Hammond linked the city's gay communities to demonic influences. They write, "Possibly, Cape Town's reputation as a 'gay capital' has its roots in something darker and uglier than the oft-touted idea that the city is liberal or free. Is Cape Town a homosexual stronghold because of sexual 'liberation' or because of sexual bondage and abuse?" (McCafferty and Hammond 2001: 114). In this framework, Cape Town is a place where demons sexually prey on people and seek to get them to sexually "fall."

South African Pentecostals believed that the way a city began and who "founded" it had dramatic effects on contemporary behaviors (Kanaan n.d.). They claimed that a place's "spiritual history" influenced subsequent generations. A major piece of Cape Town's "spiritual history" was linked to imperialism and so-called illicit sexuality. Tristan said that the "culture of sailors" was significant because they "ran away" from their lives in Europe to "[sexually] misbehave." Tristan's wife Bianca added that soldiers had similar "lifestyles" and made analogous sexual choices. The couple believed that both groups contributed to the city's "[spiritual] possession" because of their sexual encounters with prostitutes, many of whom were not white, and with one another. Similarly, a few white HRM ministry members independently mentioned to me that Cecil B. Rhodes contributed to Cape Town's "homosexual spiritual covering." Rhodes was one of the founders of the Cape colony during the latter part of the nineteenth century and was widely believed to be gay (Aldrich 2003: 92; Epprecht 2004: 104). Some Pentecostals saw the presence of the Rhodes Memorial on Devil's Peak, which was part of a mountain range that dwarfed the area and looked down upon the city, in a negative light. (The Rhodes statue was removed after student protests in 2015.) They understood the memorial to be an "idol" that contributed to the city's "homosexual possession." These Pentecostals believed that "idols" like the Rhodes statue directly contributed to the intensity of "sinful" sexual desires.

Capetonian Pentecostals claimed that secular democracy made Satan stronger because "sinful" activities and lifestyles were now legal and socially acceptable. When I asked Tristan if he thought Cape Town was possessed, he answered with a yell of "Yes!" Tristan said "the spirit of homosexuality" has lived in the city since its beginnings and continues to grow and influence people. He recounted his experiences at Life-Line, a free national crisis management phone service, as proof. Tristan said that the organization had performed a city-by-city comparison to see whether there were differences in the volume of calls and the nature of problems between metropolitan areas. Cape Town stood out because "it was all very sexual, like 80–90 percent of the calls were sexually related. Rape, and child abuse, and homosexuality, and unfaithfulness in marriage, and just it was all sex, sex, sex." He compared this trend to Johannesburg, where he said callers primarily complained about emotional problems within marriages, and Port Elizabeth, where callers asked for assistance with the occult. (I could not find data to substantiate his claim.)

Tristan supported the idea that Cape Town was a "homosexual demonic stronghold" by claiming there was a lack of evidence that this was a national problem. He and other ministry members maintained that the city caused a larger number of "sexual falls." The men in HRM asserted that it was harder for them to remain sexually abstinent than for men in other cities with gay neighborhoods like Johannesburg and Durban. They saw themselves as more "vulnerable" to spiritual contamination because they claimed that their same-sex desires were partly influenced by demonic interference. A few, similar to Ivan who was discussed earlier, even said that they felt a "spiritual weight" when they entered the city. Ex-gay men used the language of "demonic temptations" and "spiritual pressure" to articulate their belief that "sinful" sexual desires were impacted by demons who controlled the city. Tristan quipped, "If you want to deal with your sexual brokenness, come to Cape Town and [laughter] be exposed to it all. You can stand it in Cape Town, you can anywhere, y'know?" In this quote, Cape Town is not just a threat but a spiritual challenge and potentially a source of spiritual strength if one succeeded in fighting off what were believed to be demonic sexual desires. Ex-gay men's selves were significantly affected by place.

Men in the ministry used spiritual maps to avoid "possessed" locations. Maps were physical and cognitive; they evolved over time. They noted where they said they felt "tempted" and passed that information to each other in casual conversations, in support groups, and during counselling sessions. The ministry's office was inside the Church of the Reborn, which was in the gay neighborhood of Sea Point and near gay bars, sex shops where pornography could easily be purchased, and an area where male prostitutes walked at night. Ex-gay Pentecostal men said that they were "in the belly of the beast," and had to monitor and alter their behaviors accordingly. They went out in groups to get coffee and lunch in order to avoid where they saw "temptations," and they tried not to be in the vicinity at night unless they were inside the church itself. Below, I discuss how spiritual mapping assisted them in "fighting" in a "battle" for their city and nation's future, which also allowed them to protect themselves from demonic contamination.

Besides learning to avoid geographic areas that they see as spiritually dangerous, spiritual mapping has also empowered many Pentecostals to "conquer" spaces they believe are demonically possessed. Many Christians across the globe participate in "prayer marches," which involve self-designated "prayer warriors" walking together into a place they have designated as a "spiritual stronghold" and performing acts of "spiritual warfare" en masse. Prayer marches may include fasting, speaking in tongues, deliverance, and boisterous singing and public prayers (McAlister 2012). The London branch of the Congolese-based Kimbanguist church has a brass band that has marched in secular parades because it "allows them to 'spread God's vibe,' to conquer more sonic and spiritual territories" and reclaim for God areas mapped as "sinful" (Garbin 2012: 435). In Knoxville, Tennessee, evangelicals hold a "Month of Prayer" that includes a "March for Jesus" to facilitate an "agenda of exorcizing, sacralizing, and reanimating the city" (Elisha 2013: 328). In Ireland, African migrants go on "Jesus walks," visiting places like banks to pray for the recession to end and to hospitals to pray for the end of budget cuts for medical services (Maguire and Murphy 2016: 852–853). Many Pentecostals view these activities as essential pieces of "winning" back areas they consider to be under Satan's control or influence.

HRM organized a prayer march at Cape Town's Gay Pride Parade in 2008 to "battle" the parade's "demonic" purpose and to "reclaim" the area for its "rightful" owner, God. A group of volunteers met at the church before the parade began. They laid hands on each other and prayed out loud for "the blood of Jesus" to protect themselves from any possible demonic interference. A small "intercession team" remained at the church to pray continuously for the rest of the group, which was composed of twenty black, white, and coloured men and women, most in their late teens and twenties. The church group walked the entire parade route performing spiritual warfare, "rebuking Satan" and his "hold" over the area.

Although these "prayer warriors" had spiritually "protected" themselves, the ex-gay men who participated in the prayer walk, and saw themselves as the most spiritually vulnerable, claimed afterward to be "demonically contaminated." Many reported feeling "tempted" because they had walked through gay neighborhoods and been in close proximity to hundreds of gays and lesbians. Hugh, an ex-gay coloured man, felt under "extreme attack" from Satan beginning on the evening after the outreach event. He explained that he started having "explicit [gay] sex dreams" after a several-month period of calm nights. Whereas one possible way of interpreting these dreams would have been through the framework of sexual attraction, he believed that the closeness to "demonic" gays and lesbians had "weakened" his willpower.

Alwyn also felt "vulnerable" after the Pride Parade and struggled with the urge to masturbate, waking up in the middle of the night to "fight off" his same-sex sexual desires. He explained, "I grabbed my Bible from my bedside table, and went into intense spiritual warfare, rebuking Satan and his demons, and calling on Jesus and the Holy Spirit to protect and cleanse me." These ex-gay Pentecostals understood their increased same-sex desires through the language and framework of spiritual mapping, in which the sins embodied in a particular place could affect and alter thoughts and desires. Like many other Pentecostals around the world, they used spiritual mapping to uncover and police areas they saw as being under demonic control. They attempted to spiritually "cast out" outsiders to "reclaim" these areas and themselves for Christ.

Conclusion

Matthew's visit, where this chapter began, triggered a demonic backlash for some of the men in HRM like Alwyn and Coenraad. It would be easy to read this opening ethnographic vignette simply as one of sexual desire and repression—that these ex-gay men were faced with the prospect of an attractive and enticing outsider in a weekend of other enjoyments like wine tasting and sightseeing, and that they had sexual feelings as a result. However, this interpretation is too simple in that it misses a whole other world of causation. For the men in HRM, like for many Pentecostals, sexual desires and activities are part of a system where demons and Satan seek to get people to "sin" and ultimately walk away from God and their faith. In this chapter, I've discussed HRM's claims that men involved in the ex-gay process were bound to "fall" because it was difficult to rid oneself of demonic interference—new behaviors and new selves took time and effort.

Pentecostal selves were individual and dividual at the same time. God and the Holy Spirit and Satan and demons were all understood to impact humans and their sexual feelings, activities, and self-making. Matthew is transformed in this worldview into a demonic outsider who has the potential to make men "fall." His selfhood is dangerous to others. For men like Alwyn, spiritual warfare was necessary for self-actualization and for men to feel like agents and not victims to Satan's "plot" to get them to "sexually sin." However, their claims to clear demonic discernment had tensions and contradictions, with the psychological (detailed in earlier chapters) also affecting how men saw themselves and their self-work. These ex-gay men were caught in a cycle that was hard to exit where they were both agents and victims. They had to be careful not to blame Satan for everything, since this made them seem suspect and as not taking responsibility for their actions. However, at the same time, they were expected not to be in denial of the supernatural and the power of the Enemy. If they denied Satan was acting in their lives and on their sexual desires, they could be under a cloud of suspicion as being possessed. In the next chapter, I examine the ways that men sought to cultivate sexual feelings through hard work, an accompaniment to the spiritual warfare work they so diligently performed.

MASTERING ROMANCE
AND SEXUAL FEELINGS

Because ex-gay men are well tuned in fashion, looks, and measuring their masculinity visually, they use her [a girlfriend] as a project. The more hot she appears,
the more it will add to their perception of their perceived masculinity. She, without
knowing it, is molded to prove our masculinity to ourselves, our church, or other
straight men who we measure ourselves with. —ALWYN on ex-gay dating

Tristan, a white longtime HRM leader, was one of the ministry's success
stories because he had been married to a woman for fifteen years and they
had two children. His wife, a spirited white woman named Bianca,[1] said that
ex-gay men in the ministry undergo a "restoration" process to become an
"original," "God-ordained" heterosexual; this is not the replacement of one
kind of desire for another, but a personal transformation into a new self.
Bianca compared the formation of sexual attraction to women to learning
to like new foods that are better for one's body. She used the analogy of
learning to change one's craving for chocolate to apples. One may initially be
more "satisfied" by eating chocolate because it provides a "rush." However,
the satisfaction quickly subsides and the person is left feeling let down and
still hungry.

Bianca said that when one eats apples over a long period of time, the
craving or even interest in chocolate, or homosexuality, subsides. However,
liking apples required a concerted effort. Bianca explained, "What you're
doing is, I need chocolate, I need chocolate, I need chocolate, I need—I actually don't need so much chocolate. Actually, I don't need any chocolate.

Actually, I don't like chocolate. But you know, these apples that I've been eating . . . Ooh, this one is really crunchy. Ooh, these apples are sour. This is sour. Oh, this one's a sweet apple. You get different tastes of apple. Oh. Wow. These apples are fabulous. And that's how it happens. It doesn't go from I love chocolate [to] I love apples overnight." Bianca told me that Tristan's "success" was evident in how his sexual interest in her and other women, or the apples in her analogy, had steadily increased over time. Although he was initially attracted to Bianca only, Tristan began to see other women as desirable as he continued in his "healing" process. The goal of ex-gay men's desire work was sexual attraction to women. In this chapter I address how ex-gay men attempted to develop opposite-sex desire and heterosexual selves through hard work on themselves.

The men in HRM limited their access to people, situations, and places marked as fraught with "gay" temptations. Ex-gay ministries around the world placed followers under group surveillance and taught them how to react to "ungodly" desires. For example, Tanya Erzen studied men at a residential ex-gay ministry in northern California who were under numerous constraints to curb same-sex desire. They were not allowed to spend one-on-one time with other men lest they be sexually tempted, and if they broke rules they lost privileges (Erzen 2006: 53, 99). They were also forbidden to use the internet because of the easy availability of pornography, and they could not sleep in the nude (Erzen 2006: 93, 100). Similarly, in her interviews with American ex-gay men, Lynne Gerber found that the men were taught to remove themselves from possible temptations in everyday life. She writes, "Some ministries advise members to physically look away from temptations . . . Mark's [an ex-gay man] practice of training his eyes away from that which might tempt him is a variation on the advice frequently given to ministry members: in the face of temptation, flee" (Gerber 2012: 127). The ex-gay men I worked with in South Africa also put restrictions on themselves, like not using the locker room at the gym so naked male bodies would not tempt them. However, merely following these restrictions did not lead to the development of opposite-sex desire. Instead, ex-gay men had to perform daily productive desire work, part of the alignment of their spiritual and sexual selves.

Although ex-gay men may have initially arrived for counseling and support groups at the HRM office in Cape Town hoping for a quick fix for their same-sex desires, they soon learned that there was a detailed list of sequential and behavioral prescriptions they had to undergo if they wished to alter their attractions. Ex-gay mean learned to understand their desire work as a daily practice, one that involved constant self-surveillance and emotional and physical toil on the self. It was a process of intense self-realization. A new self was only possible through entering into productive and active processes of desire work. In this chapter, I address how ex-gay men attempted to develop sexual desire for women through following a set of prescribed behaviors. HRM taught men that a key part of being heterosexual was always to initiate contact with women, and thus, the first stage of desire work was to offer to open doors and carry heavy objects. From there, men moved on to other stages of desire work, masturbating to women's images, dating, limited physical touch, and ideally, heterosexual marriage. Ex-gay Pentecostal behavioral change projects were enacted to alter an interior state; their practices of bodily discipline inclined them to be heterosexual and pious and to lessen the extent and intensity of their same-sex desires.

Sex in Pentecostal Life

For the men in HRM, sex within the confines of a heterosexual marriage was the end goal of all their hard work on their desires and selves. Ex-gay Pentecostal desire work in South Africa was part of the larger therapeutic ethos of the faith, in which churches imparted new models for romantic and sexual relationships along with the skills necessary to achieve them (van Dijk 2015). Many African Pentecostals sought "companionate marriages," an ideal in which marriages are based on romantic courtship and love, emotional closeness and care, and sexual intimacy and faithfulness (Hirsch and Wardlow 2006), and they looked to their churches for guidance in fashioning these relationships. For example, young Pentecostals in the Brazilian Kingdom of God Church in Mozambique attended "therapy of love" sessions in which they were coached in showing physical affection and attuning their feelings and bodies to feel and express romantic love (van de Kamp 2016). Pentecostals who attended "love therapy" classes in Mozambique and practiced heterosexual desire work in South Africa altered their behaviors to facilitate a transformation into new selves.

Besides training men and women how to be more emotionally intimate and romantically available, African Pentecostal churches coached congregants to discuss sex in explicit ways. Men and women were taught that sex should be enjoyable for both partners in the context of heterosexual marriage (van Dijk 2013; Frahm-Arp 2012; Mate 2002). For example, Nigerian couples were instructed in foreplay and sexual positions and how to practice open communication so both husband and wife were sexually satisfied (Pearce 2012: 356). In Benin, married Pentecostal women were taught "the art of seduction" and that they should also initiate sex with husbands (Quiroz 2016: 6–7). HRM taught men that women needed more kissing and foreplay to be sexually satisfied than they did, often using an analogy of microwaves and crock-pots. They said men were sexually like microwaves, ready to have sex in an instant, but that women needed a longer "warming up" period. These African Pentecostal practices stand in stark contrast to the preaching of abstinence-only messages or the silence on sexual matters that characterized most African churches before the HIV epidemic (Burchardt 2010).

African Pentecostals, like evangelicals, charismatics, and Pentecostals around the world, said that sex should be joyfully experienced and claimed that saved sex is the best sex. Amy DeRogatis discovered that sexual fulfillment was linked to salvation for many American evangelicals. She writes, "Sex is a salvific act. It is both a sign and an outcome of being a 'true' Christian. The ultimate human joy of 'true' sexual ecstasy in marriage will only occur among the saved" (DeRogatis 2005: 132). Pentecostal men in Cape Town frequently said that born-again men and women had more multiple orgasms than the unsaved. In 2008, Afrikaans HRM leader Alwyn said that he longed to access the kind of sexual pleasure promised in the Bible in the Song of Songs. He explained, "He speaks about her breasts being so beautiful, and that it's dripping with honey. And that her hair's like goats running, and I'm thinking . . . I'm getting horny just by reading this." He imagined that sex with a saved woman would be far superior to his prior sexual experiences with other men. Pentecostals claimed that God provided sexual rewards for His faithful flock. Desire work had physical and sexual returns.

HRM believed that God created sexual activity for Christians to enjoy within the confines of what they saw as appropriate sexual expression — heterosexual monogamous marriage. In their courses, they taught that God designed our bodies, sexual organs, and even nerve endings for pleasure. White HRM leader Glen told me over coffee in 2008 that he hoped for a great deal of sexual pleasure in his marriage. He had recently gotten engaged and was looking forward to his sex life once he was married. He explained, "You know, when I look at her [fiancée], there's nothing more that I want to do, [I] just want to lie her down. And I don't feel at all condemned. Because I love her. And that's what God has done." Glen saw marriage as the place where he was able to have "God-ordained" sexual pleasure.

In HRM workshops, complementarianism was key to what was understood as God's intentionality for sex, gender roles, and sexuality. South

African Pentecostals believed that sex mirrored God's plan for distinct roles for men and women in life—women were said to receive and men to initiate. For these Pentecostals, the act of sex mimicked the roles that God put into gendered bodies. They claimed that the masculine was "ordained" to be in charge in and outside the bedroom and the feminine was constructed by God to respond to and follow men. Pentecostals at the church and in the ministry often said that God made Eve from Adam. Sex was said to "naturally" draw men and women together to form "one flesh," thus reflecting God's "divine plan." To support their ideas, they often cited Matthew 19:6: "So they are no longer two, but one flesh. What therefore God has joined together, let not man put asunder (separate)" (Amplified Bible 1987).

HRM believed that God blessed sexual encounters in marriage by putting a "spiritual covering" over them and giving believers otherworldly orgasms and a deeper way to connect spiritually with their spouses and Him. Liesl and Faan were a born-again Afrikaans couple who happily discussed their sex lives with me. They explained that they saw sex as a "communion before God" and described it as a form of prayer. The two knew each other a long time before becoming a couple and had what they described as "awful" sex when they met many years earlier in Ireland. They remained friends, and when they started dating they agreed to not even kiss before getting married. They understood their original sexual encounter as not "blessed" by God and saw their excellent sex life after marriage as proof of His love for them, their marriage, and a reward for being faithful. Within the framework of Pentecostalism, sex was a key piece of connecting with one's spouse, as well as a way to exhibit the embodiment of appropriate gender and sexual roles.

Compliments, Courtesies, and Evaluation: Objectifying Women

Men began to form new heterosexual selves by learning how to objectify women, not by dating them. Ex-gay men who entered the ministry were encouraged to begin the ex-gay process by practicing small masculine behaviors. These practices included complimenting women's femininity, performing chivalrous acts such as opening car doors, paying for tea and coffee, and offering to carry heavy items. For example, the first time I met Brian in 2004 he took me out to lunch a few blocks away from the church. After walking a few steps, he stopped and said that we needed to switch places so he was closer to the street. When I asked him why, he said it was the gentlemanly way to act.[2] Other ex-gay men I spent time with also repositioned themselves when walking with me, making sure they were closer to the dangers of the street.

Heterosexual attraction was not the outer expression of an inner feeling. Instead, repeated acts of chivalry were supposed to assist in forming the disposition itself. Exterior actions therefore had effects on interior formation (Mahmood 2005). Ex-gay American writer Alan Medinger, whose ideas were used in HRM courses, suggests that ex-gay men "practice some of the traditional male courtesies shown to women" such as walking closer to the curb. He writes, "We are changed by what we do! Our actions can change our thinking and our perspectives. Act as though a woman is something special, and she will become that to you" (Medinger 2000: 202). HRM actively coached ex-gay men to see women as "others" with "God-ordained" bodily and emotional differences who needed men to guide and protect them, a key part of Pentecostal gender ideals in which men should spiritually and physically safeguard women.

Paying close attention to women's looks was a key aspect of the ex-gay process. Some men in the ministry liked to practice how to compliment women with me so they could naturalize their speech for later use in romantic relationships with other women. I did not always enjoy this practice because they paid a lot of attention to how I looked and moved, and their comments, especially at first, felt insincere and forced. For example, if I wore makeup, someone in the ministry office would tell me abruptly in the middle of a conversation on another topic that I should do it more often because it made me *mooi*, or pretty. Over time, they became better at complimenting me and other women, and giving compliments became central to their desire work. Instead of interrupting a conversation on the Bible to give a positive affirmation, they would tell a woman who came into the office at her entrance how *mooi* she appeared that day. Ex-gay men attempted to be in new relationships with women through beginning to see them as in need of male affirmation and support, part of fulfilling the gendered ideal of men as protectors and initiators.

Compliments were one part of a larger focus in HRM on women's looks. Ex-gay men put women's appearances under surveillance and made constant comments about how they looked and acted. Women in HRM were expected to be feminine as "proof" that they were also invested in the ministry's ideologies of conventional gender roles and the complementarity of the sexes. By conventionally feminine I mean wearing skirts, dresses, and makeup, having longer hair, and deferring to male ideas and authority.

Those who were outside this frame were viewed negatively. For example, in 2005 I told Brian I would volunteer at the ministry's annual fundraiser, which was being held at a local restaurant, with other ministry members. Brian asked me what I was going to wear. I gestured to my outfit for the day, which was khaki pants and a black shirt and said it would be something similar to what I had on, reminding him how I had come from the United States for the summer with one bag. Brian then told me that if I came to the fundraiser dressed in a similar way that I would embarrass the ministry. My lack of a feminine appearance was read as dangerous to HRM's credibility.

Ex-gay men in HRM used women physically and emotionally to attempt to achieve heterosexuality. They learned that women were less powerful and important than men, and this contributed to their views of women as "others" to be used toward aspirational heterosexuality. I rarely heard men, even the ones who dated women, spend considerable time discussing one individual woman's uniqueness. The men were more interested in seeing the embodiment of appropriately feminine behaviors in these women, such as wearing makeup and jewelry.

HRM read exteriors for evidence of internal workings. The more masculine ex-gay men were, the further along in their healing they were assumed to be. The same was true for the small number of ex-lesbians in the ministry. Margot was an ex-gay Afrikaans woman in her midtwenties. She was described as a "success" because of her altered self-presentation. I met Margot a few times in 2004 and 2005, where she was the most stereotypically recognizable lesbian-looking woman in the ministry. She had short spiky hair and a nose ring and wore only T-shirts and jeans. Before her transformation into the "true feminine," others talked about her as "butch" and characterized her as an angry man-hater. When I met Margot again in 2007 she had longer hair, wore makeup and dresses and had let her piercings close up. HRM leaders read her feminine attire and demeanor as proof of significant spiritual growth and commitment to the ministry's program of change. Margot was interpreted as having achieved a new and improved self through her hard work on her appearance and affect.

Women's Experiences in HRM

Although there were some women in the ministry leadership and women attended meetings, classes, retreats, and social events, the leadership remained mostly men. There were a small number of women involved long-term in HRM, and those women who did stick it out often expressed frustration with the ministry's focus on ex-gay men, despite its claim to address and "heal" all kinds of "brokenness." Women's voices, discussed in more detail below, were often ignored and their ideas not taken seriously by male leaders. Women's role in Pentecostalism as followers of men's leadership meant that women were expected to take a backseat in ministry affairs. Women were usually given feminine tasks to do for HRM like secretarial work, decorating at fundraisers, and cooking at retreats, jobs that they did not usually find rewarding over time.

Heterosexual women usually joined the ministry to deal with their own "brokenness," which ranged from dealing with the aftermath of abuse to promiscuity to not feeling feminine enough. (Lesbians came to HRM to address their same-sex attraction.) These women often had very conflicted relationships toward men because of pasts full of their own heartbreak and trauma. To these women, the men in HRM were attractive because they were working so hard on themselves and their masculinities. Ex-gay men were appealing because they self-consciously challenged South African hegemonic gender norms and were much more open than other men about their shortcomings and weaknesses. This made them desirable to women whose past experiences with men were largely negative. The women in HRM often had crushes on ex-gay men, viewing them through starry eyes as new kinds of men to be in relationships with, especially when the men in their pasts were closed-off emotionally, distant, and/or abusive. Ex-gay men's desire work transformed them, in some women's eyes, into ideal emotional partners. However, women who had crushes or entered into flirting or emotionally intense relationships with ex-gay men often got their hearts broken when these men were incapable of being the boyfriends that the ministry claimed they could be taught to be: emotionally available and physically affectionate.

Over time, women often expressed frustration with ex-gay men and the ministry because their voices were ignored. Women said that HRM was really just focused on ex-gay men's struggles, despite claiming that it helped to heal all kinds of "brokenness" for both genders. Antjie, a white Dutch missionary, felt that there was "bias" against her for being a woman in the ministry. She saw a clear disconnect between how her work was represented in newsletters and public events and how she was treated in her time working in HRM's office. She told me, "I felt treated like a second-grade citizen in a way. I mean in meetings and on paper I was praised into the heavens [but] I must admit in practice by the founder and other staff I felt treated like a second-grade citizen." Antjie was angry that she was seen as less than the men in the ministry and that they saw her ideas as less valid. She felt silenced and discounted during her years in HRM. Similarly, Afrikaans leader Elisabe explained that she frequently felt left out of HRM because the ministry, despite claiming to be for everyone and for all kinds of "brokenness," was so focused on ex-gay men. "It was weird because sometimes I felt special for being a woman and sometimes I felt patronized [laughter, long pause] . . . Sometimes you feel like you're a token, like a token female 'cause the focus was mainly on the ex-gay boys." Like Antjie, Elisabe felt both special and othered by the men in HRM. Ministry rhetoric called for women to be put on pedestals and treated as "God's princesses," but this was rarely actualized in practice. Willa, an Afrikaans woman who was married to an ex-gay man, felt angry that women were excluded and that when they spoke up they were patronized. She told me, "Women are not heard in the ministry. The only person who makes herself heard is said to be having an 'episode.'" These women were ostracized through the exclusive focus on ex-gay men, despite rhetoric to the contrary. The men in the ministry either ignored or chastised women when they pushed on a topic.

Women were also expected to submit to male authority. Elisabe explained to me in 2013 that during her two years in the ministry she felt the pressure to submit to HRM beliefs and leaders, which included a conventional gender presentation. She told me that she did not feel comfortable challenging any of the ministry's ideologies or leadership structure. She explained, "I felt like I had to conform. I couldn't give my opinions back then unless they were in line with HRM beliefs . . . And the fact that I didn't speak up made me fit in . . . I had good femininity [laughter] because of the whole submission thing. I appeared to be submissive and therefore a good woman . . . There was a certain standard of femininity that was expected . . . [that] when you're 'whole' you'll be a certain kind of woman." Elisabe referred to her femininity as "good" and "acceptable," and said that her agreeability allowed her to fit into the ministry easily. Her "wholeness" was read off her feminine bodily presentation and submissive behavior. Women's commitment to the ministry and to Pentecostal gender roles and norms became suspect if they did not conform. Men and women's levels of self-transformation and the desire to leave "brokenness" behind were read off the body and its appearance.

HRM leaders encouraged men who were struggling with same-sex desire to note and comment on how women looked and dressed because critiquing women's bodies was a way to practice fashioning heterosexual feelings and was evidence of working hard on the self. Ex-gay men were coached on how to appreciate and judge women's bodies, particularly their breasts and buttocks, to help them determine what "type" of women they found attractive. The idea was that if men determined what was aesthetically pleasing to them about women, for example large breasts versus small breasts, they would start to view women through a new sexualized lens. For example, I attended a ministry-led Wednesday night Life Group meeting in 2004, where I was the only woman. The rest were ex-gay men, and a few were new to the ministry. Afrikaans group leader Jaco decided to perform an icebreaker with the group, asking, "What is your type of woman . . . blondes, brunettes, or red-heads?" Everyone in the group then had to answer with not only a hair-color but also what other specific characteristics they appreciated in women's appearances. If a man stumbled or clammed up, Jaco gently guided him through the process of constructing his ideal women, prompting him with further questions such as, "Does she have long hair? Is she tall or short? How does she dress?" The men all described women who were stereotypically feminine and conventionally attractive, with longer hair and slimmer bodies. Jaco instructed the men in the ministry's process to see women as "others" with whom they could acquire attraction by discussing and evaluating their bodies. Men noticing and commenting on women's bodies and femininity was part of the work of forming desire, not evidence of its successful outcome. A new self was formed through hard work and the performance of stereotypically sexist male behaviors.

It was considered proof of moving forward in one's healing to judge women for being too fat or for being not conventionally attractive enough. (All the men in HRM expected to marry attractive and slim heterosexual women.) Brian frequently mocked women's bodies. Fat women, in particular, were discussed as disgusting. He also enjoyed telling sexist and anti-Semitic jokes. Two I heard him repeat over a dozen times in various settings included: "What does a Jewish princess say when having sex? 'Beige, I want beige on the ceiling,'" and "How do you know when a Jewish princess climaxes? She drops her nail files." Sexist humor, especially about the act of sex, was a form of masculine performance. Men's practices of objectifying women's bodies further heightened the existing sexism in the ministry and led women to feel ostracized from the ministry's male and heterosexually aspiring culture.

Ex-gay men who were further along in their "healing," such as Jaco, who had a girlfriend, or were married, like Tristan, positioned themselves as mentors for other ex-gay men in earlier phases of the ex-gay process. These men used their personal knowledge about sexual activities with women in conversations with other men to exhibit masculine growth and to teach them about women's bodies and sex. Frederik was an ex-gay Afrikaans man who had been out of "the [gay] lifestyle" for years and was married to Willa. One afternoon, a group of HRM leaders gathered at his house with the stated purpose of installing ceiling fans. Instead, they ended up at a bar, where Frederik gave the group of ex-gay men, who were in various stages of their desire work, a lesson on women's pleasure, specifically on the existence of the G-spot and female ejaculation. Although Damon, a longtime coloured ministry member who was easily embarrassed, kept stage whispering to everyone to keep it down, the other men were intrigued and asked Frederik numerous clarifying questions such as "What does it feel like? Is it like she is peeing on you?" This conversation was relayed to me later because two of the men wanted to know more about women's orgasms. This discussion was one of many on this topic. Ministry members frequently asked me questions about what women liked sexually, for example whether women could have orgasms from vaginal stimulation alone. They said that these questions were motivated by an interest in their future wives' sexual pleasure. Although this was probably true, part of the impetus for these conversations was to accumulate information on women's bodies and sexual preferences to use in conversations with other men to demonstrate their own heterosexual growth. Ex-gay men used the discussion of women's bodies as a way to exhibit that they were moving toward a heterosexual self and leaving homosexuality behind them.

Masturbation

For the ex-gay men in HRM, the next step of their desire work to achieve a new self was to substitute women for men as objects of their sexual activities. Many confided that they sometimes "compulsively masturbated" while watching gay pornography. Masturbation was a moral gray area for ex-gay Pentecostal men. On the one hand, their recovery was directly linked to developing an attraction toward women, and masturbation could help to foster this attraction. On the other hand, they had to be careful not to commit what they called the "sin" of lust and become addicted to pornography and masturbation.

There was disagreement in the larger transnational ex-gay movement about whether masturbation was acceptable for the development of opposite-sex desire. Some ministries viewed masturbation as problematic, while others saw it as a potential part of "recovery." For example, in their Exodus International published pamphlet *Holding On to Sexual Purity: Finding*

Freedom from Masturbation and Impure Sexual Thoughts, American Christian writers Bob Davies and Lori Rentzel explain that masturbation can significantly set Christians back in their healing. They write, "Some men and women have found that the guilt and separation from God they sense after masturbating opens them up to spiritual warfare on other issues" (Davies and Rentzel 1993: 11). Masturbation led some Christians to feel far away from God and "opened" doors to the demonic, as discussed in the previous chapter. Alan Medinger, mentioned earlier, believes that ex-gay men can masturbate without "sinning." He writes, "For most men whose primary sexual attractions are homosexual, the creation of heterosexual fantasies is often such hard work that it does not produce the escape we often associate with lust" (2000: 218). For Medinger, work on desires was in a separate category from the "sin" of lust. In Pentecostalism, lust is understood as a "dangerous sin" because sex was one of the main "tools" used by Satan to get Christians to "fall" and ruin their lives (Moore 2002). For other men at the Church of the Reborn, masturbation was a "lustful" activity to be avoided because it was spiritually dangerous. The ex-gay exception to this general attitude toward masturbation was unique.

Masturbation was acceptable in HRM as long as it was not "compulsive," a term that remained vague and undefined. When Hendrik, a new Afrikaans ministry member, nervously asked what counted as "compulsive" in the packed ministry office one evening before a class, the room erupted in jokes. "If you can go from nine to five without doing it, you're fine," was the response that received a great deal of laughter, followed by another quip: "Do you need to go to the bathroom?" In general, ministry members' discussions of masturbation were full of joking and "camp" but masked a lot of anxiety. Adrian, with whom I began this book, was a painfully shy ex-gay coloured man who was in and out of ministry classes and support groups for years. He felt bad about watching pornography, both heterosexual and gay male, and said that he feared committing the "sin of lust" by masturbating. When he replaced gay pornography with heterosexual content, he worried that he was not learning to desire women in a way in which God would "approve." He explained, "While you're masturbating [to heterosexual imagery], you know you're working towards something. When you're done, you feel really bad and you don't want to do it anymore." He used the language of "work" to explain his practice of masturbation to heterosexual pornography, but he often felt ashamed for masturbating despite viewing it as a necessary part of his desire work and achieving a heterosexual self.

Hendrik had also tried substituting heterosexual pornography for the gay pornography he used to masturbate. He believed that using heterosexual pornography was "not how God works" because all pornography use fell under the category of "lust." He called his attempts at pornography substitution as "sick," saying it led him to begin to see women as "objects." He explained, "They [women] are a creation and a gift from God. That's how God wants you to see them. How can you be a husband to a wife if you see your wife as an object?" Hendrik wished to see women as he felt God wanted him to. This was similar to ministry ideology that said that women were "God's princesses and queens" at the same time that women were seen and treated as lesser than men. Other men also believed that masturbation was a "sexual sin" and publicly decried it while admitting it was a problem for them in private. For example, Glen called it "not a holy thing" and said that it caused distance in one's relationship with God. He claimed that it was something that "men are meant to overcome" at the same time that he admitted that since becoming a born-again Christian he was not able to stop masturbating completely. Instead, it decreased in frequency for him. Similarly, coloured ministry member Jayden called masturbation a "sexual sin" but admitted he still masturbated because it was difficult to give up.

Jaco believed that "implicating other people in your fantasies" was actually "violating" them. He said that he masturbated only when thinking about nothing, just feeling the physical pleasure. Other men thought this was a ridiculous claim, although a few had tried it unsuccessfully, saying they lost interest and could not climax. Church and ministry members laughed at me when I mentioned Jaco's strategy of masturbating without fantasy to avoid committing any "sins." One man told me that the idea was "bogus" and another laughed for a minute or two before he asked me if I was serious.

South African Pentecostals believed that God designed men and women to have different kinds of needs for sexual release. Men were thought to struggle more with masturbation because of how God created their bodies. For example, popular American Christian author Gary Chapman claims that men need to ejaculate regularly because it is part of their physiology. He writes, "For the male, sexual desire is physically based. That is, the desire for sexual intercourse is stimulated by the buildup of sperm cells and seminal fluid in the seminal vesicles. When the seminal vesicles are full, there is a physical push for release. Thus, the male's desire for sexual intercourse has a physical route" (Chapman 2004: 135). He contrasts this to women, who he believes do not have the same physical need for sexual release because their sexual desires are emotional, not physical. (Again, women are desexualized.)

In HRM, wet dreams were not counted under the "sin" of lust because they were seen as outside of one's control. Some Pentecostals thought that wet dreams and the accompanying ejaculation were God's solution for sexual release without participating in "sexual sin." For example, Alwyn believed that men needed to release semen for a healthy body. He told me, "Because the seed has to be pushed out, your sperm has to come out . . . like a woman's cycle." The comparison to a woman's menstrual cycle signaled to me that he saw the release of semen as necessary for bodily equilibrium.

South African Pentecostals outside of HRM were also worried about the possible spiritual effects of masturbation. A Pentecostal young adult group visited HRM in 2007 for a special seminar on Christian sexuality. I attended with Antjie, who believed that God had "called" her to South Africa to work with the "sexually broken." The group was planning to run a camp for township youth and came to learn how to discuss sexuality with unsaved young people. Some of the group of coloured and white men and women seemed interested during the lesson, with others obviously bored, looking out the windows and staring off into space. After the teaching, the group was invited to ask questions. It was when masturbation came up that they had the most questions and were most engaged. One young white man with red hair raised his hand and asked, blushing to match his head, why "chicks" never admitted to masturbating. Antjie and I—we had invited ourselves to come and offer a woman's perspective to Jaco's teaching—both reassured him, with the room laughing nervously, that girls masturbated. One of the young coloured men who had been quiet up to this point, looking uncomfortable and playing with a pen, jumped in to ask whether it was a sin to masturbate and whether wet dreams count as masturbation. Jaco began to answer, but Antjie interrupted him. "When temptation comes and knocks on your door," she declared, rapping her knuckles loudly on the arm of her wooden chair, "it's your choice if you open the door or not. You can wake up aroused, but it is your decision to masturbate." The group nodded, but the next question asked for further clarification about whether "nightly emissions" counted as masturbation. Jaco said no, it did not count because it was out of one's control. However, if these dreams were homosexual in content and repeated, one should ask for intervention from a spiritual counselor because demonic influence could be involved. The advice given to heterosexual young people was more conservative than what the ministry believed was allowable for ex-gay men.

Pentecostal men who attended Church of the Reborn but were not part of HRM said that giving up preconversion sexual practices was the most difficult part of being saved and/or making a recommitment to God. I found that black and coloured heterosexual men felt that masturbation was more inappropriate for Christians to engage in than white men. Joshua, a Xhosa heterosexual man who worked at the church, said the hardest thing for him to give up after his born-again experience was sex with women. It took him six months after his conversion to be able to completely abstain. He was a youth group leader in his neighborhood in the township of Khayelitsha. Joshua spent a great deal of time mentoring young men, especially helping them learn how to remain sexually pure, which included abstaining from masturbation. He told me, "It's the first thing that you're fighting. Be strong, and I will tell them if you want to grow spiritually, you need to stop this [sexual activity]. If you don't stop this, you won't grow, you won't grow spiritually. You won't experience God in your life. So, you need to stop that. And if you don't, we can help you, praying for you. Fast together with you." Joshua offered the men tools like prayer, fasting, and spiritual warfare to use when they felt sexually aroused and needed a community with whom to discuss their struggles.

For ex-gay men, any heterosexual desire was an achievement to be celebrated and talked about, especially if it occurred when men were not actively working on their attractions to women. For example, I was told an anonymous story about one ministry leader who had a "wet dream" about a woman. The woman in the dream did not have a face. Instead, the dreamer saw a vagina and himself "muffing," or performing oral sex on it. He woke up and "finished off," or brought himself to orgasm. He viewed this occurrence as distinct progress in his healing and was proud because his sexual desire for the opposite sex was becoming effortless. His hard work to develop desire was paying off. Masturbation was an important substitutionary tool in desire work. It was a key piece of working toward a heterosexual self.

Dating Practices

Ex-gay men were only encouraged to begin dating women after moving through the earlier steps of desire work described above, a period that usually lasted at least a year. The ex-gay men in South Africa who attempted to date women before they had successfully mastered other parts of the ex-gay process often led them on and abandoned them, in addition to "slowing down" their own "healing" process. HRM member Hendrik decided to join an online Christian dating service in 2007 after only a few months of counseling and support group attendance. He started texting and talking to a woman who lived a few hours away and felt that they were slowly starting to build a relationship. However, after spending a few weekends together, Hendrik realized that he had made a "big mistake. Big, big mistake. I tried really hard to make it work. I tried my best. I tried to force this thing. So I told her the problem is with me and not her but she was [silence] so taken aback. I feel sorry for her because it was a huge disappointment to her." Soon after, Hendrik tried to date an ex-lesbian from the ministry, but that relationship had a similar outcome. Hendrik never used the names of the two women he had "disappointed" in conversation. Instead, he referred to each as "she," "her," or "the woman," even though he knew that I knew one of them and knew they had dated. Hendrik was one ex-gay man of many I knew who saw women as interchangeable, legitimate tools of desire work to practice on. His focus on the outcome of desire work, not the process, led him to be frustrated with himself and with God. HRM leaders presented men like Hendrik and their dating "failures" as evidence for the centrality of working through the ex-gay process in predetermined stages. A new self could not be rushed and needed to be achieved through HRM-approved stages.

Other ex-gay men in Cape Town who entered into opposite-gender relationships to realize their heterosexuality felt that they were more successful. In the summer of 2007, Afrikaans ministry leader Alwyn told me that his friendship with Afrikaans lesbian Marina, also a ministry member, was changing significantly. The two had decided to see whether they were compatible as potential marriage partners and began spending a great deal of time together. The pair discussed in detail how they were not sexually interested in each other but were trying to "nurture" and "grow" individually in their respective gender identities to foster an attraction. They used each other to practice what they considered normative heterosexual selves, spending a lot of time to get one another to embody what they saw as "appropriate" masculinity and femininity. Alwyn said he was trying very hard to be attracted to Marina, and he constantly tried to "affirm her in her femininity," an aspect that he thought was significantly lacking. He wanted to desire her physically, but he said that when he tried to look at her romantically or sexually, all he could think was "she needs grooming." Alwyn said it was hard to be attracted to someone when all he thought about was how much he wanted to give her a makeover, particularly by taking a tweezers to her eyebrows, waxing her moustache, flossing her teeth, and cleaning under her fingernails. Marina was not happy with his body either, telling him that he needed to lose weight and calling his stomach a "Buddha belly."

She also found his mannerisms to be "camp'" and disapproved of his overly feminine behavior.

Alwyn and Marina each tried to regulate the other's gender performance as led by the ministry and to begin to desire each other sexually. Like other men in the ministry, Alwyn learned to see only certain types of conventionally feminine women as attractive. He detailed how Marina's nonfeminine appearance got in the way of his ability to try to find her attractive. Notably, while he attempted to foster his attraction for Marina, he felt a large amount of desire for another ministry leader named Sarie, a tall, slim, Afrikaans woman whom Alwyn said he "desperately wanted to snog." He frequently commented on Sarie's long brown hair, well-developed breasts, and how beautiful and feminine she appeared, often giving her compliments such as, "God gave you such an innate and spiritual femininity" and "God blessed you with such beauty."

Marina and Alwyn's attempt to develop attraction was ultimately unsuccessful and they eventually stopped seeing each other. Marina was very angry that Alwyn was not willing to wait longer for her to "grow into her femininity." She told him very cruelly during their breakup that no one would ever marry him because he was not and would never be a "real man," and because of his HIV-positive diagnosis. He was hurt but believed that Marina would "slow down" his own "growth" if he kept waiting for her to change. He felt that her inability to embody an appropriately feminine physicality was inhibiting his heterosexual aspirations. However, he said that his capacity to feel sexual desire for Sarie was "proof" that his work to develop as a heterosexual was "moving in the right direction." Although Alwyn and Sarie never officially dated because he felt emasculated by statements she made, such as "I'll teach you how to be a man," his ability to desire one conventionally attractive woman gave him confidence that it could happen again and that he was "marriage material."

In 2012, I asked Alwyn, who had left the ministry two years earlier and was now living openly as a gay man, about his experiences in dating women during the seven years he was a ministry member. He told me that having an attractive and well-coiffed girlfriend was "essential" because it served as "proof" to himself and others that he was closer to his "goal" of heterosexuality. He explained, "Because ex-gay men are well tuned in fashion, looks, and measuring their masculinity visually, they use her as a project. The more hot she appears, the more it will add to their perception of their perceived masculinity. She, without knowing it, is molded to prove our masculinity to ourselves, our church, or other straight men who we measure ourselves with." For ex-gay Pentecostal men involved in a long-term self-confidence-making project of heterosexuality, dating an attractive feminine woman served as both practice for sexual attraction and as a way to prove their commitment to themselves and others to achieving newly "healed" selves, or becoming men who desired women. Below, I examine how men attempted to take the lessons they learned during earlier pieces of their desire work and apply them to facilitate their sexual arousal by women, the most difficult part of the ex-gay process.

Sexualized Heterosexual Touch

For ministry members, deriving pleasure from touching women in a sexual manner was the linchpin of their desire work and the action with the highest chance of failure. For this reason, ex-gay men who felt they were ready were provided detailed instructions on sexual touch by more experienced men who were further along in their "healing." With the exception of men such as Alwyn who had previously "been in the [gay] lifestyle," most of the men had little to no sexual experiences with men or women when they joined HRM. If they had sexual experiences with men, these had been a few one-time furtive encounters that they described as being for "physical release" with little emotional intimacy. For example, some men detailed their participation in mutual masturbation in public bathrooms or in the showers at the gym after working out. Few had previously kissed or sexually touched women. Before coming to HRM, many ex-gay Pentecostal men strategically used religious conventions of abstinence to avoid heterosexual touch. This usually took the form of an ex-gay man telling a woman who may have been interested in dating him that he was "waiting" for God to "lay it on my heart" when and who he should date and that he was "waiting" for marriage for any sexual activities, even kissing. The men in the ministry all had much later first-time sexual experiences than the majority of South African men (Black 2013; Eaton, Flisher, and Aaro 2002).

Ex-gay ministry leader Jaco began dating a woman for the first time in 2007. He was twenty-seven years old when he asked Yolandi, a slightly older white woman, to be his girlfriend. After she accepted, he received a lot of instructions about how he should physically "initiate" his first kiss with her. Jaco told me that he was both excited and nervous. He interpreted his wish to kiss Yolandi as evidence of progress in his "healing," but he feared he would not find kissing her and touching her body enjoyable. He received detailed advice from ministry members about how to kiss and touch his girlfriend. He was instructed to be sure to "be horny" before he started and "not to make it mechanical." The work Jaco was expected to do was clear in the advice he was given. Examples included, "You want to remain standing up because if you lie down, things could get out of hand . . . It's normal and good to get an erection . . . Don't shock her the first time you kiss her. Don't go for the lips first. Kiss her cheeks and forehead to warm her up and when she's ready, you kiss her on the mouth. No tongue to start! You can use it later but you must ease her into it . . . No tongue, just pressure . . . Make sure to tell her she's beautiful." Jaco's friends made sure to add that if he failed to be sexually aroused by Yolandi's body at first, he should not worry. They encouraged him by reminding him that even if he was initially unsuccessful, he just needed to keep practicing. Yolandi told me that Jaco never inquired about what kind of sexual touching she liked. He was uncomfortable and angry when she expressed sexual interest without his prompting because he felt that she was "challenging" his role as the male initiator. His focus was on performing kissing and touch for his own ends.[3] Yolandi, like many of the women who dated men in the ministry, was one part of a larger program of heterosexual rehabilitation and a means to an end.

Ex-gay men hoped that the repetition of new behaviors would become internalized and naturalized over time. Hugh, a thirty-two-year-old coloured Pentecostal ex-gay man, told me in 2008 about the day when he realized that his hard work to "restore" his sexuality was paying off. He explained, "I was standing in church one night. Now, when these things happen to me I feel like a man because it's not orchestrated. It happens naturally. That's why I know God has been working in me. [I'm] standing in the church, and there's this girl singing and she's got tight jeans on, and a nice ass. It's a black girl and the way the jeans were sitting, this thing came over me that aroused me and everything, and for me that was like, wow, that's a man. I don't think it just happens naturally and then I know I'm at the right place in my restoration." Like Bianca, Hugh employed the language of "restoration" and not replacement to explain his desire work. He contradicted himself by claiming that his desires happened "naturally" and through effort. I believe this tension arose because he wanted to draw attention simultaneously to the amount of labor he put into his desire work and to how intimately involved God was in every part of his goals and daily life. Unlike men like Adrian and Hendrik, discussed earlier, Hugh did not worry that he was participating in "lustful" activities if they were heterosexual. For him, all heterosexual desires were from God and a sign of progress in his "healing." He told me that his desire for women was becoming stronger and that he was attracted to at least one in twenty women. He was extreme, however, in that he felt that his wish to have sex with women even outside of wedlock (which went against Pentecostal ideals of premarital abstinence and chastity) was in God's plan for him. He explained, "There will be one girl walking past me and something will captivate me about that and it will arouse me. And the only thing I can think of is having sex. I can see myself penetrating this woman. I can see, I can visually see how I'm doing it to her. So that's something I never had before. That can only be God." For Hugh, the desire to have sex with women and his explicit fantasies were part of "God's plan" for his life. Although Hugh's ideas were extreme, he shared with other ex-gay men the idea that it was through sexual desires and practice that a new self was made possible.

Marriage

All the ex-gay men in HRM aspired to be in heterosexual marriages. For them, this was the ultimate realization of a new and healed self. Tristan and Bianca, who were discussed earlier, were HRM's major success story. Brian referred to them as the ministry's "pillars." They have been married since the late 1990s and have two children, a boy and a girl. The pair were friends before their whirlwind six-month courtship. At first Bianca saw Tristan as "attractive but boring," and she was not romantically interested in him. She said that all that changed, however, when God "worked" on her sexual attractions. She told me, "The Lord did something in my heart and he [Tristan] turned from this sweet nice guy that I loved, one day to a sexual being. I don't know how He did that change . . . Suddenly it was like, 'Ooo, you're attractive. I can go for you.'" Tristan went from being like a "baby brother" to a man she was strongly sexually attracted to. He was falling in love with Bianca at the same time, and they eloped six months later. The first few years of their marriage were difficult because Bianca did not trust that Tristan would remain faithful to her. She said she would have been "devastated" if he had left her for a man. However, things improved slowly because they talked frequently about her fears and over time they dissipated and finally disappeared.

Sex was another place of slow growth for the couple. At first Tristan was unclear about what to do sexually with a woman. Bianca explained, "He hadn't a clue where all the bits and parts were, and what to do with them, and it was quite scary for him." Tristan became more sexually interested in

Bianca as time progressed and began to find sex with her to be more complex and exciting. She explained, "He said actually it's far more satisfying to make love to a woman than it is to a man. And he said there is so much more to it. There is so much more complexity to it, there's so much different feelings, better feelings, and said, 'you can't get that with a man.' So in fact that has drawn him in slowly, you know, and it's like seduced him into realizing this is actually fabulous. But it's been a process, hey." Tristan's increased sexual interest was part of the larger ex-gay process, where sexualized touch was understood to be both a sign of growth and a key piece of desire work.

Accompanying Tristan's attraction to Bianca was an increase in his attraction to other women. She told me, "In the early days, there were very few women he found attractive . . . It started off with a very small pool, but as he's become more and more familiar with females and him being in the male role, funnily enough, the pool has opened up and he can appreciate women in a way that he never could before." Bianca did not feel threatened by the increase in Tristan's attractions. Instead, she saw it as positive evidence of his "healing." She categorized their current relationship after years of marriage as "consistent," "stable," and "able to go through the long haul." Tristan said that although he still occasionally got "tempted," being married and having children kept him from "falling."

Frederik and Willa were another one of HRM's success stories because they were married. However, their relationship was more fraught than Tristan and Bianca's. An Afrikaans couple in their thirties, they originally met at the Church of the Reborn. A mutual friend introduced them in 2003 and they soon began to see and greet each other at church services and events. Frederik had been out of "the [gay] lifestyle" for around a year when the two started dating. Brian, HRM's founder, was originally wary of Frederik dating because he had not been participating in the ex-gay process for a long time. He warned him to be "careful" not to allow dating to set him back, as it did with other men like Hendrik. Willa said that their relationship started after the two had a chance to talk after a prophetic meeting at the church. Unlike many American ex-gay men, who often do not divulge their pasts (Wolkomir 2006), Frederik told Willa in detail about his past sexual encounters and time in "the [gay] lifestyle." She explained, "Our first date was the time when Frederik told me absolutely *everything* about his past. And you know I kind of went home with stars in my eyes. I went this guy is special. Well he just told you all of that, you know. And I don't know how exactly but I knew that he was my guy."

Willa believed, like many other African charismatics and Pentecostals, that God had selected a specific person to be her mate. For example, young black Pentecostal women in Soweto were taught that God would communicate whom he had chosen for their spouses (Frahm-Arp 2010: 194), and in Nigeria charismatics believed that God "guided" them in choosing romantic partners (Ojo 1997: 71). Willa was not alone at the Church of the Reborn in thinking that God had "ordained" her spouse. David, a coloured man who worked at the church and who attended many HRM events and classes, dated Greta, a white woman a few years his senior until she told him that God had decided that he was not "predetermined" as her husband anymore. (The two later reconciled and married, and Greta said that she had "misheard" God.) Willa was one of many Pentecostals who claimed that God was intimately involved in the choice of a future spouse.

I shared a room with Willa at a HRM weekend retreat in 2004. One afternoon she shared with me her struggles in dating Frederik. She said that she felt like she was always the one who had to initiate physical affection and touch. She also expressed her fears about him "falling" and her frustrations with his "selfishness," explaining her belief, which HRM also taught, that "the [gay] lifestyle" was "inherently selfish." "Being gay is all about just you," she said. Frederik often talked to her about his sexual attraction for men, something that is normal in the ex-gay process, where girlfriends and wives become receivers of sexual confessions. Willa said she was "growing a tougher skin."

Willa and Frederik became engaged after a year of dating and were married a year later. Eight months before their wedding, Frederik had what Willa described as "an incident, [it] wasn't a full-on 'fall' but there was intimacy involved there." By this she meant that Frederik had had physical sexual touch with another man but not penetrative sex. She was very angry, and the two started attending counseling with Tristan and Bianca. Despite this setback, they were married and moved in together soon afterward. Willa said that in retrospect they probably should have waited longer to get married after Frederik's "incident" because he still had not addressed the underlying reasons that led to it. She characterized the first few months of their marriage as "hectic," partly from living together for the first time but also because of sexual intimacy. She told me, "For us at that stage it was mostly the intimacy thing that really rocked the boat because we didn't know what we were getting ourselves into. We had never tried it [sex] before, and it was not like we [had] suspected it was going to be like. Because we both thought we can't wait, we're waiting for the wedding day, it would be bliss. But it wasn't bliss because we weren't ready for it, we weren't mature [enough] to go there." The couple not only had purposely been abstinent but had not even kissed before marriage in order to make their wedding night special. Many people in the ministry said that the two still struggled sexually in their marriage years into it. Some members were incredulous about Frederik's heterosexual feelings and others defended him and his marriage. For example, Damon, who remained close with the couple, told Alwyn in 2013 that the pair continued to enjoy an active sex life, were trying to have a baby, and were in that process even "breaking beds," an allusion to how much Damon claimed they energetically participated in sex. The two were popularly thought not to have a sexual relationship at all, despite tales of "beds breaking." Frederik was a major source of gossip in HRM. In 2013 a former ministry member shared with me that Frederik had been having sex with men throughout his marriage. He explained that Frederik had a "process," which entailed meeting men online and arranging a meeting at a secluded place, where the two would "wank off," or masturbate, together.

Willa herself categorized her relationship with Frederik as "not normal." When I asked her to elaborate on why she felt this way she said it was because neither had good gendered role models growing up. In her family, her mother was "very submissive" and her father "dominant" and she said that she struggled with swinging between "being very submissive and being very pathetic" and "too dominant." After marriage, the couple started seeing a heterosexual couple for gendered mentoring, so they could learn how they should respond to each other and embody Christian gender roles. Willa said, "And I assume I've been very prominent in the relationship because if I wasn't there to encourage him and stand by him for a very long time he wouldn't have continued maybe his whole, you know, course of getting over his old lifestyle. I'm not saying I'm the only one, just that I was an integral part of it. And I do think maybe in some places I might have been filling more than my female role. Maybe I've been more dominant than was necessary." Her biggest fear was that Frederik would return to being "out" and gay, and this led her to behaviors that she saw as negative and not embodying the kind of Christian woman she wanted to be, a woman who was an "encourager," soft, and happy to have and follow a masculine Christian husband. Although marriage was the ideal for ex-gay men, in practice it was often difficult and involved a lot of pain on the part of women who became confessors to ex-gay men's desires for other men. Despite knowing that couples like Willa and Frederick struggled with sexual attraction and having sex, ex-gay men still focused their desire work on the achievement of marriage as proof of realizing an ideal heterosexual selfhood.

Conclusion

Ex-gay Pentecostal men in South Africa who practiced desire work used it as a way to get to know their "natural" and "real" selves better. The men who joined HRM aspired to new heterosexual selves that controlled desire, took initiative, and found women to be physically attractive. They performed desire work, which involved micropractices of feeling and physical performance, to produce new selves. By following predetermined sequential phases, through long-term productive labor, the ex-gay men at HRM attempted to feel aroused by women, but this had a diversity of outcomes. In the next chapter, I look at one of the most common outcomes of desire work long-term, that of heterosexual failure.

"I DIDN'T FALL. I'M FREE"
Leaving Healing Revelation Ministries

Everybody popped out of the closet like nobody's business!
Like mushrooms on an autumn day, seriously [laughter].
—Ex-ministry leader on ministry members "coming out"

The Gay Weekend Away

HRM closed its South African branch in 2010 when Brian moved back to the United States to get married to a woman, finances for running the African office dried up, and most of the leadership team had returned to "the [gay] lifestyle." The ministry no longer has any African affiliations and is now American-based. In July 2013 I returned to South Africa after a five-year absence. I was eager to see in person the men and women I had worked with and known for a decade after keeping in touch through the internet and the phone. I was especially excited for a weekend away where I would see Alwyn and Coenraad, now out, and Damon and Adrian, both of whom were still ex-gay despite the ministry's closure. Damon had bought a backpackers[1] a few hours outside Cape Town, and Alwyn, Coenraad, and I took a fun road trip there together, laughing and joking, reminiscing about people we knew, comparing notes on who was still an ex-gay Pentecostal and who had left HRM in the past few years and was living an openly gay life. I wondered how the weekend would pan out, mixing together ex-ministry members. Even though the ministry was no longer in existence in South Africa, Damon and Adrian were still ex-gay and hoping and praying for heterosexuality. They continued to perform desire work. Alwyn and Coenraad had left HRM and were now seeing themselves in new ways, using the language of "wholeness" to describe their sexualities. Along with leaving HRM, they had also left the search for pious heterosexuality behind.

I was little prepared for the strangeness of the weekend. When we arrived at the backpackers, Damon at first seemed glad to see us, though he did stick us in an unswept and dusty room with bunk beds and no sheets, for which we had to ask him. As we settled in, I sought him out and tried to engage him in conversation; each time, he got up and walked away. It also turned out that the backpackers had a few other visitors. Damon initially said they were prebooked paying guests, but it turned out they were his Pentecostals friends. They seemed on high alert and were also not eager to talk to us. Although Adrian has not seen Damon since 2009, he also came from Cape Town to spiritually support him. This pattern, of Damon and the other guests ignoring us, continued for the entire weekend, and I became frustrated. Alwyn asked me to see it from Damon's perspective. He had invited other people to spiritually and physically protect himself from us and probably had people in the area and in the United States in prayer and spiritual warfare for him all weekend. They thought that Damon was in spiritual danger from proximity to Alwyn and Coenraad (and by extension myself), who in ministry terms had "fallen" and were possible dangerous spiritual contaminants. Alwyn's points, which I had not thought of when the weekend was planned, made sense to me, but I was still shocked by Damon's rudeness. I asked Damon if he was still ex-gay and he got up and left the room, saying he needed a glass of water. When Alwyn asked him the same question, he said, "I'm looking forward to marriage and children."

Damon did have words with Alwyn when we first arrived at the backpackers. Alwyn went inside to ask Damon if he needed help preparing dinner, and Damon confronted Alwyn, telling him that he was upset because Alwyn had "rejected" him since he came out. Alwyn said that he was not trying to rebuff Damon but respect his "recovery." Damon again said that Alwyn had rejected him, reminding him, "We always love those who have fallen." To which Alwyn replied, "I didn't fall. I'm free."

Damon did share with us that he was currently in spiritual counseling with a Christian couple who had diagnosed him with multiple personalities. He had originally gone to the couple for deliverance, and they told him he was not demonically possessed. Instead, they explained that he had multiple people living inside of him. He said that the personalities had formed at different times due to childhood trauma. For example, the first personality formed at the age of four when he was first sexually abused. Damon explained that he used to think he was crazy because he would lose time. He would go on a two-hour drive and only remember an hour of it or go to the supermarket to do shopping for the backpackers and find his trolley full of candy and not remember putting it in the cart. He said that the goal of his new counseling work was to "integrate" his personalities. They had "house meetings" where they would all talk together; now when he goes to the store he tells the others that they must stay in the car and he will get them some candy. Damon claimed that he felt more in control since beginning his "integration" work.

Damon's refusal to engage with Alwyn, Coenraad, and me was based on ideas about the dangers of "sexual falls" for other ex-gay Pentecostal men. Although Damon had invited us to stay at the guesthouse, he also invited a number of other Pentecostals to help him remain spiritually strong in the face of possible spiritual and sexual temptations, which Alwyn and Coenraad represented. Perhaps he originally saw the weekend as a way to evangelize, to try to get Alwyn and Coenraad back into the ex-gay fold, or maybe he was motivated by the desire to see how friends he had known well over a period of years were doing as "out" gay men. Regardless, for Damon and his friends, Alwyn and Coenraad were not only moral outsiders but also possible spiritual contaminants.

In this chapter, I explore why and how ex-gay Pentecostal men left HRM and their search for a pious heterosexual self. I am interested here in looking at why the ex-gay process broke down for men who spent years attempting to achieve heterosexuality. Instead of believing that opposite-sex desire was the end result of a long transformation, ex-gay men in HRM claimed that a new pious heterosexual self was achieved through working on the interior and exterior simultaneously. In her work, Saba Mahmood discusses how the pious self is not the outcome of a completed interior state of being. Instead, she draws attention to how disciplinary practices, like the desire work outlined in this book, and the pious self are "mutually constitutive." She writes, "The mosque participants do not understand the body as a sign of the self's interiority but as the means of developing the self's potentiality. (Potentiality here refers not to a generic human faculty but to the abilities one acquires through specific kinds of embodied training and knowledge)" (Mahmood 2005: 166). Ex-gay Pentecostal desire work was also a process of interior and exterior changes that occurred at the same time. They were also involved in "mutually constitutive" processes. This, as Mahmood discusses, means that piety is never achieved once and for all but must always be strived for— there is always room for improvement. The worldly gets in the way of the pious self and work must be undertaken to reach one's full "potentiality." Ex-gay Pentecostal men, like Egyptian Muslim women, had to train their bodies, minds, and spirits to be pious. However, ex-gay desire work was less successful than Muslim piety work, as I show below. Why were men like Damon and Adrian the exceptional "successes" and men like Alwyn and Coenraad the more typical "failures" of ex-gay desire work? What led to the differences in pious outcomes when both groups do work to achieve new, improved selves? What leads most ex-gay men to return to "the [gay] lifestyle" and abandon desire work?

As the title of this chapter illustrates, men saw themselves through a different vocabulary and lens after they came out. Out gay men like Coenraad and Alwyn saw themselves as now embodying their "natural" sexualities, which were expressed as "wholeness" and the "integration" of their spiritual and sexual selves. They saw their time in HRM as one in which they had lived in a false ex-gay self, one that involved a large degree of effort and suffering. Their new selves and the more recent ways they were living no longer involved the same amount of hard work. Openly gay ex-ministry members believed that they could now be who they "really were" without trying so hard. However, they did not view their time in HRM negatively. Most ex-ministry members saw their time in HRM productively and as part of building their new openly gay selves. Men viewed themselves as being in better places emotionally after being in HRM. Most of the data in this chapter comes from HRM's "failures," by which I mean men who "fell" and left the ministry. Those still living the ex-gay lifestyle largely would not talk with me because I was supportive of the now out ex-ministry members. Below I discuss how Pentecostal desire work allowed most ministry members to become new selves, just not heterosexuals.

The Fall of HRM

HRM began its slow demise in 2008 when people began to become disillusioned with the ministry and the way it was run. Two years later, most of the leadership was out or about to come out and HRM had closed its doors in Africa permanently. Theoretically, the whole ministry was supposed to "submit" to Brian, HRM's founder. However, the men in the HRM leadership team were able to question and challenge him without being lectured on submission. Below, I detail a significant incident in my fieldwork that occurred when HRM decided to attend the 2008 Gay Pride festivities for an evangelistic outreach.[2] Brian and I had a major disagreement about ethics, as well as his contention that I was "sowing dissension" in the ministry by questioning the ethics of the outreach and his decision-making about it.[3] This outreach was the only time the ministry did evangelism with the LGBTI community. It was also the last time I was allowed to be an official part of HRM. I detail this because it is one part of a larger story on how authority worked in HRM and the Church of the Reborn, as well as the beginning of the end of HRM. It illustrates the ways in which sexism and homophobia operated. "Sexual falls" were seen as less dangerous than questioning the ways things were run. The Pride Parade outreach also divided my fieldwork into two distinct phases. In the first, I spent a lot of time at the HRM office and the church. In the second, after I was dismissed from HRM, I spent more time shadowing individual ministry members in their everyday lives and had people visit me and spend time with me in my apartment. Being a ministry outsider was ultimately helpful to my work, as it allowed other HRM members to share with me their own struggles with Brian, ex-gay methods, and ministry norms. People left or were forced out for a variety of reasons, some of which I detail below.

The idea to perform a self-proclaimed "outreach" at the 2008 Gay Pride Parade was developed by a newer member of the leadership team. A man in his early thirties with thinning blond hair, Matt was a beefy-looking white man with the well-defined muscles of a weightlifter; he dressed to show off his physique in form-fitting shirts and vests. He was originally from Johannesburg and had moved to a suburb of Cape Town with his wife the year before, though he had known Brian for a longer period of time. Matt was a self-declared recovering gay party boy, and he sent an email to the ministry's Executive Team in June 2007 to convey an idea that God had "laid on his heart" two years earlier. He wanted the ministry to "help" those who were going to the Pride festivities. Matt rode on a parade float in the Johannesburg Gay Pride parade in 1999 and was shocked to see the Christian protesters on the parade route screaming at him and others and saying that they were going to "burn in hell" unless they repented. He believed that God wanted the ministry to offer a more "loving" option to those "struggling" with same-sex attraction. Matt's original proposal was to hand out cards with the ministry's contact information and an invitation to attend church on the Sunday after the parade. The goal was to provide gay people with an opportunity to learn that not all Christians were hurtful and condemning. The outreach was constructed as a way to reach out from a nonjudgmental place of love and compassion, as opposed to the disapproval that gays often received from Christians.

HRM's leadership and its members were very aware of the LGBTI politics and social life in Cape Town. The ministry was within walking distance of the "Gay Village" and even across the street from a restaurant that turned into a hopping gay bar at night. HRM leaders talked negatively about the Triangle Project, the city's LGBTI center, and they feared that it, along with the vibrancy of the gay community in general, would "corrupt" ministry members into leaving and rejoining the "the [gay] lifestyle." I was initially surprised that the ministry would choose to perform outreach at Cape Town's 2008 Gay Pride parade because they were in many ways frightened of the LGBTI community and its political and social influence in Cape Town. However, the ministry was also emboldened by LGBTI politics and their claims for space, public recognition, and rights, which also made a place for HRM to advocate for their own rights, claims to an identity, and visibility. The ministry members did not hide their ex-gay selves and desire work. Instead, they proselytized in churches, told their stories in conservative Christian magazines, on websites, and in radio shows, and were "out" about being "ex-gay." The choice to do outreach at Pride was part of a larger politics of visibility and the claiming of space for ex-gays in Cape Town's diversity of sexual subjectivities.

While it may seem counterintuitive, for HRM Gay Pride was a place where they believed they were justified to be. They saw themselves as offering a "solution" to LGBTI men and women, who were often condemned by religious groups, particularly conservative Christian ones. HRM said that the ministry provided a "loving" alternative to other antigay Christian groups, who told LGBTI people that they were going to literally burn in hell (at the parade itself, there were a few vehement and angry antigay protesters, who interceded with marchers in ways that involved vitriol or hate speech, and at times, they almost became violent). HRM saw themselves, as detailed in chapter 3, as also reclaiming Cape Town for Christ by walking through the parade and engaging in spiritual warfare. They understood themselves as taking back what they saw as contaminated gay spaces for God, who they believed was the city's rightful owner.

The Executive Team approved the outreach, though the details were significantly changed. Fears of a "homosexual backlash" by the gay community, in particular, the Triangle Project, led to a decision not to use the ministry's name on any of the printed materials to be distributed at the parade. Leader and Executive Team member Tristan said that in other countries there were major problems when ex-gay ministries approached people who were not seeking help and provided them with unsolicited information.

According to him, this evangelism led to negative publicity, lawsuits, and death threats. (I could find no evidence of this.) In an effort to keep HRM out of the spotlight, a decision was made to create a website name that was not directly affiliated with the ministry. The website ConQuers.com was developed to answer basic questions about God's love and sexuality and to offer a space to ask for further information. These questions were: "Do you feel lonely at times? Feel happy in your relationship? Feel content with your life/sexual orientation? Wonder if God loves you? Do you need someone to talk to?"

As a self-proclaimed "expert" on "the [gay] lifestyle," Matt stated that the information needed to be on a small piece of paper that could easily slide into a pocket or purse. Alwyn, Matt, and Jaco designed a small hot-pink card to hand out that claimed to be a website for a "Sunday After-Party."[4] Matt's idea was that an attractive card and a search for the next party would lead people to log onto the website after the parade.

Ministry policy was that the person who wanted help had to get in touch with the office and make an appointment. During my time volunteering in the ministry office I answered a few calls from a hysterical friend or relative asking for someone from HRM to come and intervene with a loved one.[5] The protocol for answering one of these calls was to let the person tell his or her story and then explain that the ministry did not help those who were not actively seeking it. Accordingly, I disagreed with the decision to give out cards with "After-Party" on them for two reasons. First, it was wrong because it was a lie.[6] Second, the outreach went against the ministry's own values and mission only to help those who sought it.

I found the decision to "trick" those at the parade to be especially hypocritical because everyone in the ministry incessantly discussed "spiritual abuse" and "spiritual manipulation." The book *The Subtle Power of Spiritual Abuse: Recognizing and Escaping Spiritual Manipulation and False Spiritual Authority within the Church* was passed around in 2008 by some of the staff at the Church of the Reborn and HRM leadership team members. In it, American Christian authors David Johnson and Jeff VanVonderen write, "Spiritual abuse can occur when a leader uses his or her spiritual position to control or dominate another person . . . Power is used to bolster the position or needs of the leader, over and above who comes to them in need" (Johnson and VanVonderen 1991: 20–21). In spiritual manipulation, the manipulator puts his or her needs and desires above God's.

Whether Brian was guilty of spiritual abuse was hotly debated. Spiritual manipulation and abuse were a part of everyday discourses on respecting boundaries and engaging in emotional honesty in HRM. "Spiritual manipulation" was a term that was used when a person was trying to get personal needs met through abusing religious authority. It also applied in situations where someone attempted to use otherworldly explanations for poor decision-making or behavior. Brian was often accused of spiritual manipulation because of his tendency to talk too much in meetings, not giving anyone else a chance to speak, and later to claim that he was filled with the Holy Spirit, not ego.

For example, at a 2007 leadership prayer session before a ministry class, Brian took over forty minutes of an hour-long meeting to narrate where God had communicated to him the ministry was going in the future. However, this was not the appropriate time for a monologue. The leadership meetings had a strict format, beginning with each leader explaining personal struggles, as well as any difficulties or "breakthroughs" from the prior week's classes. Between leaders and guest speakers, there were usually from eight to ten people present who were supposed to speak for three or four minutes each. At this meeting, no one else had time to speak and afterward people complained about Brian's taking over the meeting.

The day after the leadership prayer session, two leaders talked to Brian about the previous evening, bringing me into the conversation because I was also in the cramped and stuffy ministry office. Brian's tendency to overtalk, not listen to others, and spiritually manipulate were problems he sometimes acknowledged, and were cited as some of the reasons why people had left the ministry, not feeling there was space for them to bring in new ideas. The decrease in leadership around this time led to an agreement that if Brian talked too much he would stop. To assist him, Jaco was supposed to signal to him by subtly pulling on his earlobe. In this instance, Brian adamantly refused to take responsibility for taking over the meeting and ignored the fervent ear tugs that I saw out of the corner of my eye during his monologue. He said that it was the Holy Spirit overtaking him that caused him to speak for so long, and as the ministry's founder and leader there had to be room for God to communicate through him. He denied that he was being "spiritually manipulative." If people had a problem with this, he went on angrily, they should not be in HRM. What others in the ministry interpreted as disruptive, he saw as out of his control, claiming that the Holy Spirit was speaking through him. To try to silence him when filled with the Spirit was to try to silence God. It was the group, he claimed, that acted inappropriately in not prayerfully listening. Soon after, one of Brian's counselees arrived, and he left the room. The remaining leaders discussed how he was being spiritually manipulative and how wrong it was to try to claim divine causation for inappropriate behavior.

I thought that the 2008 Pride outreach was also spiritual manipulation. I spoke with ministry leaders about my concerns before the outreach, and they explained that it was not deceit but "trickery" and "disguise" for a greater good. I told them that I doubted God would agree with these kinds of methods, and that manipulating people to become Christians was not the appropriate way to represent the faith.

The situation finally came to a head at a weekly staff meeting a few weeks before the outreach, when Tristan brought up his own discomfort with printing "after-party" on the Pride outreach cards. Brian, who even at the calmest of times was likely to throw his hands in the air and yell "Oh my word," started in his seat. "What? No one told me!" he declared. Tristan brought up the same concerns I had and said he had also communicated this through email (which Brian claimed he never received) and spoke up at the Executive Team meetings where the outreach event was discussed.

Brian, while still rattled, went on to claim that Tristan should have been more vocal. He said it was obvious that Tristan's discomfort had not been important since it had not registered in his memory. He said dismissively that Tristan was the only person to raise any concerns about the outreach. I felt my face turning red, and I began to explain, in what I hoped was a calm voice, that I had repeatedly raised the same concerns for the past month.[7] Brian denied having heard anything like that. "Then you were not listening," I responded. He then proceeded to try to start playing "Bible chicken" with me. "Melissa," he said solemnly, "don't you think that saving even one soul makes it all worth it?" Did I not know the passages, which he proceeded to name and recite until I stopped him, about God's call for Christians to go out and proclaim His word?

I interrupted in a louder voice than I meant to. I replied, "I don't think that God wants to lie to people to get them to the Kingdom." I asked Brian whether he thought that people were really going to remain saved after they realized they had been manipulated into it. "Does God like lying?" I asked testily. Before Brian could admonish me further and bring in more scripture, Tristan intervened with one of Brian's standard lines. "Manipulation is witchcraft," he chimed in, "and the ministry does not want to be involved in anything from the Enemy [Satan]." The meeting ended; I went outside for a walk to cool down and decided to leave the Pride outreach alone. I felt that I had crossed a boundary where I was interfering in ministry matters, and I was embarrassed for being so emotional.

The day after our disagreement I went into the main church office to talk to Pastor Jurie's personal assistant. Brian was also there and called me into the large conference room to look at something. On the wood table was an open copy of the most recent *Joy Magazine*, a popular conservative South African Christian publication. He asked me to sit and read, "Is the Church Adopting the Language of Babylon." In it Errol Naidoo, the director of the South African Family Policy Institute, claimed that Christians were too politically correct and that "secular humanists, New Age philosophers and homosexual activists" were taking over South African society. He writes, "Babylonian terms like gay, homophobic, tolerance, celebrating our diversity, holistic, interfaith, common humanity, positive energy, peace gardens, hate crimes, human rights, etc[.] all conspire to undermine and refute Biblical commands and principles . . . When the humanists and their allies demand tolerance what they are actually demanding is that we tolerate sin, all manner of sin" (Naidoo 2008: 29–30). Cultural relativity and the acceptance of diversity were presented as negative, leading Christians to "tolerate sin" because of fears of being perceived as bigots.

I skimmed the article, placed it back on the table, and asked Brian what exactly he wanted me to comment on. "What do you think?" he asked. I answered that it sounded like the usual arguments made all over the world about how Christians are losing ground to liberals. Desmond Tutu was mentioned in the article because he had publicly compared homophobia to apartheid and recently said in a BBC interview, "If God, as they say, is homophobic, I wouldn't worship that God" (BBC 2007). In the interest of not fighting more with Brian, I said that I really respected Archbishop Tutu.

Brian interrupted me and, with a stern disapproving look, told me I could not like Tutu and gave me an analogy to consider. "If I give you a glass of clear, *clean* [his emphasis] water like you just bought at Woolie's [Woolworth's], you wouldn't hesitate to drink it. Now, if I use the same glass of water, but take a pinch of dirt from the plant over there and dropped it in, it would get cloudy and you wouldn't want to drink it. That is what Desmond Tutu has done to the truth." After making this declaration, he rested his intertwined hands on his stomach and leaned back in his chair, waiting for what I can only assume was agreement. I replied that I still liked Tutu, to which Brian told me again that I could not.

I figured that this back-and-forth on Tutu could go on indefinitely, so I told Brian I was hurt by what he had said the day before at the staff meeting. I had told him my concerns on at least three separate occasions, which I proceeded to list, and detailed where we were and who else was present during the conversation. He replied, "I am so sorry that you are hurt, but I don't remember you ever bringing it up at all." He asked me again to think about how many people's lives could be changed. He "hoped" I was "a big enough person" to see that I was wrong, and that I would still attend the day of the outreach to pray and intercede. He told me that as a member of the ministry, I had to submit to his leadership and stop "sowing dissent" by challenging his decisions. (I also heard later from other ministry members that Brian accused me of bringing "witchcraft" into HRM.)

The conversation then quickly switched to my own relationship with God, and Brian questioned the origin of my ideas on the outreach. "Are you listening to God about this?" he bluntly asked. He continued loudly, saying that while he knew that I "read a lot of books," it was not the same thing as communicating with God and "really listening" to what He wanted. He admitted that before yesterday he had not personally inquired of God about the outreach, but he was now completely convinced that God fully supported it. "I just kept hearing, your will is not my will over and over again during my personal time with God this morning." Brian concluded by telling me that I may have book knowledge but that I was "missing a lot." He told me that I needed to spend more time in prayer and less time trying to "influence" others. Brian believed that God had communicated directly with him and that my opinions were only human ideas and lacked the same weight as his.

Brian also asked me whether I thought it was acceptable for me to disagree with the male leadership,[8] especially when God clearly wanted women to submit to men.[9] He recited Ephesians 5:22 to me, "Wives, submit yourselves to your own husbands as you do to the Lord" (Amplified Bible 1987). My choice not to listen to Brian was therefore unbiblical, as well as disrespectful of his authority in the ministry, which he believed was arranged by God's hand. I ended the conversation by claiming I had a meeting to attend. The disagreement over the Pride outreach and my refusal to submit to Brian's leadership led to my dismissal from the ministry. I was asked not to come into the office, though I still sometimes attended ministry social events with leaders as a guest. I was removed from ministry communications and thanked for all my hard work. At this time, I was one of a few people who either left the ministry on his or her own volition or was forced out for "sowing dissent" or for not conforming to ministry norms. I detail this story to illustrate the consequences for not toeing the ministry line and challenging the leadership, as well as to point to the ministry's own "fall."

Some people left the ministry in 2007 and 2008 when I was in the field and others left in subsequent years. I felt very naive when I spent time with Alwyn and Coenraad at the backpackers that weekend in 2013. They detailed for me how some of the men, men I had been close to, spent a lot of time with, and interviewed in 2007–2008, had been having "sexual falls" and not told me about them, though they had detailed for me and confessed to other so-called sinful sexual practices and habits. For example, when they were still in the ministry, Hendrik, Coenraad, Jaco, and Alwyn all went wine-tasting together. They got intoxicated and told a lot of gay sex jokes. Hendrik was laughing and giggling along with the rest, "camping" it up. However, a few days later, Coenraad, Alwyn, and Jaco got called into the ministry office by older ministry leaders, including Brian. They were told that because of their behavior, Hendrik had had a sexual "fall" and that it was their fault because they had been "camping" and talking about gay sex. Coenraad rolled his eyes as he told me this story, explaining that Hendrik was always having "falls" and always blaming it on him. Hendrik, whom I had interviewed twice and spent time with socially, had never told me about these "sexual falls," though he had told me about masturbating and watching gay pornography. I imagine this was for many reasons, for example, that I was a woman and that he wanted me to see him in a certain way, perhaps as still masculine or godly. According to Coenraad, Hendrik mutually masturbated at the gym with other men and had participated in other "sexual sins." I felt naïve that I had not known that people were "falling" when I was previously in the field. The stories they may have told themselves and told others differed throughout the ex-gay process.

When HRM closed, Alwyn went to work as a counselor in the Church of the Reborn, where HRM had its offices. He and his girlfriend at the time, an ex-gay Pentecostal woman, decided to take a marriage course together at the church. While doing the Bible study, Alwyn began to see that even Pentecostals had different interpretations of the Bible. This was a surprise for him because he was, in his own terms, "very legalistic." Seeing the multiplicity of possible biblical interpretations started to "soften" him a bit. He decided that he and his girlfriend should break up and just be friends. At around the same time, he wrote to the Good Hope Metropolitan Community Church, an open and affirming congregation, for materials on homosexuality and the Bible. Alwyn had begun to doubt that the Pentecostal interpretation that gayness was a sin was correct or the only interpretation. Soon after, Dorothy, the youth pastor at the Church of the Reborn, came to him and said that a man had come in with same-sex attraction. She asked Alwyn to meet with him and to tell him that homosexuality was a sin from which he could recover. Alwyn replied that that was not his job. He thought that his job as a counselor was to listen and to counsel each person toward wherever and whatever was best for him. You tell him, he implored Dorothy, you're the youth pastor. After going back and forth, Alwyn stayed firm, which led Dorothy to report Alwyn to the church leadership at the next ministerial meeting. Jurie, the Church of the Reborn's head pastor, came to Alwyn and told him that he had a week to recant his position, which was only doubt that there was one biblical interpretation for homosexuality. Alwyn and Dorothy went through all the relevant scriptures together. (For example, Leviticus 18:22, "You shall not lie with men as with women. It is abomination.") He brought in the interpretations from Good Hope Metropolitan Community Church and she agreed with him that except for one scripture in Paul, there was a lack of clarity about the "sinfulness" for homosexuality. Alwyn told Jurie that he remained doubtful about homosexuality being unbiblical and a "sin." Jurie then fired him. After years of working on and off at the church and HRM, Alwyn was told he could never be in leadership again, though he was still welcome to come to church and to "recommit" his life to Christ. Jurie also called all of Alwyn's counselees and told them that Alwyn was not allowed to talk to them anymore. Alwyn was excommunicated because he dared to question the idea that homosexuality was sinful and wrong. Alwyn was one of the last of the former HRM leadership to "come out." Below, I detail how leaving HRM changed ex-gay men who participated in desire work for years.

New Selves

In 2013 I was able to spend time with and reinterview a few of the men and women I originally worked with during my previous periods of fieldwork. None were still affiliated with HRM. These men now self-identified as gay and were largely out, though some not to their families. Men went from claiming that God was helping them transform their gender and sexual selves to believing that these transformations were either impossible or very difficult, only accessible to a small population, of which they were not a part.

The men in HRM experienced significant changes in their religious lives. They moved from a deep and intense relationship with the Holy Spirit and Jesus Christ and heavy spiritual warfare practices to a more spiritual and less doctrinal connection to God, if they still had a relationship with Him at all. These changes manifested themselves in three ways: the men became less legalistic and doctrinal, they were less sure about the existence of God and how He operated, and they made a move away from reading and believing in the Bible. Alwyn was the ministry member who had been most involved in spiritual warfare, as detailed earlier in this book. When I asked him in 2013 about his involvement in spiritual warfare practices he explained to me that he thought that there was an emotional piece to his and the ministry's spiritual warfare work. He told me that he thought "in a way we worked ourselves up. We got emotionally charged [pause] to the point of convincing ourselves . . . I don't know, I think that the spiritual world is a world where we'll just never have enough proof, or enough knowledge to say that we 100 percent understand it or that we are correct in our interpretation of the spiritual world." This lack of certainty in the spiritual world and God's plan, which men previously claimed to know, manifested itself in a lack of believing in or reading the Bible. When I asked Jaco how his faith had changed since he left the ministry, came out as gay, and had gotten married to a man, he told me he was "less constrained by scripture and bylaw . . . Living connected lives [is] much more important than blindly reading the Bible. It's almost like the scales fell from my eyes."

Coenraad also stopped reading the Bible and began to meditate to connect with God, which he was surprised to say made him feel even more close to Him than he felt while a Pentecostal Christian. However, his relationship with God was a process. When he could not alter his sexuality he said he felt "disappointed with Him [God], the fact that I've really trusted Him to make a change in my life and it's not like I haven't tried or lived a double life or anything. I've really tried. So I was disappointed with Him. And just to once again make peace with the fact that God isn't a slot machine." Coenraad had begun to see that God was not going to "reward" his "good" and pious behavior as a Pentecostal with heterosexuality. His idea of God as a "slot machine" expressed his belief that if he played the game right and tried over a long period of time, he would eventually win, or in this comparison, achieve heterosexuality. Coenraad was initially disappointed and felt disconnected from God because he did all the right things to shed his same-sex attractions and they still remained. It was only when he left the ministry and realized that God did not operate in a quid-pro-quo way that he was able to begin to feel close to God again. When we spoke in 2013 he was involved in a period of not reading the Bible because he did not want to invite doctrine into his life. "Because my whole life I've strived and tried to be and always be the good Christian boy. And I've stopped that. I just want to be."

Alwyn still prayed sometimes but his prayer practices changed dramatically. He went from an ideology of "falling in love" with Jesus, detailed ear-

lier in this book, to not praying to Jesus at all anymore. Instead he sometimes prayed to God and did not even know if he still self-identified as a
Christian. Elisabe, who used to be an HRM leader, no longer self-identified
as a Christian after leaving HRM. "My beliefs are less rigid and sometimes
I don't feel like I have any beliefs anymore. I pray occasionally, and I still
would like to believe in God but there are times when I don't actually know
if I believe in God. And when I pray I do feel more . . . [pause] it's not such
an experiential thing anymore as back in those days [in HRM] . . . I miss the
experiential thing." Elisabe felt sad that she had lost her connection with
God and the feelings that accompanied it. Similarly, after leaving HRM, Simon's relationship with God also changed. He categorized it as moving from
being "super religious" to being "very different [now]. I don't do anything
because I have to. Like purely just say how I'm doing . . . [Now I] just ask
for strength. I used to always, I felt it was a constant must do this or I must
apologize for this. Now I'm all right." A close relationship with God and
Jesus Christ, so central to men's desire work, disappeared along with their
strivings to be heterosexual.

Both ex-gay men and heterosexual ex-ministry members noted that the
most positive pieces of their experiences in the ministry were in learning
about dysfunctional family systems and that this was leading to their becoming more "integrated" people. Elisabe said that five years after she left the
ministry she still used HRM ideas to deal with her current family relationships. She talked to me about triangulation[10] in particular, saying she applied
this idea she learned in HRM to her daily life. She not only noticed when it
was happening but also now tried to change the situation. Her time in HRM
provided her with the therapeutic language and skills necessary to combat
common dysfunctional familial dynamics between herself, her mother, and
her younger sister. Alwyn still also used the therapeutic ideas and practices
from the ministry, telling me that HRM helped him learn about and process
his own "dysfunctional" family, learning what were his "issues" and what
belonged to them. "So in that sense I learned a lot about the psychological
part about growing up in a dysfunctional family, learning about codependency and narcissism. So it opened up a whole new world for me." Similarly,
being in HRM was a way for him to experience counseling for the first time
when secular counseling was too expensive for him and seen as outside of
the norms of respectable Afrikaans culture. "It [HRM] definitely softened
me, or prepared me for therapy . . . It was cheap, it was accessible, and it was
very empathetic in the sense of I could speak the unspeakable shame. So it
broke the ground for me in that I could enter into therapy. So it opened the

door for me that psychological obstacle of accessing real therapy." He mentioned in particular how HRM provided the language and tools to deal with "childhood trauma" in its counseling and classes.

Coenraad also found the classes and psychological ideas he learned in HRM helpful. He discussed childhood trauma and the need to release it. He believed that he would not have dealt with his "issues" without his time in HRM, which contributed to his "being a more whole person. So my reason for being there was to get straight, but in the process there's a lot of positive things that did happen." For Jaco, the ministry helped him become more "integrated." He explained, "[The] irony is that all of that [HRM] brought me to a healthier place, evolved me into a healthier place. Even things that are chaos are part of the process. Those things brought me [finally] to emotional health. [I have] a feeling of gratitude, I'm grateful because it started me off to a healthier place in some respects. I had to focus on myself, what was good and what was not, what to work on, self-awareness, [begins crying] and all those things, I'm mostly grateful for it. I don't want to erase it because I wouldn't trust that I would be in the same place I am today . . . if I become very judgmental and bitter about those years. It will also be something I do to myself . . . It didn't destroy me, it's all a part of me." Jaco was grateful for his time in HRM because it led him on a journey that ended with him marrying another ex-gay Pentecostal man and emigrating to Canada to live with him. Coenraad also said that he "didn't want to throw the baby out with the bathwater" and that while some people may have been scarred emotionally from HRM, he was not and largely has taken positives from his years in the ministry. His sexuality was not transformed but other parts of his life improved.

Similarly, Liam was "thankful" for the psychological theories he learned, specifically naming "codependency and family of origin and shame, and even mother and father wound to a degree, although one could go into abstraction on all these things, that's what most people did, but it was useful information and the type of stuff generally people don't get to come across . . . so I definitely think I'm healthier. I'm happier for that information but it wasn't a healthy environment." Liam found that HRM provided him with key information in addressing his problems but found the context this was provided in to be troubling and dysfunctional. Unlike Coenraad, Jaco, and Liam, Simon didn't feel that the counseling piece of HRM was helpful. When I asked him about it he told me, "In the end, no. 'Cause I was lied to and was lying . . . like I was not honest in how disillusioned I was feeling about the fact the things I was thinking all the time. That things hadn't changed . . . all I could think about was men." Liam's experience was that HRM lied to him about his sexuality being changeable. Unlike most of the men, he felt that the ministry was damaging. Most ex-HRM members looked back on their time in the ministry positively, particularly because it provided them with ways to perform productive labor on bodies, minds, and spirits. Though their desire work was ultimately unsuccessful, they found working on themselves to be productive; it eventually led to improved selves and better lives.

Success Rates and Failures

Over the past few years, many "strugglers" have left HRM and the fantasy of a heterosexual life. They no longer practice heterosexual desire work. Unlike many ex-gay men who leave American ex-gay ministries, who often remain angry and traumatized by their experiences (Schlanger and Wolfson 2014; Toscano n.d.), the men who left HRM expressed a common belief that it was part of their "journey" and helped them become more "integrated" and "whole" men. The failure of desire work became a part of their new narratives as openly gay men.

Ex-ministry members had different and overlapping reasons for why they no longer believed that being ex-gay works. Alwyn was adamant that being ex-gay was not possible because it was trying to change something too fundamental about a person's selfhood. He also thought that it was extremely painful to attempt, telling me, "It's just so traumatic to try and change your sexuality. It's like trying to change your skin color . . . Back in the day [when in HRM] I just remember this wrestling inside of them [ex-gays], this inner war within themselves. This craziness, this anxiety, this suffering. And I think it was more traumatic trying to change." While in the ministry he thought that changing his sexuality was possible and part of "God's plan" for his life. Alwyn's comparison of skin color signaled to me that he had moved to seeing homosexuality as an unchangeable essence, a part of "naturalness," which it is impossible or very difficult to change. In the ministry's worldview, sexuality was both changeable and an essence. Heterosexuality was buried, a core awaiting rediscovery that God had "ordained," but also something that could be altered with hard work. Alwyn had moved from one essentialist understanding of sexuality to another. He noted that attempting to be ex-gay led to immensely negative feelings, employing the language of "trauma," "suffering," and an "inner war," which he claimed he experienced himself and saw and heard about from his counselees and other ex-gay Pentecostal men. For him, the ex-gay process was an impossible bind, one that involved immense amounts of pain and one that was doomed to fail because ultimately ex-gay Pentecostal men were trying to change something that was an essential part of their make-up.

When I asked Jaco if he thought being ex-gay was possible, he answered me with a decisive NO. He pointed me back to looking at ex-gay rhetoric. He explained very adamantly, "So nobody can change their sexual orientation. All the people in the ministry, support group[s], one-on-one counseling, Exodus [International], and all those ministries, it's basically a fact, not even an opinion: you just have to manage your attractions, so a resounding no." He continued, "The effort is to try to kill a part of you, there has to be an assassination of half of who you are, so no!" He believed that even ex-gay ministries were fooling themselves with their own rhetoric, where the focus is on the transformation of one's activities and from there, hopefully, an interior transformation would emerge. He also thought that being ex-gay was a way to have a half or lesser life, so that one could not reach his full potential while involved in ministries like HRM. Like Alwyn, he used strong language of violence to the self. Alwyn used the term "inner war" and Jaco employed the word "assassination." Both men agreed that they had had to kill a part of themselves when involved in HRM.

For ex-ministry leader Antjie, people's behaviors were evidence that although they were working hard, the ex-gay process was not successful. She used the term "dysfunctional" to categorize HRM members who, despite laboring hard on themselves, were unable to change, leading to "acting out." She explained, "I saw lots of people actually start to develop certain things like alcoholism, anger issues, and they became—it seemed like they became more and more frustrated because they couldn't be what they feel they are, in my opinion. And that manifested itself in abuse of alcohol, anger issues, passive-aggressiveness. Stuff like that." According to her logic, if God had been working in these people's lives the way He was supposed to be, then this would have led them to happier, more satisfied, and better selves. Instead, she saw people becoming neurotic, feeling out of control, and "acting out" with various substances and emotions, proof that the ministry's promise of a new and better self was failed and bankrupt.

Coenraad and Liam both said that while being ex-gay did not work for them they did not believe that it meant it was impossible for everyone. Each said he could only speak from his own experiences. Coenraad said that he saw sexuality as a "pendulum" where some people were able to move back and forth in their sexualities. He was uncomfortable using his own experiences in not being able to change his sexuality as a "mold because I think sexuality is much more complex than yes or no." He continued, saying that there were couples in HRM that seemed happily married, and while he did not know the inner workings of their relationships and lives—he was no longer in contact with them—their existence was proof of the complexities of sexualities and the possibilities that there were some pendulum swingers. Liam said that someone else with "less family trauma" might have turned out differently. "But if the same person had been born in just a different set of circumstances, maybe I would have popped out, have gone the heterosexual route, but that's not how my life [turned out]. I've analyzed myself inside out, back to front and times four hundred . . . Who's to say that if you've thrown different circumstances into the pot some different me would have popped out?" Unlike Alwyn, who used the comparison of something that he saw as unchangeable like skin color, Liam and Coenraad both saw sexuality as more fluid and dependent on the person. They both acknowledged that for other people maybe changing sexuality was an easier process than it was for them, though they both noted that it would be a difficult process for anyone. For Liam, a different kind of childhood experience or family structure might have led him to be heterosexual. He saw himself, including his sexuality, as a product of his experiences, both positive and negative.

For Willa, who was married to an ex-gay Pentecostal man, the problem with desire work was that it was never finished. When I asked her about what she thought of HRM's methods, something that she knew intimately through her marriage, she said that she thought that being ex-gay needed to be seen as a "stage" and not a type of lifestyle. She explained, "I do think you need to move on. Look, it'll never be normal but it will be normal because you call it [that] . . . Some people wear it [being an ex-gay Pentecostal] like a fighter pilot's jacket, like badges, not a raincoat to wear it and then take it off." According to Willa, the problem with HRM was that being ex-gay led to subject-formation as a particular type of person. She found that frustrating because she felt that it meant that men got stuck in always seeing themselves through the lens of working toward something, of never arriving there. She characterized living an ex-gay lifestyle as both abnormal and normal, acknowledging that same-sex desire and "sexual falls" would always separate ex-gay Pentecostal men from heterosexual men. However, she also pointed out that part of being in HRM was to "act as if," to use exterior transformations to initiate interior ones. She thought that men in HRM, including her husband, needed to act in "normal" ways and that this would affect their interiors. Her comparison of kinds of jackets is telling as well. She compared being an ex-gay Pentecostal man to wearing a unique type of jacket, that of a fighter pilot, where the outside is covered in badges, or patches. These patches can be read as being evidence of the men's "brokenness," which they were taught they must always be ready to talk about and revisit. Willa saw this as a problem because it meant that ex-gay Pentecostal men never took off these jackets and focused too much on their badges, or brokenness. She instead advocated for using the ex-gay process when it was needed, similar to how one puts on and takes off a raincoat. It was there when one needed help but wearing it all the time was self-defeating.

Elisabe said she also had "suspicions" while she was involved in HRM because of some of the men's behavior. She told me, "Just the whole thing about them massaging each other and all that . . . It seemed like a little of hero worship. And that seems to often be an indication where there's like hero-worship going on between the guys. You're like 'hmm . . . okay . . .' [laughter] . . . Latent homosexuality, what is going on here? [laughter]." When I asked her if she was surprised when so many of the men came out in the past few years she said that she was "purely because they were so adamant that they were healed. On the other hand, they did keep slipping up as well . . . I think in the beginning when I first started with HRM I had, you know, I had quite rose-colored glasses on, and I didn't realize that people were struggling so much . . . I guess I was a bit naive . . . I wasn't aware of everything that was going on under the surface. It seemed like a happy family to me, and that's what drew me in." Elisabe was surprised, like I had been, that there were so many "sexual falls" going on beneath the surface. While the ministry claimed to be open, there were layers of "issues" for men going on at the same time. I asked Tristan and Bianca, long-time HRM leaders, if they were surprised about who came out and left HRM. They told me no, that the main group—Liam, Jaco, Coenraad, and Alwyn—had been "coming out" for a long time. They thought that these men had used the ministry to come out of the closet. Everything was a gay joke to them or had sexual innuendo. They thought these leaders were living the single gay lifestyle without the sex during the time they were involved in the ministry. This is markedly different than the way these individuals spoke about their own experiences in HRM.

The sequential phases of desire work involved concerted, long-term effort that took years of practice and performance. This effort led many ex-gay men to express frustration that their labors were not moving them fast enough toward heterosexuality. Most ministry members moved slowly through the steps with simultaneous hope and exhilaration, combined with fear and dread that they would never reform and "fix" what they called their "broken" sexual attractions. The ministry informed ex-gay men that until their same-sex desires were reoriented toward women, they would period-ically have "sexual falls."

Ex-gay Pentecostal men who "fell" blamed themselves for not working hard enough or being "good enough." Their "hope" for heterosexuality was often transformed into despair. They frequently expressed anger at them-selves and God after their "falls;" in some, falls led to self-hatred and in-tense anxiety about ever realizing heterosexuality. For example, Coenraad attempted to transform his sexual desires for twenty years before he began to live openly as a gay man at forty-five. He was a part of HRM for many of these years. He explained to me in 2013 that being ex-gay was, "exhaust-ing. I was tired all the time with all the effort of being the perfect Chris-tian boy. I had all the self-loathing and self-hatred. I've slipped again, I've messed up, I'm not supposed to mess up at all. I tried to live this pure life, but now I've watched porn again, [and I feel] all that anxiety and weight." Once he "finally ended" his heterosexual desire work and "integrated" his (homo)sexual and religious selves, he began to feel "well-rested" for the first time in years. Coenraad experienced his desire work as emotionally ardu-ous, and it frequently left him angry with himself for "not going ['healing'] fast enough" and at God for not "rewarding" his hard work. Like Coenraad, Hendrik felt distressed and exhausted because of his "failed" attempts at dat-ing women. After neither of his relationships worked out, he began "falling back into my old ways of thinking and self-hatred, and all these things of I'm not good enough, I'm too bad, and I'll never amount to anything. [I'll] be single and never have a woman." For Hendrik, dating was part of a cycle where he ended up having "sexual falls" and hating himself. His desire work did not pay off.

Some men who experienced these dejected feelings fell into a cycle of "sexual falls," which continued despite detailed and full confessions to HRM leaders, more time in counseling, and social time spent exclusively with other ex-gay Pentecostals for support. Simon was twenty-four when he ini-tially joined HRM in 2004. He spent four years in the ministry, believing for most of it that heterosexuality was "God's perfect will for my life." However, he started a cycle of "falls" in the last two years of his time in HRM, brought on by his fears that his desire work would never be successful. He told me that he would go from being "a wonderful good boy" who had "honeymoon periods with God" to "very bad sexual behavior. It progressed in a very addictive way. It would get worse [over time]. More alcohol, more sinister meetings." Simon began to have blackouts from drug and alcohol use and had unprotected sex with other men to "punish" himself for his same-sex desires. After each "fall," Simon "confessed" in detail to Brian, HRM's founder. Brian did not reprimand or excommunicate Simon; he reframed the "falls" as a productive part of his larger journey towards heterosexuality. When Simon told Brian in frustration, "I just like to screw men," Brian replied with, "That's good, then you'll like to screw women too." Although HRM presented "falls" as part of the ex-gay lifestyle, men like Simon found them emotionally painful and debilitating. The inability to foster heterosexual attraction was why most ex-gay men eventually "returned to the lifestyle," some after many years of self-surveillance and physical and emotional discipline. For example, Simon is now "out" and married to a man.

The ministry measured "success rates" despite its focus on process in building a heterosexual orientation over time. HRM collected these statistics for two reasons. The first was to facilitate financial contributions from donors to pay for office space and salaries. The second was to encourage ex-gay men. HRM leaders said they used "success rates" to "empower" "strugglers," an ex-gay term for gay men having trouble resisting gay "temptations." The ministry told men that if they were "highly motivated" and followed a pre-determined sequential order of emotional and behavioral change, as detailed earlier in this book, that they too could get married and have children.

Alwyn told me in 2008 that he thought "success rates" were around 30 percent for people who were under thirty-five when they first came to the ministry. He said that older men were "too stuck in their ways" to make significant, lasting changes. Alwyn amended this number when we spoke in 2013. He explained that he had conducted an "informal research project" in 2009 when he first began to have doubts about ex-gay "success." He pulled one hundred random files of ex-gay men who had come for counseling since the ministry opened in 1997. Out of the hundred, he said, only five of the men were "still living heterosexual lives," which Alwyn believed was because each was married. He told me, "Of those five, how many of their sexual orientation has changed? I believe zero, and that to me was the answer of how successful this gay reparative therapy was. Some of them have claimed they have changed sexual orientation, but if we look at the facts, how many of them still struggle with looking at pornography of people of the same gender? Have experiences where they have mutual masturbation in the bushes with people of the same gender? That just says to me the sexual orientation just doesn't change." Alwyn did not see evidence of long-lasting change in the majority of men involved in the ministry.

Why Does Desire Work Fail?

Ex-gay Pentecostal men in South Africa who practiced desire work used it as a way to get to know their "natural" and "real" selves better. They share this in common with other individuals who use sexual desire and practices to realize their "true" selves, a diverse group that includes lesbians in Namibia (Lorway 2015), Muslim youth in Turkey (Ozyegin 2015), and BDSM practitioners in America (Weiss 2011).[11] South African ex-gay men shared with these groups participation in activities that require specialized learning and repeated practice over time to achieve one's "natural" self. Desire work illustrates how sexual desires, not only sexual subjectivities, are socially and historically located. It demonstrates how heterosexuality has a history; it is not universal or timeless and changes depending on cultural context (Blank 2012; Katz 2007). Sexual desire also remains an individual process, which leads some ex-gay men to "succeed" in heterosexual desire work and others to "fail."

Ex-gay Pentecostal men who joined Healing Revelation Ministries in Cape Town, South Africa, aspired to new heterosexual selves that controlled desire, took initiative, and found women to be physically attractive. They performed desire work, which involved micropractices of feeling and spiritual and physical performances to produce their "natural" selves. By following predetermined sequential phases, through long-term productive labor, the ex-gay men at HRM attempted to feel aroused by women, though this had a diversity of outcomes.

Ex-gay men experienced their bodies and emotions as pliable and molded them to assist in meeting heterosexual goals. The renewed focus on the empowered self, its habits, its dispositions, and the personal realm, was part of a larger African Pentecostal response to economic and political despair, detailed in the introduction to this book. Although attaining the heterosexual self remained elusive for many ex-gay men, the new confident and aware selves they built were a part of broader African Pentecostal practices that offer a variety of directions, tools, and relationships to build new, authoritative, and hopeful selves, despite daily struggles and political and economic uncertainties.

With two important differences, my observation that behavioral changes come before, and are meant to cause, internal changes in piety and heterosexuality is similar to what Saba Mahmood (2005) found in the aforementioned study of a religious piety movement in Egypt where women aimed to become more devout. First, Muslim women covered themselves to create internal piety, and ex-gay Pentecostal men opened themselves up to the others to gain God's blessings of heterosexuality: men publicly flirted with women, masturbated to their images, and engaged in sexualized touch with women. Second, Mahmood is convinced that this process works, and I am not. So why are the women in the Egyptian Muslim piety movement "successful" and most South African ex-gay Pentecostal men "unsuccessful" in their projects of pious transformation when both do arduous work to cultivate interior changes? The dedication and daily work are similar, and yet for ex-gay men, the interior changes brought by ex-gay processes usually either were short-lived or did not take place at all. I account for this finding by addressing three differences between these religious self-formation projects: the national context, gender, and the type of change sought.

In Egypt, women in the piety movement had the support of a wider Muslim community, and in South Africa, ex-gay men were abject despite the gay rights protections in the constitution. Ex-gay Pentecostal men felt profoundly ostracized. They saw themselves as outside the norms of the gay community because of their piety and desire for change. They felt othered by the Christian community because of their struggles with their "sinful" gender subjectivities and (homo)sexualities. They also perceived themselves as outside the realm of normative South African society due to the national disapproval of homosexuality. In South Africa, gayness is stigmatized and interpreted as "un-African," and gay men, even those seeking "help" to "heal" their homosexual desires, are ridiculed and humiliated by the larger society and other Pentecostals. HRM members were the subject of much homophobic joking and sarcasm, with few church staff and members publicly or privately supporting the men. Many at the Church of the Reborn were upset that HRM was affiliated with their church. Despite their desire for piety, ex-gay Pentecostal men were often seen by others as incapable of achieving it due to their "sinful" desires. By publicly admitting to same-sex desire and to needing help, ex-gay men presented themselves as more similar to stereotypical ideas of women, a negative characteristic in South Africa, where dominant heterosexuality is linked to men having power over women and their bodies, and not by sharing traits with them.

The second reason for the difference in effectiveness of the movements in Egypt and in South Africa is their gender. The women in Mahmood's study fulfilled normative Muslim gender roles by covering their bodies and learning to be shy and submissive (Mahmood 2005: 157–158). However, ex-gay men in South Africa were acting unmasculine by admitting that they needed assistance in learning to be heterosexual. They disclosed that they shared women's desire for male sexual partners, which is contextually negative. Normative masculinity in South Africa is linked to the control of women's bodies and coercive sex, violence, alcohol and drug use, risk taking behavior, and being unemotional (Morrell, Jewkes, and Lindegger 2012; Walker, Reid, and Cornell 2004). Men in HRM sought to embody a pious form of masculinity where they had feelings, were nonviolent, followed religious norms, and did not consume addictive substances, and while they sought to be leaders, they claimed not to want to oppress women like other South African men. There was little support for this type of Christian masculinity outside the faith. However, even inside the faith other Christians, as noted above, viewed ex-gay men as suspect and unable to be "real" pious masculine men because of their same-sex desires.

Third, women in the piety movement were involved in a project of controlling their bodies and emotions with God's "help." Ex-gay men shared the control of affect with women in Egypt, but during their time in HRM, their new pious selves were also heavily dependent on how others responded to them, especially women. A major piece of desire work was learning how to engage with other people in new ways, detailed in chapters 2 and 4. Ex-gay men were taught how to see and treat other men less as potential sexual objects and more as nonsexual peers that they could be emotionally intimate with without sexualizing these feelings. This meant that men were dependent on how other men responded to them, which was a challenge, especially in their dealings with heterosexual men, who often viewed them with suspicion. Similarly, ex-gay men were also dependent on how women responded to them. Women's reactions to the men's new heterosexual behaviors, such as compliments and sexual advances, were outside of the men's authority. Women could halt the production of desire work and men's transformations by refusing to engage with them or by mocking them, reifying their positions as abject. There were multiple relationships in play besides the relationship between one person and God.

Conclusion

Ex-gay men who left HRM were largely positive about their time in the ministry. They felt that it had offered them tools to be new kinds of healthier, more balanced, and aware selves than they were before they joined the HRM. However, their same-sex desires, their reason for being in HRM, did not change over time, despite years of labor on their affect, bodies, and spirits. As heterosexuals they "failed," but as people they felt successful in that they left HRM with the tools to process emotions. They saw themselves through a new lens—as being capable of having deep relationships with themselves and with others. They learned a new language of self-making that drew from psychology, theology, NGOs, literalist readings of the Bible, and self-help. For the men who left, their selves were more successful despite their heterosexual failures.

For ex-gay Pentecostal men, desire work was the only way to achieve what they considered a rewarding and "godly" life. They are an especially poignant example of what Lauren Berlant calls "cruel optimism," in which what they desired (heterosexuality) impeded their achievement of a more satisfying and happy life. Berlant writes that "optimism is cruel when it takes shape as an affectively stunning double bind: a binding to fantasies that block the satisfaction they offer" (Berlant 2011: 51). Desire work is a form of cruel optimism in that ex-gay Pentecostal men were bound to the fantasy of heterosexuality that was always out of reach. That fantasy got in the way of their flourishing by impeding their recognition that desire work was largely unsuccessful. For example, the built-in nature of "sexual falls" meant that men would "fall," and instead of seeing this as evidence that ex-gay methods were flawed or not working for them, they were taught that "falls" were part of their journey to heterosexuality. Desire work was an impediment to ex-gay men flourishing. The time they spent obsessively paying attention to and managing their desires took away from their living a satisfying life. Ex-gay men were bound to a fantasy that offered them joy but often delivered despair and failure instead.

In the documentary *God Loves Uganda* (2013) filmmaker Roger Ross Williams follows young evangelical missionaries who travel from the United States to Uganda in the hope of "saving" Africans from "sexual immorality," namely homosexuality. In the film, the mostly white missionaries from the International House of Prayer in Kansas City, Missouri, plan to do "God's work" in Africa. They prepare well. In their home church, they pray in front of world maps and lay hands on the continent of Africa, uttering pleas for its peoples to be saved and redeemed, washed in the blood of Jesus. They task prayer teams from the church with praying around the clock for God to intercede in the lives of so-called sinners all over the world. Men and women shake and cry as they are filled with the Holy Spirit, eager to bring what they see as God's love and salvation to a generically needy "African," who risks temptation into sexual immorality and remains spiritually adrift from a personal relationship with Jesus Christ. On the ground in Uganda, the film captures the missionaries at work, at rest, and en route—traveling to remote villages, laughing and singing, and then turning serious as they urge Africans to accept Jesus Christ as their Lord and Savior.

What was striking about this film to me was not the intensity of the missionaries' focus on "saving Ugandans" from Satan's pull, but that this Satanic plot was so squarely centered on homosexuality. These evangelical missionaries come not only to "save" Africans from spiritual degradation but specifically from "sexual sins," in particular the "sin" of homosexuality. The American pastors in the film have no qualms about their entitlement to be in Uganda to do "God's work" and to "save" Ugandans from the apparent pull of what they consider to be abhorrent sexuality. They hold prayer vigils, workshops, and crusades. They urge Ugandans to reclaim their nation from "sexual sin" and to pass the "Anti-Homosexuality Bill" to make homosexuality punishable with jail time and even death.[1] They do not waver, bold and secure in their knowledge that homosexuality is a "sin," un-African, against God's desires and dictates, and wrong for Ugandans.

As I watched the film for the first time, I was struck by the similarities and differences between the people in the film and in Healing Revelation

Ministries. Both groups were engaged in projects of personal and community "liberation" and "healing" from what they consider to be a universal sin. They share one faith and the fervor to stop so-called sexual sins in Africa. Each group expresses varying forms and levels of homophobia, racism, and misogyny. My own reactions to these two interconnected yet distinct projects and populations were also very different. In *God Loves Uganda*, I was uncomfortable not only with the fervor of the white evangelicals in the film but also with the one-sidedness of their representation by the filmmaker, who cast them almost as caricatures of themselves. When I showed the film in an upper-level African Studies course, students laughed at the portrayal of these Americans, not able to take these mostly white and very religious missionaries seriously. As I drafted this manuscript, I wanted to give readers a chance to like, or at least understand, the people in these pages who sought to transform their desires and selves through hard work. I reflected on the film as I wrote: how different were its projects and how similar was its protagonists' homophobia?

One of the key differences was that the men in HRM attempted to change themselves, not other Africans.[2] The men in HRM (with the exception of Brian, HRM's founder) were all South African, hard at work on themselves and at their own bidding rather than invited, coerced, or manipulated into another's project. The missionaries in the film, however, were focused on transforming the lives of others. How effective they were in saving souls and altering morality is debatable. As detailed in the introduction to this book, homophobia is pervasive in most of Africa, including South Africa, where the LGBTI community is legally but not socially protected from cultural sanctions and violence. How different are the men in HRM from other homophobes? Does it ultimately matter that they claimed not to be homophobic and were working on themselves and not others? These are questions I struggled with during my fieldwork and in writing this book. I liked the men whose lives are detailed in these pages, counting many of them as friends, and grappled with how to understand them and write about them. I did not seek to excuse their homophobia, misogyny, and racism but to understand it in context. This book sought to answer the questions of why and how ex-gay men sought to be heterosexual.

HRM's work did not take place in a cultural vacuum. The ministry drew its rhetoric and practices from the popular literature on self-help and twelve-step groups like Alcoholics Anonymous (AA). These included self-cultivation and self-care in pursuit of an ideal and grounding oneself in a community to help with that new subject formation. In my time working with HRM, I knew very few men who were successful in desiring only women over the long term. In this way, the ministry was comparable to other groups that focused extreme attention on the self, as was the failure to achieve the sought-after subjectivity. In the article "Secret of AA: After 75 Years, We Don't Know How It Works," Brendan Koerner struggles to understand AA's popularity and international growth, despite its failures for a majority of those who attempt it (Koerner 2010). Weight Watchers also provides a useful comparison to ex-gay programs, because it focuses attention on the individual's body, teaching participants how to chart and record the minutiae of what they eat, as well as having them publicly confess a variety of "falls." These and other weight-loss techniques are employed in a long-term process of personal care to transform into an ideal self, fashioning the person in accord with particular moral precepts and goals. In Weight Watchers, this goal and moral ideal is a thin, attractive, and healthy body. In her work on Weight Watchers, Cressida Heyes writes, "Weight Watchers' rhetoric cultivates both positions—that the care of the self implicit in successful dieting will improve one's self-knowledge and that knowing oneself is central to weight loss" (Heyes 2006: 140). The care of the self involved in becoming heterosexual is also a major way to fashion an informed and aware subject.

Alcoholics who drink, dieters who leave Weight Watchers, and men who have "sexual falls" return to these programs again and again over time. Although much of the work on the self that individuals undertake "fails" in the long term, it still has effects on people's lives. Bianca, who was involved in the ministry for many years and was married to an HRM leader, said that the success rate was "an incredibly, incredibly, low amount . . . I think we got a zero success rate. However, if we say how many people have we affected, how many people's lives have been changed even slightly, then I think it's huge." Ex-gay men's selves were significantly transformed by their time in the ministry, some according to ministry precepts and others ultimately in opposition to them. In the long term, most of the men in the ministry failed in their work to become heterosexual, but for a time they were ex-gay and lived lives where they were involved in challenging physical, emotional, and religious work. The ministry also had some unexpected consequences, a major one being that many ex-gay men who had never been in "the [gay] lifestyle" used the ministry as an alternative way of "coming out," even though this process usually took years. Most men in these pages have returned "to the [gay] lifestyle." Some ultimately married other men, and others remained single. A few continue to be married to women and have children. As detailed in the previous chapter, most saw their time in the ministry as productive and as part of forming new and improved, if not necessarily heterosexual, selves.

The purpose of my work in this book was not to prove that ex-gay men are failures or successes or to reinscribe ideas that sexual desires are innate and natural/biological. I was interested in a close reading of the processes of transformation, the work employed, and what these meant for a particular group of men in Cape Town in the first decades of the twenty-first century. This book studies the formation of subjectivities; it does not assess them and whether they "work." A wide range of polarized literature exists on ex-gay therapies, success, and the politics involved in changing sexuality. In this book, I focused on why South African Pentecostal men chose to work so hard on themselves, putting themselves under personal, community, and what they viewed as godly surveillance.

For ex-gay men in South Africa, gender and sexual selves were fluid, changeable aspects of the achievement of subjectivity. Like many other groups and individuals, these Pentecostal men in South Africa sought to change national norms of masculinity, seeing their work as redeeming manhood by changing the frequently violent and oversexualized masculinity that had become normative at the beginnings of democracy. The men in HRM understood themselves as actively involved in transforming their masculinities in a Christian context where God was said to be able to make anything possible. Changing sexual and gender subjectivities made sense within this framework.

I began this book with Adrian, an ex-gay coloured man, who over time and with HRM's guidance was able to alter his voice (making it lower and more masculine sounding), posture, and walking. He told me, "I think I have worked that [effeminacy] off. I don't even know how I used to walk because I've totally lost the ability to walk like that [pause] I think." Adrian believed that with physical and affective labor, what I call desire work, he would be able to transform himself into a heterosexual, masculine man. However, also contained in his quote is tentativeness and uncertainty, a pause, followed by "I think." Adrian, despite years of working the ex-gay process, was still in many ways unsure about its eventual outcome and the certainty of his arrival at his desired goal—a new, transformed, and what he considered to be a better self.

Adrian was a flexible self, intent on trying out a number of tools and embracing new ideologies to arrive at his ideal self. He was however also inflexible in his belief that his goal was "God-ordained" and the only solution to a life full of despair and social marginalization. HRM promised ex-gay men like Adrian a new self and a new heterosexual life. However, as the last chapter illustrates, success for men like Adrian was varied and complicated by the difficulties of achieving a new self because of the continuation of same-sex attraction and the seemingly unavoidable "sexual falls." Ultimately, Adrian, like many of the other men in HRM, remained a self in flux, one always in process and in a not very promising process, regardless of his hard work on the self. At the time of this writing, though, Adrian remains committed to being ex-gay and the promise of a new self. Personal failures and the failures of the men around him have not gotten in the way of his deeply ingrained desire for heterosexuality.

Preface

1 The name of the ministry, church, and people are pseudonyms.
2 I followed a number of ex-gay ministries when I was in graduate school, and few of them exist today. However, more continue to pop up.
3 HRM broke away from its affiliation with Christian Uplift in 2002 because the male founder had a very public "sexual fall" that hurt its credibility; it closed soon afterward.
4 In 2016 Exodus Global Alliance had two African ministries listed on their website, one in South Africa, Living Waters South Africa, and the other in Egypt, Life Ministry. In 2017, it had one ministry listed, Journey South Africa.

Introduction

1 *Moffie* has a variety of meanings. It translates from Afrikaans as sissy. It is also often used to say someone is gay/effeminate (Cage 2003: 82). The men in HRM understand it negatively and used it in a demeaning way. Some South Africans have reclaimed the term *moffie* as positive, similar to how many in the United States have reclaimed "queer." Adrian means *moffie* negatively here.
2 Ken Cage defines "camp" as "a form of humor popular among gay people, using satire and sometimes downright mean . . . [to] mimic the opposite sex; to be witty and clever" (Cage 2003: 61).
3 GEAR was a form of what is usually coded as neoliberalism. (See Ferguson 2009 for a discussion of the problematics of this term, especially in the African context.)
4 The 2011 census found that the population in Cape Town broke down racially as 43.2 percent coloured, 39.4 percent black, 16 percent white, and 1.4 percent Indian/Asian (Statistics South Africa 2012: 11).
5 Pentecostal forms of Christianity are similar to evangelical and charismatic forms of the faith in sub-Saharan Africa (Omenyo 2014; Asamoah-Gyadu 2007). Charismatics are often similar to Pentecostals in ecstatic religious expression but remain members of mainline churches. Evangelicals also share much in common with Pentecostals, for example, the importance of the born-again experience, but downplay or do not believe in the more miraculous pieces of Pentecostal identity like speaking in tongues or miraculous healing. That said, this self-definition can vary and depends on the person and his/her self-definition.
6 The 2011 South African census did not pose questions about religion.

7   Conversion is frequently more ambiguous for women than men, in that it can lead to both empowerment and disenfranchisement in the public and private realms (Soothill 2014; Parsitau 2011; Soothill 2007; Mate 2002).

8   This familial destruction was brought on by apartheid practices like migrant labor, which separated men, often for years, from their families.

9   The 1966 Forest Town Raid (outside of Johannesburg) was the largest and most public police presence in gay life in South Africa at the time (Cage 2003: 12).

10 Gayle was not the only "gay language" in South Africa. There is also *isingquomo*, township gay slang, which is heavily Zulu-based and thought to have originated in Durban (McLean and Ngcobo 1995).

11 Ronald Louw explains that "*isitabane* . . . is a derogatory word (except where it has been appropriated by those whom it describes)" (2001: 292).

12 For example, Anglican bishop Michael Lugar of the Diocese of Rejaf said, "In the Sudan we know nothing of homosexuality. We only know the Gospel and we proclaim it" (Hoad 2004: 60).

13 Bishop Benjamin Kwashi of Nigeria said that Africans were "oppressed with this Western imposition [homosexuality]" (Hoad 2004: 61).

14 The question asked was, "Do you think it is wrong for two adults of the same sex to have sexual relations?" Possible answers were "always wrong," "almost always wrong," "wrong only at times," and "not wrong at all." The percentages per year answering "always wrong" were 84 percent (2003), 83 percent (2004), 85 percent (2005), 83 percent (2006), and 82 percent (2007).

15 One leader was thought to make the small group seem too much like counseling. Ideally, the assistant learned how to facilitate a small group in order to be a leader the next time the class was offered. That person could train someone else so that over time more leaders with the appropriate skills were created for the ministry.

16 "Bible chicken" is my term for the biblical equivalent of drivers trying to force each other off the road and get the other person to give up and crash. For many Pentecostals, quoting relevant biblical passages is a verbal art of competition. The way it works is that one person will answer a question or start an argument referring to or quoting a Bible passage. For Bible chicken to begin, the other person must answer back in an identical fashion. This can go on until one person crashes, runs out of biblical references. For example, if someone says that God doesn't care whether people are gay, a ministry member may answer with, "Doesn't it say in Leviticus that a man shouldn't lie with another man?" Or "Look at Leviticus 18:22." The first person then has to come back with another passage, maybe something about the dietary laws in Leviticus that Christians no longer follow, stating that if we do not follow those taboos, why the ones on homosexuality? And so on.

1. Cultural Convergences

1   I am not interested in critiquing or commending the commission here. My focus is on how the commission popularized new ideas about trauma and healing (see Ross 2008 for a critique of the commission). Although TRC trauma discourses

were not universally embraced—for example, they caught on much more with urban than rural citizens—they were well known throughout the country.

2 Apartheid was supported by the Afrikaner Christian theologies of the Dutch Reformed Church and also resisted by antiapartheid Christian activists across race and ethnicity, who used their faith for social justice work (Anderson and Pillay 1997; Balia 1989; Moodie 1975).

3 HRM's staff were not legally "counselors." The ministry used the term "discipleship" on all of its official forms. They also made everyone affiliated with the ministry, including me, sign a liability form that acknowledged that they knew that participation in HRM "discipleship" was not professional therapy. However, they still referred to themselves as "Christian counselors."

4 People attending other twelve-step groups started sex addiction support groups simultaneously throughout the United States in the 1970s. The major groups dealing with compulsive sex are Sex and Love Addicts Anonymous, begun in 1976, Sex Addicts Anonymous (1977), and Sexaholics Anonymous (1979).

5 Personal correspondence with a South African sex addiction counselor, 2010.

6 The names of well-established American ministries, people, and programs remain.

7 Salt does not stand for anything. I am assuming it has to do with the idea of "salt of the earth." Salt is an American program, but I could not find any accompanying program on Desert Stream's website for Pepper. It may be a South African innovation. It also did not correspond to a group's name.

8 Cape Town had more Co-Dependents Anonymous (CODA) meetings than other parts of country. Of the meetings listed on CODA South Africa's website in 2008, there was one in the Eastern Cape in Port Elizabeth, one in Gauteng province in Johannesburg, and six in the Western Cape—all in Cape Town or the surrounding suburbs. The national CODA Steering Committee Meeting also met near Cape Town. This was still true in 2017.

9 Racially, Salt and SAA were also almost exclusively white. Petrus, an ex-gay Afrikaans leader in Salt and member of SAA, thought the membership in both groups was 2–5 percent black and between 10 and 20 percent coloured in 2008.

10 I am referring to the AIDS denialism that marked the Mbeki administration (see, for example, Fourie and Meyer 2010; Cullinan and Thom 2009).

11 See Waidzunas (2015) for a survey of ex-gay studies and Bailey et al. (2016) for a survey of studies on sexual orientation.

12 Reparative therapy has been made illegal in California for minors (Eckholm 2012a, c).

2. Building Godly Emotional Intimacy

1 I find using the term "cannibal" is problematic in the African context because of colonial ideas that Africans were "primitive" and in need of colonization. However, it was not interpreted as a problem by the ministry.

2 This concept comes from the work of Christian "expert" on masculinity, Leanne Payne, who claimed that she learned about cannibalism from a missionary (Payne 1996 [1981]: 42).

3 Wouter refused to apologize in 2007 when Jaco asked his brother why he had not protected him. Wouter dismissed the incident as "traumatic," going so far as to say it was necessary to "toughen you [Jaco] up."

4 Many ex-gay men said that being in the ministry improved their relationships with their earthly fathers and father figures.

5 Glen struggled with "compulsive masturbation," not same-sex attraction. People with same-sex attraction were usually assumed to have little control over their desires and behaviors. Ex-gay testimonies almost always mentioned pornography use and masturbation as major obstacles to overcome.

6 This is an example of the overlapping use of God and Jesus.

7 Falling in love with Jesus is a concept that has historical precedents in the context of Catholic ascetics and monastic life, but it is also expressed in contemporary evangelical and Pentecostal discourses in new and different ways. For centuries within monasticism, nuns have ceremonially married Jesus, worn veils, and/or covered their heads as proof of being a monogamous faithful wife. In the modern era, at the profession of vows ceremony, women also wear a veil and are given a gold ring that signifies this marriage.

3. Becoming Spiritual Warriors

1 Pentecostals diagnosed demonically possessed individuals through drastic changes in personality and behavior that could not be attributed to external stresses like job loss, a death in one's family, or separation/divorce. Most Pentecostals I knew were unlikely to claim that a person with a history of mental illness was possessed because they recognized that psychological conditions could alter behavior. For example, the Church of the Reborn's first course of action if a member was acting abnormally was to send him or her to the doctor for professional evaluation and/or arrange for counseling with church staff.

2 David was unique at the church and the ministry for his down-to-earth approach to dealing with the supernatural. David was known at the church for his straightforward manner and refusal to listen to any *kak*, an Afrikaans term that means "rubbish" or "shit." For example, a woman came in for counseling, claiming that God had given her the "gift" of prophecy. She wanted to start a ministry that would be financially supported by the church. Knowing the counselee's personal history and struggle with addiction, David firmly but kindly told her that the church was not interested. Furthermore, he said, it was the large amount of cough syrup she drank on a daily basis that was responsible for her hallucinations, which she was reading as visions from the Holy Spirit. He offered her the church's resources to help combat her substance abuse problem.

3 Bynum is most known for her best-selling and highly influential DVD *No More Sheets: The Truth about Sex.*

4 Bynum usually discusses heterosexual sex, except to name homosexuality as a "spirit of perversion."

5 I also heard Zimbabwe's rapid collapse blamed on Robert Mugabe's demonic possession. During a tea break at a HRM Strategic Planning Day in 2007, I overheard

ministry members discussing the rapidly deteriorating political and economic situation there. One man posited that the root of the troubles was Great Zimbabwe: that it was possessed by the spirit of greed, which was passed down through time to Mugabe.

4. Mastering Romance and Sexual Feelings

1 Bianca was a biological woman. The men in HRM were all married to biological women.
2 This practice is not unique to Pentecostalism. It used to be a common practice when the streets were dangerous because of horses and buggies (Post 2004).
3 The couple dated for almost a year before breaking up.

5. Leaving Healing Revelation Ministries

1 "Backpackers" is another term for hostels.
2 The first Gay Pride parade held in Cape Town was in 2001 (De Waal, Manion, and Cameron 2006). The first Gay Pride parade in South Africa was in 1990 in Johannesburg (Donham 1998: 418).
3 This was not the first time Brian and I had an argument or the first time I was angry about a ministry decision.
4 The paper was the size of a business card. The website name was centered in the middle of the card, with "Sunday After-Party" directly underneath. The "Q" in conQuers was larger than the other letters and was topped by a five-pointed crown. Before I saw the card it was described to me as "provocative and enticing," because of its loud pastel color and the focus on the "Q," which the creators said could stand for "queer" or "queenie."
5 The most notable of these calls occurred on a day that I was alone in the office for a short period of time. I answered the phone and listened to a hysterical woman who called to say that her fiancée's brother was almost suicidal after his father dragged him very publicly out of a popular gay bar during peak hours. The father's drastic response was a result of an anonymous phone call from a self-proclaimed "concerned friend." The woman I spoke to on the phone wanted someone from the ministry to come to the family's house and intervene before the brother hurt either himself or the person he thought had called his father. After letting her get the story off her chest, I explained that there was little the ministry could do for her soon to be brother-in-law, as the policy was only to help people who wanted it. This meant that no one could call and make an appointment for someone else and that the ministry did not get involved in interventions or other intimate family matters. I sent the woman on the phone to the ministry website and gave her the phone number for Cape Town's Suicide Help Line.
6 I refused to give out any cards. I went to the outreach and took photographs and notes. I thought the outreach should have been canceled. Theoretically, I would have had less of a problem with the ministry handing out their information and stating why they were there, though I do not think this would have turned out well.

There were Christian protesters on the Pride parade route and there was a great deal of yelling back and forth between marchers and the protesters that at points almost became violent.

7 I was told afterward by other leadership team members present that I had over-reacted and was chastised for being "too aggressive" and not having a "teachable spirit," a term used to insult someone for being stubborn and not listening to others.

8 At the time there were two women and four or five men on the Executive Team.

9 All the men in the ministry shared this idea.

10 Triangulation occurs when one person refuses to communicate with another. Instead, he or she draws a third person in to do the communication.

11 BDSM stands for bondage, dominance and submission, and masochism.

Afterword

1 Key stakeholders continue to pursue the passage of a bill to criminalize homo-sexuality.

2 One exception was the ministry's Pride Parade outreach.

Adams, Ty. 2006. *Single, Saved, and Having Sex*. West Bloomfield, MI: Walk Worthy.

Africa, Statistics South. 2004. *Census 2001: Primary Tables South Africa, Census '96 and 2001 Compared*. Pretoria: Statistics South Africa.

Africa, Statistics South. 2012. *Census 2011 Municipal Report: Western Cape*. Pretoria: Statistics South Africa.

Agana, Wilfred Asampambila. 2016. *"Succeed Here and in Eternity": The Prosperity Gospel in Ghana*. Bern: Peter Lang.

Aldrich, Robert F. 2003. *Colonialism and Homosexuality*. London: Routledge.

Amnesty International. 2013. *Making Love a Crime: Criminalization of Same-Sex Conduct in Sub-Saharan Africa*. London: Amnesty International. www.amnestyusa.org /wpcontent/uploads/2017/04/making_love_a_crime__africa_lgbti_report_emb_6 .24.13_0.pdf. Accessed November 1, 2017.

Amplified Bible. 1987. Grand Rapids, MI: Zondervan.

Anderson, Allan. 2005. "New African Initiated Pentecostalism and Charismatics in South Africa." *Journal of Religion in Africa* 35 (1): 66–92.

Anderson, Allan. 2014. "Evil, Witchcraft, and Deliverance in the Pentecostal Worldview." In *Pentecostal Theology in Africa*, edited by Clifton R. Clarke. Eugene, OR: Pickwick.

Anderson, Allan H., and Gerald J. Pillay. 1997. "The Segregated Spirit: The Pentecostals." In *Christianity in South Africa: A Political, Social, and Cultural History*, edited by Richard Elphick and T. R. H. Davenport, 227–241. Berkeley: University of California Press.

Ankerberg, John, and John Weldon. 1994. *The Facts on Homosexuality*. Eugene: Harvest House.

Anonymous. n.d.-a. "A Man to Hug Me." HRM, Cape Town.

Anonymous. n.d.-b. "The Pursuit of Intimacy." HRM, Cape Town.

Asamoah-Gyadu, J. Kwabena. 2007. "Pulling Down Strongholds: Evangelism, Principalities and Powers and the African Pentecostal Imagination." *International Journal of Mission* 96 (382–383): 306–371.

Ashforth, Adam. 2005. *Witchcraft, Violence, and Democracy in South Africa*. Chicago: University of Chicago Press.

Bailey, J. Michael, Paul L. Vasey, Lisa M. Diamond, S. Marc Breedlove, Eric Vilain, and Marc Epprecht. 2016. "Sexual Orientation, Controversy, and Science." *Psychological Science in the Public Interest* 17 (2): 45–101.

Balia, Daryl. 1989. *Christian Resistance to Apartheid: Ecumenism in South Africa 1960–1987*. Braamfontein, South Africa: Skotaville.

Ballard, Richard. 2004. "Assimilation, Emigration, Semigration, and Intergration: 'White' Peoples' Strategies for Finding a Comfort Zone in Post-Apartheid South Africa." In *Under Construction: "Race" and Identity in South Africa Today*, edited by Natasha Distiller and Melissa E. Steyn, 51–66. Johannesburg: Heinemann.

Barker, Gary, and Dean Peacock. 2009. "Making Gender Truly Relational: Engaging Men in Transforming Gender Inequalities, Reducing Violence and Preventing HIV/AIDS." In *Working with Men and Boys: Emerging Strategies from across Africa to Address Gender-Based Violence and HIV/AIDS*, edited by Orly Stern, Dean Peacock, and Helen Alexander, 8–22. Cape Town: Sonke Gender Justice Network.

Baxter, Mary K., and T. L. Lowery. 1998. *A Divine Revelation of Heaven*. New Kensington, PA: Whitaker House.

BBC. 2007. "Tutu Chides Church for Gay Stance." *BBC News*. http://news.bbc.co.uk/2/hi/africa/7100295.stm. Accessed March 26, 2011.

Berger, Jonathan. 2008. "Getting to the Constitutional Court on Time: A Litigation History of Same-Sex Marriage." In *To Have and to Hold: The Making of Same-Sex Marriage in South Africa*, edited by Melanie Judge, Anthony Manion, and Shaun De Waal, 17–28. Sunnyside, South Africa: Fanele.

Berkowitz, Paul. 2013. "South Africa's Unemployment Rate Rises to Near-Record Levels." *Daily Maverick*. www.dailymaverick.co.za/article/2013-08-02-sas-unemployment-rates-rise-to-near-record-levels/#.Wf3LsIYkrBI. Accessed December 27, 2013.

Berlant, Lauren Gail. 2011. *Cruel Optimism*. Durham, NC: Duke University Press.

Besen, Wayne R. 2003. *Anything but Straight: Unmasking the Scandals and Lies behind the Ex-Gay Myth*. New York: Harrington Park.

Besteman, Catherine. 2008. *Transforming Cape Town*. Berkeley: University of California Press.

Bieber, Irving, and Toby Bieber. 1979. "Male Homosexuality." *Canadian Journal of Psychiatry* 24 (5): 409–421.

Black, Dorothy. 2013. *The Student Village Sex Survey 2013*. Cape Town: Student Village.

Blackwood, Evelyn. 1999. "Tombois in West Sumatra: Constructing Masculinity and Erotic Desire." In *Female Desires: Same-Sex Relations and Transgender Practices across Cultures*, edited by Evelyn Blackwood, 181–205. New York: Columbia University Press.

Blank, Hanne. 2012. *Straight: The Surprisingly Short History of Heterosexuality*. Boston: Beacon.

Blee, Kathleen M. 2002. *Inside Organized Racism: Women in the Hate Movement*. Berkeley: University of California Press.

Bloomberg, Charles, and Saul Dubow. 1989. *Christian-nationalism and the Rise of the Afrikaner Broederbond in South Africa, 1918–48*. Bloomington: Indiana University Press.

Borer, Tristan Anne. 1998. *Challenging the State: Churches as Political Actors in South Africa, 1980–1994*. Notre Dame, IN: University of Notre Dame Press.

Bornstein, Erica. 2005. *The Spirit of Development: Protestant NGOs, Morality, and Economics in Zimbabwe*. Stanford, CA: Stanford University Press.

Boyd, Lydia. 2015. *Preaching Prevention: Born-Again Christianity and the Moral Politics of AIDS in Uganda*. Athens: Ohio University Press.

Brakke, David. 2006. *Demons and the Making of the Monk: Spiritual Combat in Early Christianity*. Cambridge, MA: Harvard University Press.

Brandes, Stanley H. 2002. *Staying Sober in Mexico City*. Austin: University of Texas Press.

Brestin, Dee, and Kathy Troccoli. 2001. *Falling in Love with Jesus: Abandoning Yourself to the Greatest Romance of Your Life*. Nashville: Thomas Nielson.

Brusco, Elizabeth E. 1995. *The Reformation of Machismo: Evangelical Conversion and Gender in Colombia*. Austin: University of Texas Press.

Burchardt, Marian. 2009. "Subjects of Counselling: Religion, HIV/AIDS and the Management of Everyday Life in South Africa." In *AIDS and Religious Practice in Africa*, edited by Felicitas Becker and P. Wenzel Geissler, 333–358. Leiden: Brill.

Burchardt, Marian. 2010. "Ironies of Subordination: Ambivalences of Gender in Religious AIDS Interventions in South Africa." *Oxford Development Studies* 38 (1): 63–82.

Burchardt, Marian. 2013. "'Transparent Sexualities': Sexual Openness, HIV Disclosure and the Governmentality of Sexuality in South Africa." *Culture, Health and Sexuality* 15 (sup4): S495–S508.

Burchardt, Marian. 2015. *Faith in the Time of AIDS: Religion, Biopolitics, and Modernity in South Africa*. New York: Palgrave Macmillan.

Burke, Timothy. 1996. *Lifebuoy Men, Lux Women: Commodification, Consumption, and Cleanliness in Modern Zimbabwe*. Durham, NC: Duke University Press.

Bynum, Juanita. 2000. *No More Sheets: The Truth about Sex*. Lanham, MD: Pneuma Life.

Cage, Ken. 2003. *Gayle: The Language of Kinks and Queens—A History and Dictionary of Gay Language in Southern Africa*. Houghton, South Africa: Jacana Media.

Campbell, John. 2013. "Declining Poverty Rates in South Africa." *Council on Foreign Relations*. www.cfr.org/blog/declining-poverty-rates-south-africa. Accessed December 12, 2013.

Campbell, Susan. 2009. *Dating Jesus: A Story of Fundamentalism, Feminism, and the American Girl*. Boston: Beacon.

Carey, Benedict. 2012. "Psychiatry Giant Sorry for Backing Gay 'Cure.'" *New York Times*, www.nytimes.com/2012/05/19/health/dr-robert-l-spitzer-noted-psychiatrist-apologizes-for-study-on-gay-cure.html. Accessed May 18, 2012.

Carnes, Patrick. 2001. *Out of the Shadows: Understanding Sexual Addiction*. Center City, MN: Hazeldon.

Carnes, Patrick, with Joseph Moriarity. 1997. *Sexual Anorexia: Overcoming Sexual Self-Hatred*. Center City, MN: Hazelden.

Carr, E. Summerson. 2011. *Scripting Addiction: The Politics of Therapeutic Talk and American Sobriety*. Princeton, NJ: Princeton University Press.

Carrillo, Héctor. 2002. *The Night Is Young: Sexuality in Mexico in the Time of AIDS*. Chicago: University of Chicago Press.

Chapman, Gary D. 2004. *The Five Love Languages: How to Express Heartfelt Commitment to Your Mate*. Chicago: Northfield.

Cheney, Kristen. 2012. "Locating Neocolonialism, 'Tradition,' and Human Rights in Uganda's 'Gay Death Penalty.'" *African Studies Review* 55 (2): 77–95.

Chetty, Dhianaraj. 1995. "A Drag at Madame Costello's: Cape Moffie Life and the Popular Press in the 1950s and 1960s." In *Defiant Desires: Gay and Lesbian Lives in South Africa*, edited by Mark Gevisser and Edwin Cameron, 115–127. New York: Routledge.

Chitando, Ezra, and Adriaan van Klinken, eds. 2016a. *Christianity and Controversies over Homosexuality in Contemporary Africa*. London: Routledge.

Chitando, Ezra, and Adriaan van Klinken. 2016b. "Introduction: Christianity and the Politics of Homosexuality in Africa." In *Christianity and Controversies over Homosexuality in Contemporary Africa*, edited by Ezra Chitando and Adriaan van Klinken, 1–17. London: Routledge.

Cock, Jacklyn. 2005. "Engendering Gay and Lesbian Rights: The Equality Clause in the South African Constitution." In *Sex and Politics in South Africa*, edited by Neville Hoad, Karen Martin, and Graeme Reid, 188–209. Cape Town: Double Storey Books.

Cole, Jennifer. 2010. *Sex and Salvation: Imagining the Future in Madagascar*. Chicago: University of Chicago Press.

Coleman, Simon. 2006. "Materializing the Self: Words and Gifts in the Construction of Charismatic Protestant Identity." In *The Anthropology of Christianity*, edited by Fenella Cannell, 163–184. Durham, NC: Duke University Press.

Colvin, Christopher. 2000. "The Angel of Memory: 'Working Through' the History of the New South Africa." In *Between the Psyche and the Polis: Refiguring History in Literature and Theory*, edited by Anne Whitehead and Michael Rossington, 157–173. Burlington, VT: Ashgate.

Colvin, Christopher. 2008. "Trauma." In *New South African Keywords*, edited by Nick Shepherd and Steven Robins, 223–234. Johannesburg: Jacana.

Comaroff, Jean, and John Comaroff. 1996. *Of Revelation and Revolution: The Dialectics of Modernity on a South African Frontier*. Vol. 2. Chicago: University of Chicago Press.

Comaroff, Jean, and John Comaroff. 2000. "Privatizing the Millenium: New Protestant Ethics and the Spirits of Capitalism in Africa, and Elsewhere." *Afrika Spectrum* 35 (3): 293–312.

Constitution of the Republic of South Africa. 1996.

Covington, Stephanie, and Liana Beckett. 1988. *Leaving the Enchanted Forest: The Path from Relationship Addiction to Intimacy*. San Francisco: Harper & Row.

Csordas, Thomas J. 1997. *The Sacred Self: A Cultural Phenomenology of Charismatic Healing*. Berkeley: University of California Press.

Csordas, Thomas J. 2002. *Body/Meaning/Healing*. Contemporary Anthropology of Religion. New York: Palgrave Macmillan.

Cullinan, Kerry, and Anso Thom, eds. 2009. *The Virus, Vitamins, and Vegetables: The South African HIV/AIDS Mystery*. Sunnyside, South Africa: Jacana Media.

Currier, Ashley. 2012. *Out in Africa: LGBT Organizing in Namibia and South Africa*. Minneapolis: University of Minnesota Press.

Curtis, Brent, and John Eldredge. 2001. *The Sacred Romance: Drawing Closer to the Heart of God*. Nashville: T. Nelson.

Dallas, Joe, and Nancy Heche. 2009. *The Complete Christian Guide to Understanding Homosexuality*. Eugene, OR: Harvest House.

Daswani, Girish. 2011. "(In-)Dividual Pentecostals in Ghana." *Journal of Religion in Africa* 41: 256–279.

Daswani, Girish. 2015. *Looking Back, Moving Forward: Transformation and Ethical Practice in the Ghanaian Church of Pentecost*. Toronto: University of Toronto Press.

Davies, Bob. 1998. *History of Exodus International: An Overview of the Worldwide Growth of the Ex-Gay Movement*. Seattle: Exodus International–North America.

Davies, Bob, and Lori Rentzel. 1993. *Holding On to Sexual Purity: Finding Freedom from Masturbation and Impure Sexual Thoughts*. Seattle: Exodus International–North America.

DeBarros, Luiz. 2015. "NG Kerk Decision: Gay People Could Still Face Rejection." *Mamba Online*. www.mambaonline.com/2015/10/15/ng-kerk-decision-gay-people-still-face-rejection/. Accessed November 4, 2017.

Denzin, Norman K., and John M. Johnson. 1993. *The Alcoholic Society: Addiction and Recovery of the Self*. New Brunswick, NJ: Transaction.

DeRogatis, Amy. 2005. "What Would Jesus Do? Sexuality and Salvation in Protestant Evangelical Sex Manuals, 1950s to the Present." *American Society of Church History* 74 (1): 97–137.

DeRogatis, Amy. 2015. *Saving Sex: Sexuality and Salvation in American Evangelicalism*. New York: Oxford University Press.

De Waal, Shaun, Anthony Manion, and Edwin Cameron. 2006. *Pride: Protest and Celebration*. Johannesburg, South Africa: Fanele.

de Witte, Marleen. 2011. "Touched by the Spirit: Converting the Senses in a Ghanaian Charismatic Church." *Ethnos* 76 (4): 489–509.

Domonoske, Camila. 2016. "Anglican Leaders Censure Episcopal Church for Stance on Homosexuality." NPR, *The Two-Way*. www.npr.org/sections/thetwo-way/2016/01/14/463085910/anglican-leaders-censure-episcopal-church-for-stance-on-homosexuality. Accessed November 4, 2017.

Donham, Donald L. 2002. "Freeing South Africa: The 'Modernization' of Male-Male Sexuality in Soweto." In *The Anthropology of Globalization: A Reader*, edited by Jonathan Xavier Inda and Renato Rosaldo, 410–427. Malden, MA: Blackwell.

Drescher, Jack, and Kenneth J. Zucker, eds. 2006. *Ex-gay Research: Analyzing the Spitzer Study and Its Relation to Science, Religion, Politics, and Culture*. New York: Harrington Park.

Dugard, Frankie. 2008. "Power to the People? A Rights-Based Analysis of South Africa's Electricity Services." In *Electric Capitalism: Recolonising Africa on the Power Grid*, edited by David A. McDonald, 264–287. Cape Town: HSRC Press.

Du Pisani, Kobus. 2001. "Puritanism Transformed: Afrikaner Masculinities in the Apartheid and Post-Apartheid Period." In *Changing Men in Southern Africa*, edited by Robert Morrell, 157–175. Scottsville, South Africa: University of Natal.

Du Pisani, Kobus. 2012. "Shifting Sexual Morality? Changing Views on Homosexuality in Afrikaner Society during the 1960s." *Historia* 57 (2): 182–221.

Dworkin, Shari L., Christopher Colvin, Abbey Hatcher, and Dean Peacock. 2012. "Men's Perceptions of Women's Rights and Changing Gender Relations in South

Africa: Lessons for Working with Men and Boys in HIV and Antiviolence Programs." *Gender and Society* 26 (1): 97–120.

Eaton, Liberty, Alan J. Flisher, and Leif E. Aaro. 2002. "Unsafe Sexual Behavior in South African Youth." *Social Science and Medicine* 56: 149–165.

Eckholm, Erik. 2012a. "'Ex-Gay' Men Fight Back against View That Homosexuality Can't Be Changed." *New York Times*. www.nytimes.com/2012/11/01/us/ex-gay-men-fight-view-that-homosexuality-cant-be-changed.html. Accessed November 1, 2012.

Eckholm, Erik. 2012b. "Rift Forms in Movement as Belief in Gay 'Cure' Is Renounced." *New York Times*. www.nytimes.com/2012/07/07/us/a-leaders-renunciation-of-ex-gay-tenets-causes-a-schism.html. Accessed November 1, 2012.

Eckholm, Erik. 2012c. "California Is First State to Ban Gay 'Cure' for Minors." *New York Times*. www.nytimes.com/2012/10/01/us/california-bans-therapies-to-cure-gay-minors.html. Accessed November 1, 2012.

Edelen, Dan. 2007. "Nowhere Men." *Cerulean Sanctum*. ceruleansanctum.com. Accessed December 5, 2010.

Eldredge, John. 2001. *Wild at Heart: Discovering the Secret of a Man's Soul*. Nashville: T. Nelson.

Eldredge, John, and Stasi Eldredge. 2005a. *Captivating: A Guided Journal to Aid in Unveiling the Mystery of a Woman's Soul*. Nashville: Nelson Impact.

Eldredge, John, and Stasi Eldredge. 2005b. *Captivating: Unveiling the Mystery of a Woman's Soul*. Nashville: Nelson Books.

Elisha, Omri. 2013. "The Time and Place for Prayer: Evangelical Urbanism and City-wide Prayer Movements." *Religion* 43 (3): 312–330.

Engelke, Matthew. 2004. "Discontinuity and the Discourse of Conversion." *Journal of Religion in Africa* 34 (1–2): 82–109.

Engelke, Matthew. 2007. *A Problem of Presence: Beyond Scripture in an African Church*. Berkeley: University of California Press.

Engelke, Matthew. 2010. "Past Pentecostalism: Notes on Rupture, Realignment, and Everyday Life in Pentecostal and African Independent Churches." *Journal of the International African Institute* 80 (2): 177–199.

Ensley, Mike. 2005. "True Love Changes You: How Jesus Christ Loved Me Out of Homosexuality." *Exodus Impact* 3 (9).

Epprecht, Marc. 1998. "The 'Unsaying' of Indigenous Homosexualities in Zimbabwe: Mapping a Blindspot in an African Masculinity." *Journal of Southern African Studies* 24 (4): 631–651.

Epprecht, Marc. 2004. *Hungochani: The History of a Dissident Sexuality in Southern Africa*. Montreal: McGill-Queen's University Press.

Epprecht, Marc. 2013. *Sexuality and Social Justice in Africa: Rethinking Homophobia and Forging Resistance*. London: Zed Books.

Erasmus, Zimitri. 2001. "Introduction: Re-imagining Coloured Identities in Post-Apartheid South Africa." In *Coloured by History, Shaped by Place: New Perspectives on Coloured Identities in Cape Town*, edited by Zimitri Erasmus, 14–28. Cape Town: Kwela.

Erzen, Tanya. 2006. *Straight to Jesus: Sexual and Christian Coversion in the Ex-Gay Movement*. Berkeley: University of California Press.

Fausto-Sterling, Ann. 1997. "How to Build a Man." In *Science and Homosexualities*, edited by Vernon A. Rosario, 219–225. New York: Routledge.

Ferguson, James. 2009. "The Uses of Neoliberalism " *Antipode* 41 (S1): 166–184.

Foucault, Michel. 1988. "Technologies of the Self." In *Technologies of the Self: A Seminar with Michel Foucault*, edited by Luther H. Martin, Huck Gutman, and Patrick H. Hutton, 16–49. London: Tavistock.

Foucault, Michel. 1990. *The History of Sexuality, Volume 1: An Introduction*. New York: Vintage Books.

Fourie, Pieter, and Melissa Meyer. 2010. *The Politics of AIDS Denialism: South Africa's Failure to Respond*. Burlington, VT: Ashgate.

Frahm-Arp, Maria. 2010. *Professional Women in South African Pentecostal Charismatic Churches*. Leiden: Brill.

Frahm-Arp, Maria. 2012. "Singleness, Sexuality, and the Dream of Marriage." *Journal of Religion in Africa* 42: 369–383.

Freeman, Carla. 2014. *Entrepreneurial Selves: Neoliberal Respectability and the Making of a Caribbean Middle Class*. Durham, NC: Duke University Press.

Freeman, Dena. 2012. "The Pentecostal Ethic and the Spirit of Development." In *Pentecostalism and Development: Churches, NGOs and Social Change in Africa*, edited by Dena Freeman, 1–40. New York: Palgrave Macmillan.

Garbin, David. 2012. "Marching for God in the Global City: Public Space, Religion, and Diasporic Identities in a Transnational African Church." *Culture and Religion: An Interdisciplinary Journal* 13 (4): 425–447.

Garner, Robert. 2000. "Safe Sects? Dynamic Religion and AIDS in South Africa." *Journal of Modern African Studies* 38 (1): 41–69.

Gerber, Lynne. 2012. *Seeking the Straight and Narrow: Weight Loss and Sexual Reorientation in Evangelical America*. Chicago: University of Chicago Press.

Gershon, Ilana. 2011. "Un-Friend My Heart: Facebook, Promiscuity, and Heartbreak in a Neoliberal Age." *Anthropological Quarterly* 84 (4): 865–894.

Gevisser, Mark. 1995. "A Different Fight for Freedom: A History of South African Lesbian and Gay Organisations from the 1950s to the 1990s." In *Defiant Desire: Gay and Lesbian Lives in South Africa*, edited by Mark Gevisser and Edwin Cameron, 14–86. New York: Routledge.

Giddens, Anthony. 1991. *Modernity and Self-Identity: Self and Society in the Late Modern Age*. Stanford, CA: Stanford University Press.

Gifford, Paul. 2001. "The Complex Provenance of Some Elements of African Pentecostal Theology." In *Between Babel and Pentecost: Transnational Pentecostalism in Africa and Latin America*, edited by André Corten and Ruth Marshall-Fratani, 62–79. Bloomington: Indiana University Press.

Gifford, Paul. 2014. *Christianity, Development, and Modernity in Africa*. London: C. Hurst & Co.

Ginsburg, Faye D. 1989. *Contested Lives: The Abortion Debate in an American Community*. Berkeley: University of California Press.

Gontek, Ines. 2009. "Sexual Violence against Lesbian Women in South Africa." *Outliers* 2: 36–53.

Gray, Mary L. 2009. *Out in the Country: Youth, Media, and Queer Visibility in Rural America*. New York: New York University Press.

Griffith, R. Marie. 1997. *God's Daughters: Evangelical Women and the Power of Submission*. Berkeley: University of California Press.

Griffith, R. Marie. 2004. *Born Again Bodies: Flesh and Spirit in American Christianity*. Berkeley: University of California Press.

Gunda, Masiiwa Ragies. 2010. *The Bible and Homosexuality in Zimbabwe: A Sociohistorical Analysis of the Political, Cultural and Christian Arguments in the Homosexual Public Debate with Special Reference to the Use of the Bible*. Bamberg: University of Bamberg Press.

Harding, Susan Friend. 2000. *The Book of Jerry Falwell: Fundamentalist Language and Politics*. Princeton, NJ: Princeton University Press.

Hausman, Ken. 2001. "Furor Erupts over Study on Sexual Orientation." *American Psychiatric Association* 36 (13): 20.

Haustein, Jorg. 2011. "Embodying the Spirit(s): Pentecostal Demonology and Deliverance Discourse in Ethiopia." *Ethnos* 76 (4): 534–552.

Haynes, Naomi. 2012. "Pentecostalism and the Morality of Money: Prosperity, Inequality, and Religious Sociality on the Zambian Copperbelt." *Journal of the Royal Anthropological Institute* 18: 123–139.

Haynes, Naomi. 2017. "Learning to Pray the Pentecostal Way: Language and Personhood on the Zambian Copperbelt." *Religion* 47 (1): 35–50.

Hefner, Robert W. 2013. "Introduction: The Unexpected Modern—Gender, Piety, and Politics in the Global Pentecostal Surge." In *Global Pentecostalism in the 21st Century*, edited by Robert W. Hefner. Bloomington: Indiana University Press.

Henderson, Elizabeth Connell. 2000. *Understanding Addiction*. Jackson: University Press of Mississippi.

Herwitz, Daniel. 2003. *Race and Reconciliation: Essays from the New South Africa*. Minneapolis: University of Minnesota Press.

Heuser, Andreas, ed. 2015. *Pastures of Plenty: Tracing Religio-Scapes of Prosperity Gospel in Africa and Beyond*. Frankfurt: Peter Lang.

Heyes, Cressida J. 2006. "Foucault Goes to Weight Watchers." *Hypatia* 21 (2): 126–149.

Hirsch, Jennifer S., and Holly Wardlow. 2006. "Introduction." In *Modern Loves: The Anthropology of Romantic Courtship and Companionate Marriage*, edited by Jennifer S. Hirsch and Holly Wardlow, 1–31. Ann Arbor: University of Michigan Press.

Hirschkind, Charles. 2001. "The Ethics of Listening: Cassette-Sermon Audition in Contemporary Egypt." *American Ethnologist* 28 (3): 623–649.

Hlaka, Kay. 2007. "Wanted: Good Black Men." *Drum*, October 4, 2007.

Hoad, Neville. 2004. "Neoliberalism, Homosexuality, Africa, and the Anglican Church: The World Conference of Anglican Bishops at Lambeth, July 18–August 9, 1998." In *Producing African Futures: Ritual and Reproduction in a Neoliberal Age*, edited by Brad Weiss, 54–78. Leiden: Brill.

Hoad, Neville. 2007. *African Intimacies: Race, Homosexuality, and Globalization*. Minneapolis: University of Minnesota Press.

Hoad, Neville Wallace, Karen Martin, and Graeme Reid, eds. 2005. *Sex and Politics in South Africa*. Cape Town: Double Storey.

Hodzic, Saida. 2017. *The Twilight of Cutting: African Activism and Life after NGOs*. Oakland: University of California Press.

Holland, Dorothy, William Lachicotte, Deborah Skinner, and Carole Cain. 1998. *Identity and Agency in Cultural Worlds*. Cambridge, MA: Harvard University Press.

Holvast, René. 2009. *Spiritual Mapping in the United States and Argentina, 1989–2005: A Geography of Fear*. Leiden: Brill.

HRW. 2011. "'We'll Show You You're a Woman': Violence and Discrimination against Black Lesbians and Transgender Men in South Africa." Human Rights Watch. www .hrw.org/sites/default/files/reports/southafrica1211.pdf. Accessed November 4, 2017.

Hunter, Mark. 2010. *Love in the Time of AIDS: Inequality, Gender, and Rights in South Africa*. Bloomington: Indiana University Press.

Illouz, Eva. 2003. *Oprah Winfrey and the Glamour of Misery: An Essay on Popular Culture*. New York: Columbia University Press.

Irvine, Leslie. 1999. *Codependent Forevermore: The Invention of Self in a Twelve Step Group*. Chicago: University of Chicago Press.

Jewkes, Rachel, Jonathan Levin, Nolwazi Mbananga, and Debbie Bradshaw. 2002. "Rape of Girls in South Africa." *Lancet* 359: 319–320.

Jewkes, Rachel, Yandisa Sikweyiya, and Kristin Dunkle. 2009. "Understanding Men's Health and the Use of Violence: Interface of Rape and HIV." Pretoria: Medical Research Council. www.mrc.ac.za/gender/interfaceofrape&hivsarpt.pdf. Accessed November 4, 2017.

Johnson, David, and Jeff VanVonderen. 1991. *The Subtle Power of Spiritual Abuse: Recognizing and Escaping Spiritual Manipulation and False Spiritual Authority within the Church*. Grand Rapids, MI: Bethany House.

Johnston, Sandy. 2008. *Under the Radar: Pentecostalism in South Africa and Its Potential Social and Economic Role*. Johannesburg: Centre for Development and Enterprise.

Jones, Rochelle. 2013. "The Transnational Ex-Gay Movement." *AWID*. www.awid.org /news-and-analysis/transnational-ex-gay-movement. Accessed September 10, 2014.

Jones, Stanton L., and Mark A. Yarhouse. 2007. *Ex-Gays? A Longitudinal Study of Religiously Mediated Change in Sexual Orientation*. Downers Grove, IL: IVP Academic.

Jones, Tiffany F. 2008. "Averting White Male Ab(Normality): Psychiatric Representations and Treatment of 'Homosexuality' in 1960s South Africa." *Journal of Southern African Studies* 34 (3): 397–410.

Kanaan Ministries. n.d. *Breaking Generational Curses over Our Cities and Their People*. Cape Town: Kanaan Ministries.

Kanaan Ministries. n.d. *Spiritual Mapping*. Cape Town: Kanaan Ministries.

Kaoma, Kapya. 2009. *Globalizing the Culture Wars: U.S. Conservatives, African Cultures, and Homophobia*. Somerville, MA: Political Research Associates.

Kaoma, Kapya. 2013. "The Marriage of Convenience: The U.S. Christian Right, African Christianity, and Postcolonial Politics of Sexual Identity." In *Global Homophobias: States, Movements, and the Politics of Oppression*, edited by Meredith Weiss and Michael J. Bosia, 75–102. Urbana: University of Illinois Press.

Kaoma, Kapya. 2014. "The Paradox and Tension of Moral Claims: Evangelical Christianity, the Politicization and Globalization of Sexual Politics in Sub-Saharan Africa." *Critical Research in Religion* 2 (3): 227–245.

Katz, Jonathan. 2007. *The Invention of Heterosexuality*. Chicago: University of Chicago Press.

Keane, Helen. 2002. *What's Wrong with Addiction?* New York: New York University Press.

Keane, Webb. 2007. *Christian Moderns: Freedom and Fetish in the Mission Encounter*. Berkeley: University of California Press.

Klausen, Susanne M. 2015. *Abortion under Apartheid: Nationalism, Sexuality, and Women's Reproductive Rights in South Africa*. Oxford: Oxford University Press.

Koerner, Brendan. 2010. "Secret of A A: After 75 Years, We Still Don't Know How it Works." *Wired*. www.wired.com/2010/06/ff_alcoholics_anonymous/. Accessed November 1, 2017.

Kurtz, Ernest. 1979. *Not-God: A History of Alcoholics Anonymous*. Center City, MN: Hazeldon.

Laing, Aislinn. 2011. "Mugabe Calls David Cameron 'Satanic' for Backing Gay Rights." *Telegraph*. www.telegraph.co.uk/news/politics/david-cameron/8912132/Mugabe -calls-David-Cameron-satanic-for-backing-gay-rights.html. Accessed November 4, 2017.

Lampman, Jane. 1999. "Targeting Cities with 'Spiritual Mapping' Prayer." *Christian Science Monitor*. www.csmonitor.com/1999/0923/p15s1.html. Accessed November 4, 2017.

Leap, William. 2005. "Finding the Centre: Claiming Gay Space in Cape Town." In *Performing Queer: Shaping Sexualities 1994–2004*, edited by Mikki Van Zyl and Melissa E. Steyn, 236–264. Roggebaai, South Africa: Kwela Books.

Lester, Rebecca J. 2005. *Jesus in Our Wombs: Embodying Modernity in a Mexican Convent*. Berkeley: University of California Press.

Lindhardt, Martin. 2010. "Mind, Self, and the Devil: Satanic Presence in Internal Conversations among Chilean Pentecostals." *Nordic Journal of Religion and Society* 23 (2): 177–195.

Lindhardt, Martin. 2015. "Men of God: Neo-Pentecostalism and Masculinities in Urban Tanzania." *Religion*: 1–21.

Loos, Jackie. 2004. *Echoes of Slavery: Voices from South Africa's Past*. Claremont, South Africa: David Philip.

Lorway, Robert. 2015. *Namibia's Rainbow Project: Gay Rights in an African Nation*. Bloomington: Indiana University Press.

Louw, Ronald. 2001. "Mkhumbane and New Traditions of (Un)African Same-Sex Weddings." In *Changing Men in Southern Africa*, edited by Robert Morrell, 287–296. Scottsville, South Africa: University of Natal Press.

Lovekin, Adams, and Newtown Maloney. 1977. "Religion Glossolalia: A Longitudinal Study of Personality Changes." *Journal for the Scientific Study of Religion* 16 (4): 383–393.

Luhrmann, Tanya. 2012. *When God Talks Back: Understanding the American Evangelical Relationship with God*. New York: Vintage Books.

Luhrmann, Tanya, Howard Nusbaum, and Ronald Thisted. 2010. "The Absorption Hypothesis: Learning to Hear God in Evangelical Christianity." *American Anthropologist* 112 (1): 66–78.

Lyonga, Frida. 2016. "The Homophobic Trinity: Pentecostal End-Time, Prosperity and Healing Gospels as Contributors to Homophobia in Cameroon." In *Christianity and Controversies over Homosexuality in Contemporary Africa*, edited by Ezra Chitando and Adriaan van Klinken, 51–64. London: Routledge.

Maguire, Mark, and Fiona Murphy. 2016. "Ontological (in)Security and African Pentecostalism in Ireland." *Ethnos* 81 (5): 842–864.

Mahmood, Saba. 2005. *Politics of Piety: The Islamic Revival and the Feminist Subject*. Princeton, NJ: Princeton University Press.

Marshall, Ruth. 2009. *Political Spiritualities: The Pentecostal Revolution in Nigeria*. Chicago: University of Chicago Press.

Martin, Emily. 1991. "The Egg and the Sperm: How Science Has Constructed a Romance Based in Sterotypical Male-Female Roles." *Signs* 16 (3): 485–501.

Mate, Rekopantswe. 2002. "Wombs as God's Laboratories: Pentecostal Discourses of Femininity in Zimbabwe." *Africa* 72 (4): 549–568.

Matza, Tomas. 2009. "Moscow's Echo: Technologies of the Self, Publics, and Politics on the Russian Talk Show." *Cultural Anthropology* 24 (3): 489–522.

Maxwell, David. 2005. "The Durawall of Faith: Pentecostal Spirituality in Neo-Liberal Zimbabwe." *Journal of Religion in Africa* 35 (1): 4–32.

Maxwell, David. 2006. *African Gifts of the Spirit: Pentecostalism and the Rise of a Zimbabwean Transnational Religious Movement*. Athens: Ohio University Press.

McAlister, Elizabeth. 2012. "From Slave Revolt to Blood Pact with Satan: The Evangelical Rewriting of Haitian History." *Studies in Religion* 41 (2): 187–215.

McAlister, Elizabeth. 2014. "Possessing the Land for Jesus." In *Spirited Things: The Work of "Possession" in Afro-Atlantic Religions*, edited by Paul C. Johnson, 177–205. Chicago: University of Chicago Press.

McCafferty, Christine, and Peter Hammond. 2001. *The Pink Agenda: Sexual Revolution in South Africa and the Ruin of the Family*. Cape Town: Christian Action.

McCray, Jan. 1997. *The Love Every Woman Needs: Intimacy with Jesus*. Grand Rapids, MI: Chosen Books.

McLean, Hugh, and Linda Ngcobo. 1995. "Abangibhamayo Bathi Ngimnandi (Those Who Fuck Me Say I'm Tasty): Gay Sexuality in Reef Townships." In *Defiant Desire: Gay and Lesbian Lives in South Africa*, edited by Mark Gevisser and Edwin Cameron, 158–185. New York: Routledge.

Medinger, Alan P. 2000. *Growth into Manhood: Resuming the Journey*. Colorado Springs: Waterbrook Press.

Meyer, Birgit. 1995. "'Delivered from the Powers of Darkness': Confessions of Satanic Riches in Christian Ghana." *Africa: Journal of the International African Institute* 65 (2): 236–255.

Meyer, Birgit. 1998. "'Make a Complete Break with the Past': Memory and Postcolonial Modernity in Ghanaian Pentecostal Discourse." In *Memory and the Postcolony: African Anthropology and the Critique of Power*, edited by Richard Werbner, 182–208. New York: St. Martin's.

Meyer, Birgit. 2007. "Pentecostalism and Neo-Liberal Capitalism: Faith, Prosperity and Vision in African Pentecostal-Charismatic Churches." *Journal for the Study of Religion* 20 (2): 5–28.

Miraftab, Farank. 2004. "Neoliberalism and the Casualization of Public Sector Services: The Case of Waste Collection in Cape Town, South Africa." *International Journal of Urban and Regional Research* 28 (4): 874–892.

Mkhize, Nonhlanhla, Jane Bennett, Vasu Reddy, and Relebohile Moletsane. 2010. *The Country We Want to Live In: Hate Crimes and Homophobia in the Lives of Black Lesbian South Africans.* Cape Town: HSRC Press.

Moffett, Helen. 2006. "'These Women, They Force Us to Rape Them': Rape as Narrative of Social Control in Post-Apartheid South Africa." *Journal of Southern African Studies* 32 (1): 129–144.

Moodie, T. Dunbar. 1975. *The Rise of Afrikanerdom: Power, Apartheid, and the Afrikaner Civil Religion.* Berkeley: University of California Press.

Moon, Dawne. 2004. *God, Sex, and Politics: Homosexuality and Everyday Theologies.* Chicago: University of Chicago Press.

Moore, Beth. 2002. *When Godly People Do Ungodly Things: Arming Yourself in the Age of Seduction.* Nashville: B&H.

Morrell, Robert, ed. 2001. *Changing Masculinities in a Changing Society: Men and Gender in Southern Africa.* London: Zed Books.

Morrell, Robert, Rachel Jewkes, and Graham Lindegger. 2012. "Hegemonic Masculinity/Masculinities in South Africa: Culture, Power, and Gender Politics." *Men and Masculinities* 15 (11): 11–30.

Morrell, Robert, and Linda Richter. 2004. "The Fatherhood Project: Confronting Issues of Masculinity and Sexuality." *Agenda* 62: 36–44.

Msibi, Thabo. 2011. "The Lies We Have Been Told: On (Homo)Sexuality in Africa." *Africa Today* 58 (1): 55–77.

Mthethwa, Bongani. 2008. "Crime's Not That Bad in South Africa: It's Worse." *Sunday Times*, 12.

Muholi, Zanele. 2004. "Thinking Through Lesbian Rape." *Agenda* (61): 116–125.

Muparamoto, Nelson. 2016. "Enduring and Subverting Homophobia: Religious Experiences of Same-Sex-Loving People in Zimbabwe." In *Christianity and Controversies over Homosexuality in Contemporary Africa*, edited by Ezra Chitando and Adriaan van Klinken, 143–156. London: Routledge.

Naidoo, Errol. 2008. "Is the Church Adopting the Language of Babylon?" *Joy Magazine* 17 (2): 29–31.

Nel, J. A. 2008. "Exploring Homophobic Victimisation in Gauteng, South Africa: Issues, Impacts and Responses." *Acta Criminologica* 21 (3): 19–36.

Newell, Sasha. 2007. "Pentecostal Witchcraft: Neoliberal Possession and Demonic Discourse in Ivoirian Pentecostal Churches." *Journal of Religion in Africa* 37: 461–490.

Ngubane, Sphelele. 2015. "Dutch Reformed Church's Radical Gay Ruling." *IOL News.* www.iol.co.za/news/south-africa/kwazulu-natal/dutch-reformed-churchs-radical -gay-ruling-1928889. Accessed November 4, 2017.

Nguyen, Vinh-Kim. 2009. "Therapeutic Evangelism—Confessional Technologies,

Antiretrovirals and Biospiritual Transformation in the Fight against AIDS in West Africa." In *AIDS and Religious Practice in Africa*, edited by Felicitas Becker and P. Wenzel Geissler, 359–378. Leiden: Brill.

Nguyen, Vinh-Kim. 2010. *The Republic of Therapy: Triage and Sovereignty in West Africa's Time of AIDS*. Durham, NC: Duke University Press.

Nicolosi, Joseph. 1993. *Healing Homosexuality: Case Stories of Reparative Therapy*. Northvale, NJ: Jason Aronson.

Nkoli, Simon. 1993. "This Strange Feeling." In *The Invisible Ghetto: Lesbian and Gay Writing from South Africa*, edited by Matthew Krouse and Kim Berman, 19–26. Johannesburg: COSAW.

Nkoli, Simon. 1995. "Wardrobes: Coming Out as a Black Gay Activist in South Africa." In *Defiant Desire: Gay and Lesbian Lives in South Africa*, edited by Mark Gevisser and Edwin Cameron, 249–257. New York: Routledge.

Ojo, Matthews. 1997. "Sexuality, Marriage, and Piety among Charismatics in Nigeria." *Religion* 27: 68–79.

Omenyo, Cephos. 2014. "African Pentecostalism." In *The Cambridge Companion to Pentecostalism*, edited by Cecil M. Robeck Jr. and Amos Young, 132–151. New York: Cambridge University Press.

O'Neill, Kevin Lewis. 2010. *City of God: Christian Citizenship in Postwar Guatemala*. Berkeley: University of California Press.

Ozyegin, Gul. 2015. *New Desires, New Selves: Sex, Love, and Piety among Turkish Youth*. New York: New York University Press.

Parikh, Shanti. 2015. *Regulating Romance: Youth Love Letters, Moral Anxiety, and Intervention in Uganda's Time of AIDS*. Nashville: Vanderbilt University Press.

Park, Jason. 2013. *Resolving Homosexual Problems: A Guide for LDS Men*. Salt Lake City: Century.

Parsitau, Damaris Seleina. 2009. "'Keep Holy and Abstain Till He Comes': Interrogating a Pentecostal Church's Engagement with HIV/AIDS and the Youth in Kenya." *Africa Today* 56 (1): 44–64.

Parsitau, Damaris Seleina. 2011. "'Arise, Oh Ye Daughters of Faith': Women, Pentecostalism, and Public Culture in Kenya." In *Christianity and Public Culture in Kenya*, edited by Harry Englund, 131–145. Athens: Ohio University Press.

Pascoe, C. J. 2007. *Dude, You're a Fag: Masculinity and Sexuality in High School*. Berkeley: University of California Press.

Payne, Leanne. 1995. *Crisis in Masculinity*. Grand Rapids, MI: Baker Books.

Payne, Leanne. 1996 [1981]. *The Broken Image: Restoring Personal Wholeness through Healing Prayer*. Grand Rapids, MI: Baker Books.

Peacock, Dean. 2013. "South Africa's Sonke Gender Justice Network: Educating Men for Gender Equality." *Agenda* 95: 1–13.

Pearce, Tola Olu. 2012. "Reconstructing Sexuality in the Shadow of Neoliberal Globalization: Investigating the Approach of Charismatic Churches in Southwestern Nigeria." *Journal of Religion in Africa* 42: 345–368.

Perkins, Cody. 2015. "Coloured Men, Moffies, and the Meanings of Masculinity in South Africa, 1910–1960." PhD diss., University of Virginia.

Pew Forum on Religion and Public Life. 2006. "Overview: Pentecostalism in Africa." Pew Research Center. www.pewforum.org/2006/10/05/overview-pentecostalism -in-africa/. Accessed December 27, 2013.

Pew Forum on Religion and Public Life. 2009. "Religion in South Africa 15 Years after the End of Apartheid." Pew Research Center. www.pewforum.org/2009/04/23 /religion-in-south-africa-15-years-after-the-end-of-apartheid/. Accessed May 1, 2011.

Pew Forum on Religion and Public Life. 2011. "Global Christianity: A Report on the Size and Distribution of the World's Christian Population." Pew Research Center. www.pewforum.org/2011/12/19/global-christianity-exec/. Accessed December 23, 2013.

Pew Research Center. 2013. "The Global Divide on Homosexuality: Greater Acceptance in More Secular and Affluent Countries." Washington, DC: Pew Research Center. www.pewglobal.org/files/2013/06/Pew-Global-Attitudes-Homosexuality -Report-FINAL-JUNE-4-2013.pdf. Accessed December 23, 2013.

Posel, Deborah. 2005a. "'Baby Rape': Unmaking Secrets of Sexual Violence in Post-Apartheid South Africa." In *Men Behaving Differently: South African Men since 1994*, edited by Graeme Reid and Liz Walker, 21–64. Cape Town: Double Storey.

Posel, Deborah. 2005b. "Sex, Death and the Fate of the Nation: Reflections on the Politicalization of Sexuality in Post-Apartheid South Africa." *Africa: Journal of the International African Institute* 75 (2): 125–153.

Post, Peggy. 2004. *Emily Post's Etiquette*. 17th ed. New York: HarperResource.

Pype, Katrien. 2011. "Confession cum Deliverance: In/Dividuality of the Subject among Kinshasa's Born-Again Christians." *Journal of Religion in Africa* 41: 280–310.

Pype, Katrien. 2012. *The Making of the Pentecostal Melodrama: Religion, Media and Gender in Kinshasa*. New York: Berghahn Books.

Queiroz, Jandira, Fernando D'Elio, and David Maas. 2013. "The 'Ex-Gay' Movement in Latin America: Therapy and Ministry in Latin America." Somerville, MA: Political Research Associates. www.politicalresearch.org/wp-content/uploads /downloads/2013/04/Ex-Gay-Movement-in-Latin-America.pdf. Accessed November 7, 2017.

Quiroz, Sitna. 2016. "The Dilemmas of Monogamy: Pleasure, Discipline and the Pentecostal Moral Self in Benin." *Religions* 7/8: 1–16.

Reay, Barry, Nina Attwood, and Claire Gooder. 2015. *Sex Addiction: A Critical History*. Maden, MA: Polity.

Reddy, Thiven. 2015. *South Africa, Settler Colonialism and the Failures of Liberal Democracy*. London: Zed Books.

Reid, Graeme, and Teresa Dirsuweit. 2002. "Understanding Systemic Violence: Homophobic Attacks in Johannesburg and Its Surrounds." *Urban Forum* 13 (3): 99–126.

Reinhardt, Bruno. 2014. "Soaking in Tapes: The Haptic Voice of Global Pentecostal Pedagogy in Ghana." *Journal of the Royal Anthropological Institute* 20 (2): 315–336.

Rivers, Jessica. 2016. "The Intimate Intensity of Evangelical Fighting Ministries." *Temenos* 52 (2): 215–237.

Robbins, Joel. 2007. "Continuity Thinking and the Problem of Christian Culture: Belief, Time, and the Anthropology of Christianity." *Current Anthropology* 48 (1): 5–38.

Robbins, Joel. 2012. "On Enchanting Science and Disenchanting Nature: Spiritual Warfare in North America and Papua New Guinea." In *Nature, Science, and Religion: Intersections Shaping Society and the Environment*, edited by Catherine Tucker, 45–64. Santa Fe: School for Advanced Research Press.

Roberts, Benjamin, and Vasu Reddy. 2008. *Pride and Prejudice: Public Attitudes towards Homosexuality*. Cape Town: Human Sciences Research Council.

Robins, Steven L. 2008. *From Revolution to Rights in South Africa: Social Movements, NGOs and Popular Politics after Apartheid*. Scottsville, South Africa: University of Kwazulu-Natal Press.

Rofel, Lisa. 2007. *Desiring China: Experiments in Neoliberalism, Sexuality, and Public Culture*. Durham, NC: Duke University Press.

Rogers, Sy. 1993. "Questions I'm Asked Most about Homosexuality." Singapore: Church of the Savior. Exodus Global Alliance. https://exodusglobalalliance.org/commonquestionsabouthomosexualityp39.php. Accessed November 3, 2017.

Rose, Nikolas S. 1999 [1989]. *Governing the Soul: The Shaping of the Private Self*. 2nd ed. New York: Free Association Books.

Ross, Fiona. 2008. "Truth and Reconciliation." In *New South African Keywords*, edited by Nick Shepher and Steven Robins, 235–246. Johannesburg: Jacana.

Ross Williams, Roger, dir. 2013. *God Loves Uganda*. Documentary film.

Ruiters, Michele. 2009. "Collaboration, Assimilation and Contestation: Emerging Constructions of Coloured Identity in Post-Apartheid South Africa." In *Burdened by Race: Coloured Identities in Southern Africa*, edited by Mohamed Adhikari, 104–133. Cape Town: UCT Press.

Sadgrove, Joanna, Robert M. Vanderbeck, Johan Andersson, Gill Valentine, and Kevin Ward. 2012. "Morality Plays and Money Matters: Towards a Situated Understanding of the Politics of Homosexuality in Uganda." *Journal of Modern African Studies* 50 (1): 103–129.

Samara, Tony Roshan. 2005. "Youth, Crime and Urban Renewal in the Western Cape." *Journal of Southern African Studies* 31 (1): 209–227.

Samara, Tony Roshan. 2010. "Order and Security in the City: Producing Race and Policing Neoliberal Spaces in South Africa." *Ethnic and Racial Studies* 33 (4): 637–655.

Sampson, Marty. 2003. *Better Than Life: Hillsong United*. Sydney, Australia.

Schlanger, Zoe, and Elijah Wolfson. 2014. "Ex-Ex-Gay Pride." *Newsweek*, May 1. http://www.newsweek.com/ex-ex-gay-pride-249282. Accessed May 15, 2014.

Schlemmer, Lawrence. 2008. *Dormant Capital: Pentecostalism in South Africa and Its Potential Social and Economic Role*. Edited by Ann Bernstein. Johannesburg: Centre for Development and Enterprise.

Seleka, Ntwaagae. 2008. "Woman Killed Dad Who Gave Her HIV/AIDS." *Sowetan*, June 19.

Sinnott, Megan. 2004. *Toms and Dees: Transgender Identity and Female Same-Sex Relationships in Thailand*. Honolulu: University of Hawaii Press.

Smilde, David. 2007. *Reason to Believe: Cultural Agency in Latin American Evangelicalism*. Berkeley: University of California Press.

Smith, Daniel Jordan. 2006. "Love and the Risk of HIV: Courtship, Marriage, and Infidelity in Southeastern Nigeria." In *Modern Loves: The Anthropology of Romantic*

Courtship and Companionate Marriage, edited by Jennifer Hirsch and Holly Wardlow, 135–153. Ann Arbor: University of Michigan Press.

Smith, David A. 2014. "Uganda Anti-Gay Law Declared 'Null and Void' by Constitutional Court." *Guardian*. www.theguardian.com/world/2014/aug/01/uganda-anti-gay-law-null-and-void. Accessed March 17, 2015.

Smythe, Dee. 2015. *Rape Unresolved: Policing Sexual Offences in South Africa*. Cape Town: UCT Press.

Soothill, Jane E. 2007. *Gender, Social Change and Spiritual Power: Charismatic Christianity in Ghana, Studies of religion in Africa*. Leiden: Brill.

Soothill, Jane E. 2014. "Gender and Pentecostalism in Africa." In *Pentecostalism in Africa: Presence and Impact of Pneumatic Christianity in Postcolonial Societies*, edited by Martin Lindhardt, 191–219. Leiden: Brill.

Spitzer, Robert. 2003. "Can Some Gay Men and Lesbians Change Their Sexual Orientation? 200 Participants Reporting a Change from Homosexual to Heterosexual Orientation." *Archives of Sexual Behavior* 32 (5): 403–417.

Spronk, Rachel. 2011. "'Intimacy is the Name of the Game': Media and the Praxis of Knowledge in Nairobi." *Anthropologica* 53: 145–158.

Stackhouse, John. 2007. "Jesus, I'm NOT in Love with You." *Stackblog*, stackblog .wordpress.com. Accessed December 5, 2010.

Stamier, Tshepiso, and Sipho Kekana. 2008. "Rescued, Then Raped." *Daily Sun*, March 20, 1.

Steffan, Melissa. 2013. "Alan Chambers Apologizes to Gay Community, Exodus International to Shut Down." *Christianity Today*. www.christianitytoday.com/news/2013 /june/alan-chambers-apologizes-to-gay-community-exodus.html. Accessed September 27, 2013.

Steingo, Gavin. 2005. "'I Am Proud to Be South African Because I Am South African': Reflections on 'White Pride' in Post-Apartheid South Africa." *African Identities* 3 (2): 195–210.

Steyn, Melissa. 2005. "'White Talk': White South Africans and the Management of Diasporic Whiteness." In *Postcolonial Whiteness: A Critical Reader in Race and Empire*, edited by Alfred J. Lopez, 119–135. Albany: State University of New York Press.

Stychin, Carl. 1996. "Constituting Sexuality: The Struggle for Sexual Orientation in the South African Bill of Rights." *Journal of Law and Society* 23 (4): 455–483.

Swarr, Amanda Lock. 2009. "'Stabane,' Intersexuality, and Same-Sex Relationships in South Africa." *Feminist Studies* 35 (3): 524–548.

Swisher, Sallie H. 1995. "Therapeutic Interventions Recommended for Treatment of Sexual Addiction/Compulsivity." *Sexual Addiction and Compulsivity* 2 (1): 31–39.

Tamale, Sylvia. 2013. "Confronting the Poliitics of Nonconforming Sexualities in Africa." *African Studies Review* 56 (2): 31–45.

Taylor, Charles. 1989. *Sources of the Self: The Making of the Modern Identity*. Cambridge, MA: Harvard University Press.

Tennant, Agnieszka. 2006. "Dating Jesus: When 'Lover of My Soul' Language Goes Too Far." *Christianity Today*. www.christianitytoday.com/ct/2006/december/17.56 .html. Accessed December 6, 2006.

Thomas, Choo. 2003. *Heaven Is So Real!* Lake Mary, FL: Creation House.

Thomas, Samuel S. 2000. "Transforming the Gospel of Domesticity: Luyha Girls and the Friends Africa Mission, 1917–1926." *African Studies Review* 43 (2): 1–27.

Thoreson, Ryan Richard. 2014. "Troubling the Waters of a 'Wave of Homophobia': Political Economies of Anti-Queer Animus in Sub-Saharan Africa." *Sexualities* 17 (1–2): 23–42.

Thorton, Brendan Jamal. 2016. *Negotiating Respect: Pentecostalism, Masculinity, and the Politics of Spiritual Authority in the Dominican Republic*. Gainesville: University Press of Florida.

Toscano, Peterson. n.d. "Ex-Gay Harm—Let Me Count the Ways." *Beyond Ex-Gay*. https://beyondexgay.com/article/harm1.html. Accessed May 1, 2014.

Travis, Trysh. 2009. *The Language of the Heart: A Cultural History of the Recovery Movement from Alcoholics Anonymous to Oprah Winfrey*. Chapel Hill: University of North Carolina Press.

Tucker, Andrew. 2009. *Queer Visibilities: Space, Identity and Interaction in Cape Town*. Chichester, UK: Wiley-Blackwell.

Tutu, Desmond. 1999. *No Future without Forgiveness*. New York: Doubleday.

Valois, Caroline. 2016. "Scandal Makers: Competition in the Religious Marketplace among Pentecostal-Charismatic Churches in Uganda." In *Christianity and Controversies over Homosexuality in Contemporary Africa*, edited by Ezra Chitando and Adriaan van Klinken, 38–50. London: Routledge.

van de Kamp, Linda. 2011. "Converting the Spirit Spouse: The Violent Transformation of the Pentecostal Female Body in Maputo, Mozambique." *Ethnos* 76 (4): 510–533.

van de Kamp, Linda. 2016. *Violent Conversion: Brazilian Pentecostalism and Urban Women in Mozambique*. Rochester, NY: James Currey.

van der Meer, Erwin. 2010. "Strategic Level Spiritual Warfare and Mission in Africa." *Evangelical Review of Theology* 34 (2): 155–166.

van Dijk, Rijk. 1998. "Pentecostalism, Cultural Memory and the State: Contested Representations of Time in Postcolonial Malawi." In *Memory and the Postcolony: African Anthropology and the Critique of Power*, edited by Richard Werbner, 155–181. London: Zed Books.

van Dijk, Rijk. 2001. "Time and Transcultural Technologies of the Self in the Ghanian Pentecostal Diaspora." In *Between Babel and Pentecost: Transnational Pentecostalism in Africa and Latin America*, edited by André Corten and Ruth Marshall-Fratani, 216–234. London: Hurst & Company.

van Dijk, Rijk. 2007. "Testing Nightscapes: Ghanaian Pentecostal Politics of the Nocturnal." *Etnofoor* 20 (2): 41–57.

van Dijk, Rijk. 2013. "Counselling and Pentecostal Modalities of Social Engineering of Relationships in Botswana." *Culture, Health and Sexuality* 15 (4): 509–522.

van Dijk, Rijk. 2015. "Faith in Romance: Towards an Anthropology of Romantic Relationships, Sexuality and Responsibility in African Christianities." University of Amsterdam, Inaugural Lecture Series.

van Klinken, Adriaan. 2011. "Male Headship as Male Agency: An Alternative Understanding of a 'Patriarchal' African Pentecostal Discourse on Masculinity." *Religion and Gender* 1 (1): 104–124.

van Klinken, Adriaan. 2012. "Men in the Remaking: Conversion Narratives and Born-Again Masculinity in Zambia." *Journal of Religion in Africa* 42: 215–239.

van Klinken, Adriaan. 2013. *Transforming Masculinities in African Christianity: Gender Controversies in Times of AIDS*. Farnham, UK: Ashgate.

van Klinken, Adriaan. 2015. "African Christianity: Developments and Trends." In *Handbook of Global Contemporary Christianity: Themes and Developments in Culture, Politics, and Society*, edited by Stephen J. Hunt, 131–151. Leiden: Brill.

van Klinken, Adriaan, and Ezra Chitando, eds. 2016. *Public Religion and the Politics of Homosexuality in Africa*. London: Routledge.

Van Wyk, Ilana. 2014. *The Universal Church of the Kingdom of God in South Africa: A Church of Strangers*. New York: Cambridge University Press.

Van Zyl, Mikki, Jeanelle de Gruchy, Shelia Lapinsky, Simon Lewin, and Graeme Reid. 1999. *The aVersion Project: Human Rights Abuses of Gays and Lesbians in the South African Defence Force by Health Workers during the Apartheid Era*. Cape Town: Simply Said and Done.

Vaughan, Megan. 1991. *Curing Their Ills: Colonial Power and African Illness*. Stanford, CA: Stanford University Press.

Verwey, Cornel, and Michael Quayle. 2012. "Whiteness, Racism, and Afrikaner Identity in Post-Apartheid South Africa." *African Affairs* 111 (445): 551–575.

Vincent, Louise, and Bianca Camminga. 2009. "Putting the 'T' into South African Human Rights: Transsexuality in the Post-Apartheid Order." *Sexualities* 12: 678–700.

Von Schnitzler, Antina. 2016. *Democracy's Infrastructure: Techno-Politics and Protest after Apartheid*. Princeton, NJ: Princeton University Press.

Waidzunas, Tom. 2015. *The Straight Line: How the Fringe Science of Ex-Gay Therapy Reoriented Sexuality*. Minneapolis: University of Minnesota Press.

Wale, Kim. 2013. "Confronting Exclusion: Time for Radical Reconciliation—SA Reconciliation Barometer Survey 2013 Report." The Institute for Justice and Reconciliation. http://reconciliationbarometer.org/wp-content/uploads/2013/12/IJR-Barometer-Report-2013-22Nov1635.pdf. Accessed November 4, 2017.

Walker, Liz, Graeme Reid, and Morna Cornell. 2004. *Waiting to Happen: HIV/AIDS in South Africa—The Bigger Picture*. Cape Town: Double Storey Books.

Wanner, Catherine. 2003. "Advocating New Moralities: Conversion to Evangelicalism in Ukraine." *Religion, State and Society* 31 (3): 273–287.

Warhol, Robyn R. 2002. "The Rhetoric of Addiction: From Victorian Novels to AA." In *High Anxieties: Cultural Studies in Addiction*, edited by Janet Farrell Brodie and Marc Redfield, 97–108. Berkeley: University of California Press.

Weiss, Margot Danielle. 2011. *Techniques of Pleasure: BDSM and the Circuits of Sexuality*. Durham, NC: Duke University Press.

Wekker, Gloria. 2006. *The Politics of Passion: Women's Sexual Culture in the Afro-Surinamese Diaspora*. New York: Columbia University Press.

Wiese, Bill. 2006. *23 Minutes in Hell*. Lake Mary, FL: Charisma House.

Wilcox, W. Bradford. 2004. *Soft Patriarchs, New Men: How Christianity Shapes Fathers and Husbands*. Chicago: University of Chicago Press.

Wilkinson, Annie Kathryn. 2011. "Cleanliness Is Holiness: Reparative Practices in Ecuador." MA thesis, Latin American Faculty of Social Sciences.

Wilson, Sherryl. 2003. *Oprah, Celebrity, and Formations of Self*. New York: Palgrave Macmillan.

Wolkomir, Michelle. 2006. *Be Not Deceived: The Sacred and Sexual Struggles of Gay and Ex-gay Christian Men*. New Brunswick, NJ: Rutgers University Press.

Wood, Kate. 2005. "Contextualizing Group Rape in Post-Apartheid South Africa." *Culture, Health and Sexuality* 7 (4): 303–317.

Wyrod, Robert. 2016. *AIDS and Masculinity in the African City: Privilege, Inequality, and Modern Manhood*. Berkeley: University of California Press.